Gene Stratton-Porter

Gene Stratton-Porter

Novelist and Naturalist

JUDITH REICK LONG

Indiana Historical Society
Indianapolis 1990

Illustrations, unless otherwise indicated, are courtesy of the Gene Stratton-Porter State Historic Sites, Indiana State Museum.

The paper in this publication meets the minimum requirements of American National Standard for Information Sciences—Permanence of Paper for Printed Library Materials, ANSI Z39.48-1984.

Library of Congress Cataloging-in-Publication Data

Long, Judith Reick, 1935-1987.
  Gene Stratton-Porter, novelist and naturalist / by Judith Reick Long.
    p. cm.
Includes bibliographical references and index.
  ISBN 0-87195-052-9 : $19.95
  1. Stratton-Porter, Gene, 1863–1924–Biography. 2. Novelists, American—20th century—Biography. 3. Naturalists—United States–Biography. 4. Indiana–Biography. I. Title.
PS3531.07345Z59   1990
813'.52—dc20
[B]   90-4740
                                                CIP

To my father, Howard Reick, with love and gratitude

Contents

Foreword

INDIANA literature has never been the exclusive domain of male authors, but probably the names of men come first to mind when the subject is broached. The so-called Big Four of Indiana literature during its most popular period were all men (George Ade, Meredith Nicholson, James Whitcomb Riley, and Booth Tarkington), as was its most famous and prolific black sheep, Theodore Dreiser. Today, too, most writers noted for ties to Indiana are male: Michael Martone, Kurt Vonnegut, Dan Wakefield. Yet women have contributed mightily to the state's overall literary output, from Sarah Bolton and Eunice Bullard Beecher in the early years of statehood through Gene Stratton-Porter and Jessamyn West, Marilyn Wall Durham, and Marilyn Augburn Sharp of more recent times.

Part of the reason for the higher male author profile is surely bibliographic. Fine biographies of Ade, Dreiser, Riley, and Tarkington have long been available to readers, and critical studies of their work are also plentiful. Not so with the women authors, but this book marks a welcome step towards the redress of that situation. Judith Long's biography of a major Indiana writer is itself a major contribution. This pub-

lication marks the first full-scale life of an author whose books
have remained popular throughout the twentieth century.
Stratton-Porter's works of both fiction and nature studies have
appeared in fourteen different languages and continue to en-
thrall new generations of young readers for whom the country life and natural beauty of the pristine Indiana landscape is
increasingly remote.

In many ways this study is a tour de force. Often Gene
Stratton-Porter's own autobiographical writings were inten-
tionally misleading or worse, but her biographer has succeeded in piecing together evidence from countless sources,
traditional and nontraditional, thereby developing a new, fascinating, and persuasive portrait. Long's Stratton-Porter is a
complex woman whose early life was marred with tragedy,
frequent moves, and unhappy educational experiences, and
whose married life with an Adams County druggist and
banker, Charles Dorwin Porter, was surely one of the most
unusual of that period. The patient tolerance and support
Porter gave his wife after she finally found her niche in life as
a writer and wildlife photographer was important, perhaps
critical, to her success, but she seems not to have recognized
it herself. Once her own income from her writings provided
the means, she moved away, first to Wildflower Woods in
Noble County, Indiana, and then to southern California.

Long's success in her efforts to interpret her subject is all
the more remarkable, for she lacked training in history and
literary criticism, instead coming to this work by way of her
rare book business in Georgia after having been fascinated by
Gene Stratton-Porter's writings and visits to her houses as a
girl living in Indiana. Indeed, one of Long's many significant
findings regarding Stratton-Porter's career is bibliographic;
Long has identified *The Strike at Shane's*, a prize-winning
story with *Animal Farm*-like characteristics anonymously
published in 1893, as her first book. This work preceded her

signed articles, beginning in 1900, and her widely hailed *The Song of the Cardinal* (1903) by nearly a decade.

With *The Song of the Cardinal* Gene Stratton-Porter was on the way to making her reputation as a "Bird Woman," a self-taught photographer of considerable talent and a champion of nature and wildlife conservation. She has been characterized as a person in the forefront of the national conservation movement and the one who, along with President Theodore Roosevelt, did most to popularize its viewpoints. During the final three years of her life, Stratton-Porter used her "page" in every issue of *McCall's* magazine to speak out on these and, often, family-related issues.

There is a sad aspect to this publication: its author did not live to see her words in print and bound between covers bearing her name. I had no idea, when a Mrs. Long from Marietta, Georgia, first sought my assistance in getting her manuscript about an Indiana author published, that there was any urgency in her request. Perhaps I should have suspected something later when she wrote in April 1987 that, "for personal reasons," it was important to "get the book placed this year," but I did not. The manuscript went through the normal review process at the Indiana Historical Society, but the letter of acceptance by Dr. Thomas A. Mason, director of publications, arrived at the Long household two weeks following the author's death, on 28 November of that year. The consoling fact is that Mrs. Long has left a legacy that will live on. Through this book others will be able to benefit from her lifelong interest in Gene Stratton-Porter—as late as March 1987 Long was in California, examining the home where "GS-P" had lived—and her valuable, gracefully written interpretation of Stratton-Porter's life and writings.

Finally, I want to express a word of gratitude to J. Edgar Long, on behalf of myself (for the invitation to write this introduction) and the editorial staff of the Indiana Historical

Society, for his outstanding cooperation in making the final revisions to his late wife's manuscript. We hope that she would have been pleased with the results.

Ralph D. Gray
Indiana University–Purdue
University, Indianapolis

Acknowledgments

I T is with much gratitude that I acknowledge the co-operation of the following individuals: Martha Wright, reference librarian, and Marybelle Burch, former manuscripts librarian, both of the Indiana Division, Indiana State Library; Virginia Brann, senior archives assistant, Archives of Indiana United Methodism, DePauw University, Greencastle, Indiana; Robert E. Zilliox, archivist, The Duggan Library, Hanover College, Hanover, Indiana; Joseph Gault, Indiana Department of Financial Institutions; Vena Simmons, Geneva Public Library; Walter Burgin, Geneva, Indiana; Kenneth E. Gray, curator, Wabash County Historical Museum, Wabash, Indiana; Maxine Lambright, Rome City, Indiana; Anne Laurie Smith, North Webster, Indiana; Mamie Schenbeck and Judith Burkhardt, Berne, Indiana; Nancy Lichtle and Lola Gould, Decatur Public Library; Mary Jane Runyon, Decatur, Indiana; Ed Breen, Marion, Indiana; William Wepler, Indiana State Museum; Robert M. Taylor, Jr., Indiana Historical Society; and Shirley S. McCord, Indiana Historical Bureau. A special note of thanks goes to Margie Sweeney and Martha Swartzlander, Gene Stratton-Porter State Historic Site, Rome City, and Rebecca M. Smith, Limberlost State Historic Site, Geneva.

Also, Robert Barclay, director, the Aurora Historical Museum, Aurora, Illinois; Judy Star, former director, American Humane Education Society, Boston, Massachusetts; Clyde M. Maffin, Ontario County historian, Canandaigua, New York; Sybil M. O'Dell, librarian, Clifton Springs Library, Clifton Springs, New York; J. O. Preston, New York State Department of Environmental Conservation; Cecil Rockwell, former executive secretary, Wayne County Historical Society, Wooster, Ohio; Ruth Williams, Wooster, Ohio; Lois Polson, Victorville, California; Nancy O'Connor, Records Department, the Hollywood Cemetery Association; Evelyn T. Jacobs, Los Angeles; and M. Beech, Erie, Kansas. Especially cooperative were the courthouse staffs of Wabash and Adams counties, Indiana, and Wayne County, Ohio. Bernard A. Bernier, Jr., acting chief, Serials Division, Library of Congress, rendered exceptional service.

It must be emphasized that all of the above persons were merely asked for information. The conclusions drawn from the data they so generously furnished are my sole responsibility.

For his pointed suggestions with respect to the manuscript in rough draft, I am much indebted to an Indiana scholar and antiquarian bookman, the late Byron Troyer of Fort Myers, Florida. For his final scrutiny of the manuscript, I am grateful for the help of Dr. Ralph D. Gray, editor, *Journal of the Early Republic* and member of the History Department of Indiana University-Purdue University at Indianapolis. Yet it is to a regional writer that I owe my greatest debt. It is to French Quinn, historian of Adams County, Indiana, that I owe my inspiration. In summarizing her years of dedication to the study of bird and plant life, Quinn once likened Gene Stratton-Porter's life story to a fairy tale: "Charley Porter ran the drug store and he brought his bride Gene Stratton there and she found the Limberlost swamp right at her cottage door and that swamp was ready and waiting to be talked about and written about and Mrs. Porter saw its glories and millions of folks know of the 'Limberlost'—some day there will be a state park there and everybody will live happily ever after."

Whether everybody has lived happily ever after is a speculative matter, although French Quinn's prediction about a future state park dedicated to Gene Stratton-Porter has now come to pass. Today there are two state historic sites, not one as Quinn envisioned, currently maintained in the memory of America's foremost bird woman—"Limberlost Cabin" in Geneva, Indiana, and "Wildflower Woods" on the shores of Sylvan Lake at Rome City, Indiana.

Judith Reick Long

Symbols

Sometimes I think a pure white flower
   A holy sign must be.
Some day, mayhap I'll gather one,
   And set its mark on me.

Sometimes I think a butterfly
   A sacred symbol, bright.
Some day, mayhap I'll lure me one,
   And worship with delight.

Sometimes I think a flying bird
   Is just a soul set free.
Some day, mayhap I'll capture one
   To wing my flight for me.

Gene Stratton-Porter
(1863-1924)

A Latter-Day Moses

S HORTLY after the turn of the century, two American giants emerged who sought to reshape the national perspective. One of these forces was Theodore Roosevelt, champion of big game and the Great Outdoors. The other was a woman, a best-selling novelist and authority on birdlife named Gene Stratton-Porter. Together, although they were personally unacquainted, the books and public works of these two powerful wildlife advocates opened a new way of thinking to millions. The first to compare Theodore Roosevelt and Gene Stratton-Porter was one of their contemporaries, author and editor Grant Overton: "Each has swayed the millions; each, beyond all possible question, has influenced human lives. Neither was oppressed by the enormous responsibility attached to such a role."[1]

The life of Theodore Roosevelt has been well chronicled. That is not the case, however, with the life of Gene Stratton-Porter, his companion crusader. Biographers have neglected this influential woman. No in-depth study of her life has been published other than a somewhat cosmetic account penned by her daughter, Jeannette Porter Meehan.[2]

The neglect of Gene Stratton-Porter by biographers is a serious oversight. By 1920 her name had become a household word around the globe. Her bibliographer writes that her books were translated variously into Dutch, German, French, Spanish, Norwegian, Swedish, Danish, Finnish, Czech, Japanese, Korean, Afrikaans, and Arabic.[3]

Gene Stratton-Porter's road to international fame was long and paved with hidden heartbreak. Her first loves were wild birdlife and the flowers of swamp and field. During her early years, however, circumstances conspired to make it difficult to indulge these passions openly. As a young adult, she was a social misfit.[4] Because she enjoyed bird-watching and other outdoor pursuits, she was regarded by her peers as an oddity. How she felt about not belonging is best illustrated by what happened to her shortly before her twenty-first birthday, in the summer of 1884, at an inland resort in the Midwest.

As she later reconstructed it, much to her discomfort, she was surrounded that summer by a multitude of fun-loving vacationers considerably different from herself. By day these merrymakers liked to play cards, and by night they liked to dance. Few explored the sandy beaches, and fewer fished. None but the hardy ventured into the nearby woods. To most of the throng here on holiday, the wall of woods encircling this resort was a place to avoid, its shadows thick with insects and its dank interior slithering with the unexpected.

Only two women at this lakeside playground shared Gene Stratton-Porter's zest for the out-of-doors. One of them would consent to search the nearby woods for orchids—but only if accompanied by a man—and, by some strange quirk, the other one could even row a boat. Otherwise, the women vacationing here were of one mind, more fearful than reverential of any kind of wildlife and utterly contemptuous of outdoor pastimes. Reared and geared as ladies, highly adept at the indoor arts of fancywork and embroidery, and just as highly practiced in the Victorian arts of fanning themselves and fainting, the women here were quite suspicious, even scornful, of anyone or anything that looked or acted as if he, she, or it belonged out-of-doors, and that included Gene Stratton-Porter. "I was considered an outcast," she remembered, "half demented because I fished in the rain one night when I might have attended a ball. One woman blasted me with scorn because I had the hardihood to offer to her a timothy straw strung with luscious big, wild red raspberries."[5]

Years later Gene Stratton-Porter was able to forgive those veranda clingers who had denounced her that long-ago summer, even going so far as to offer an excuse for their scornful behavior. She blamed it on faulty upbringing—theirs, not hers—an upbringing prone to connect the out-of-doors with acute discomfort and hardship:

> I came into the world at a time when the womanhood of our land was in fierce recoil against the hardships of pioneer life as it steadily edged its way westward. It was a common thing in my childhood to hear a mother fiercely declare that her children should not be permitted to endure the hardships that had fallen to her lot. Every effort was strained to make . . . some mysterious thing constantly referred to as a "lady" of her daughter.[6]

She apparently felt that, in their combined efforts to bring up a generation of ladies, the pioneering mothers of this nation had gone too far. She also believed that in their total revolt against the adversities associated with carving homes out of the wilderness, these pioneer women had spawned a generation of daughters at home nowhere but in the parlor or under a parasol. And indeed, unlike her hardened mother who had braved this nation's trackless forests, the typical female of the late nineteenth century was truly a poor specimen, self-consciously preoccupied with cultivating and maintaining a delicate image. Had she tramped a woods in search of berries, cast a bait until the sun burned her face, or stooped to weed

Gene Stratton-Porter in California, 1924

a garden without gloves, the typical young woman of Gene Stratton-Porter's generation would surely have endangered her reputation as a lady. Eventually, increasingly alarmed by the preponderance of women who shrieked at caterpillars and prided themselves on pale complexions, Gene Stratton-Porter began to see in this widespread disdain for the out-of-doors a great challenge, as well as an opportunity, to become a bellwether: "I came in time to believe that there might be a life work for one woman in leading these other women back to the forest; on account of my inclinations, education and rearing, I felt in a degree equipped to be their Moses."[7]

Today, such a self-comparison to Moses might seem overly presumptuous, or even sacrilegious. Before the turn of the century, however, such an analogy was unremarkable because of the black woman then widely known as Moses. Harriet Tubman's admirers referred to her as Moses because of her fearless leadership of slaves to freedom via the underground railroad. However, unlike Harriet Tubman, who did not vie for this exalted designation, Gene Stratton-Porter strove for veneration and high recognition. Her desire to command the respect and the following of a Moses was more than vigorous.

This ambitious woman did not attain any measure of fulfillment until she reached her early forties. Recognition came slowly in the wake of years of frustration and self-preparation. She first attracted national attention in 1903, at the age of forty, following the publication of an uplifting novel about a pair of loving redbirds.[8] A similar work followed one year later, a romantic, wholesome book that propelled her to worldwide fame.[9]

Gene Stratton-Porter eventually captured a vast readership by means of the light romance, narratives braided with woodlore, birdlife, and salubrious prescriptions for home happiness. And despite her original aim of appealing to America's women, this readership had no glandular basis. Men as well as women treasured the recipe in her pastoral novels for

Gene Stratton-Porter, 1903

happily-ever-after, a formula compounded of the soothing balm of the out-of-doors and embracing the sanctity of the home. Urban transplants recognized scenes in her rustic settings from their own happy rural childhoods. Lifelong city dwellers transported themselves through the pages of Gene Stratton-Porter to woodland settings of harmony and peace. Whether this nature lover ever achieved her goal of enticing the veranda-bound afield is debatable. Frederic Taber Cooper, a noted critic, doubted that her penchant for fresh air was contagious:

> It is rather pleasant to return to nature vicariously through the pages of Mrs. Porter's stories, explore the woodlands and swamps quite safely, with no danger of getting our clothing soiled or our shoes muddy, picnic on the grass, untroubled by crawling ants or persistent mosquitoes, and persuade ourselves that the Music of the Wild is very near to our hearts, when as a matter of fact if the canary sings too loudly, we usually put a handkerchief over its cage.[10]

Although most were best-sellers, the novels of Gene Stratton-Porter generally met with a negative response from the literary establishment. Early in her career, her fiction was branded as unrealistic. To the lettered, her upstanding characters seemed larger than life. One wag labeled her one of the "apostles of the Impossibly Virtuous," a knee-jerk appellation she was never able to overcome.[11] Her last novel, *The Keeper of the Bees*, was adjudged to radiate "sweetness, hope, and light with the unreasoning intensity of an August sun."[12]

Several nonfiction books also sprang from the pen of Gene Stratton-Porter. Most of these factual works dealt with wild birdlife, her central interest. Like Stratton-Porter's fiction, her bird books found small favor with the academic community, primarily because she compiled her field observations in an unscientific manner. Gene Stratton-Porter confined herself to the study of the homelife of wild birds. She was primarily interested in nest building, diet, and social behavior. She had no use for breeding censuses, complicated migration patterns, or other dry statistics. Her orientation was strictly unacademic. Nevertheless, a paleontologist was so moved by one of her nonfiction works that he named a trilobite for her, and Christopher Morley, who likened her to Jean-Henri Fabre, wrote to her that the stories in *Homing with the Birds* "refresh the sense of amazement."[13] Generally, however, the academic consensus was that Gene Stratton-Porter's field studies were of value only to those who would not read John Muir or Henry David Thoreau. A London critic, who evidently thought Gene Stratton-Porter was a man, took exception to the unscholarly thrust of *Music of the Wild*, one of Stratton-Porter's most popular nonfiction books: "We sometimes feel that he is soaring above us, and confess that we do not 'hear the Great Secret' and see the 'Compelling Vision' even when he shows us 'trees you never before have seen, flowers and vines the botanists fail to mention.' "[14]

Yet it was the critical response to her fiction that bothered Gene Stratton-Porter the most. She could not understand why the learned condemned the upstanding characters in her novels or why the critics maligned fiction based on virtuous behavior. "A thing utterly baffling to me," she wondered, "is why the life history of the sins and shortcomings of a man should constitute a book of realism, and the life history of a just and incorruptible man should constitute a book of idealism. Is not a moral man as real as an immoral one?"[15] Confronted repeatedly with reviews condemning her fiction as idealistic, at first she denounced her critics as seekers only after gloom and disparaged the academic groove from which they vocalized. Eventually, unable to combat an ever-rising tide of literary criticism, she ceased worrying about her detractors: "As to whether my work is or ever will be literature, I never bother my head. Time, the hearts of my readers, and the files of my publishers will find me my ultimate place."[16] Her place in literature was ultimately defined by Yale pundit William Lyon Phelps, who elevated her status to that of "a public institution, like Yellowstone Park."[17]

Her popularity peaked with a novel, *The Harvester*, that climbed to number one on the best-seller list in 1912. Thereafter, the demand for her books began an almost imperceptible, but steady, decline. By 1919 her status as a best-selling novelist had begun to erode seriously. Prior to this time, the United States had rallied to a dictum reflected in all of Gene Stratton-Porter's books: "Become a Self-Made Man! Produce! Achieve!" After World War I, however, the nation began to hear the rumbles of another generation: "Consume! Enjoy!" A Stratton-Porter novel released on the heels of the war failed to meet this new and growing pulsation, struggling to reach number nine on the best-seller list.[18] Only shortly before this downturn in the popularity of her novels became evident, this now famous woman had been otherwise inundated, nearly overwhelmed, by the difficulties posed by a son-in-law who was alleged to be both an alcoholic and a drug addict.[19] Thus, late in 1918, she had committed herself to a sanitarium under an assumed name. She emerged from this rest cure revitalized. Shortly thereafter she left her home in the Midwest for the sunlight of Los Angeles, there to preach the gospel of the out-of-doors from a new base. Once in California, however, she began to undergo a metamorphosis, experimenting with poetry and eventually becoming a moviemaker and an editorialist of nationwide circulation. With this branching out into unfamiliar mediums, Gene Stratton-Porter experienced her greatest personal growth, although this new three-way fragmentation of her energies further eroded her already tenuous hold on the public pulse. Only as an editorialist did her flame again flicker, and then only briefly.

At the time of her death Gene Stratton-Porter was widely mourned. A forest of ten thousand white pines was dedicated to her in the Adirondack Forest Preserve.[20] This memorial stands in the shadow of Tongue Mountain on Lake George, New York. Other commemorative services were conducted by the American Reforestation Association, which was also responsible for a memorial tree planting in each Los Angeles school yard.[21] Because of Gene Stratton-Porter's interest in and support of poetry, the College Woman's Salon of Los Angeles established an annual poetry award in her memory. Throughout the United States, obituaries observed her death, including several in national magazines such as *McCall's*, to which she had been a substantial contributor, and *Outdoor America*, a publication of the Izaak Walton League.[22]

According to her publishers, Gene Stratton-Porter did not possess "an aptitude for personal publicity."[23] Lack of "aptitude" does not begin to describe her dislike for personal publicity. Late in 1924 she did grant a rare personal interview to a reporter, but this interview failed at that time to make its way into print. Published after her death, it reveals Gene Stratton-Porter's feelings about a subject important to every modern generation. During the last three years of her life she was consumed with this timeless subject: the conflicting roles of women in a free society.

> What are women going to do with their natural instincts for love, marriage and children? That is the problem. Everywhere I see young women deliberately crushing down their normal desires for fundamental human things in order to take up some life work that will raise them above the level of "mere wifehood" and allow them to grasp the awards they conceive belong to man. Women are tearing themselves apart in their search for both lives—the sex and the mental. It is literally a travail of spirit. The cultured, modern woman is keen to do something worthwhile. She emerges from college all armored like a knight of old to do battle with the world. She has acquired the ideal of creative accomplishment; she endeavors to suppress her elementary instincts in order to attain it. The fun-

damental desires often prove too strong. She marries and has children—spends the next twenty-five years in the home. Then what? She is middle-aged. The middle-aged woman is, along with the flapper, the revolutionist of today. She is demanding her place in the world. But in the case of the middle-aged woman rebel, her seclusion has put her out of touch with life and opportunity and there are but few places she can really fill.[24]

During the 1920s, as Gene Stratton-Porter well understood, not all of America's women were flappers who rolled their stockings and spent their Saturday nights in a speakeasy getting high on bathtub gin. Contrary to popular legend, the vast majority of the nation's women at this time led a less glittering existence. Some of these women were formally educated; some of them, like Gene Stratton-Porter, were not. These were the secluded middle-aged women about whom she was so concerned, and for whom she felt a need to write of the deeper and uplifting things of life. These were women who hung out the wash every Monday and who depended for personal enjoyment upon a quiet swing on the front porch every night after supper—after they canned the pickles, emptied the ice pans, filled the lunch pails, and ironed the shirts. During the mid-1920s, these homemakers of America found justification for their existence every month of the year on page two of *McCall's* magazine under the byline of Gene Stratton-Porter. Editorials written by her expressed a homey brand of sanity predicated on common sense and the sanctity of the home. Through these editorials Gene Stratton-Porter eventually achieved to her own satisfaction her goal of being a Moses, at least from a literary standpoint. As a teacher of God's laws, Moses instructed his followers in the laws of physical and moral cleanliness, brotherly love, and tabernacle specifications, maintenance, and sanctification. Likewise, Gene Stratton-Porter instructed America's women in the laws

of physical and moral cleanliness and brotherly love, although
her specifications and laws for maintenance and sanctification
revolved around a different tabernacle, the American home.

By contrast with her thoughtful concern for women, Gene
Stratton-Porter's attitude toward men was charged with hostility. She felt the women of her generation, in terms of mental
development and appreciation of beauty, could back men "off
the map."[25] At times her writings clearly display her negative
feelings toward the male gender. In one instance she deplores
the shooting and stuffing of the rare Kirtland's warbler, a
northeastern North American bird that breeds in Michigan.
Asking if a woman would leave undisturbed this ornitho-
logical wonder, she declares: "A woman would; but did the
man?"[26] And in 1924, shortly before her death, she charged:
"Men are not the fine physical specimens they were forty years
ago, and neither are they the fine mental specimens; . . . they
are not writing better books or transacting business as honestly and fairly, while as to physical and moral courage most
of them have gone completely white-livered."[27]

Seldom did Gene Stratton-Porter permit herself such a ran-
corous outburst toward the opposite sex. Ordinarily she kept
her hostility toward men well hidden. A highly secretive person, she seldom revealed her innermost thoughts and feelings,
and then often unwittingly. One such rare exposure occurred
during the last twenty-four hours of her life, shortly after her
return home from a week's vacation along the California
coast. To all outward appearances, she seemed rested. According to her longtime secretary: "Her eyes were shining. I
was struck especially by their clearness and their untroubled
depths. She seemed at peace with the world."[28]

That evening, as her secretary later related, while studying
an issue of *Poetry* magazine, Gene Stratton-Porter discovered
a poem that struck a deep personal chord. The next morning,
after concluding her business dictation, she turned again to
this poem and read it aloud. Then again that evening, at din-

ner, she quoted from this poem for the third time, not knowing that she was reciting her own epitaph. Less than an hour later Gene Stratton-Porter met her death in a traffic accident near her home. Because of its special personal significance, this poem was recited at her funeral. It is a poem spoken by a mother to her infant, and it gives us a rare glimpse of the inner Gene Stratton-Porter:

> God is every lovely word
> You want to hear and haven't heard.
> And if you should need a place,
> After searching everywhere,
> To hide a secret, or your face—
> You could hide it there.
> God is much the safest place
> To hide a secret—or your face.[29]

Gene Stratton-Porter's best-kept secret had to do with her father, Mark Stratton. To him, more than anyone else, she said she owed much, and indeed, because of her father, she became a writer. He was a charismatic person whose persuasive powers bordered on the hypnotic, and his influence cannot be overemphasized. He was also the major source of her lifelong conflict.

Not all of Gene Stratton-Porter's statements about her father carry the weight of evidential authority. Many of her assertions about him are highly suspect. The first debt she maintained she owed her father had to do with his honorable English name, Stratton, although her statements with respect to her father's supposedly untarnished name are overdone. She protests too much, as if she were afraid she might be contradicted, or as if she might inadvertently contradict herself.

> My first debt to my father—and the one for which I think I should be more devoutly thankful for than any other—is the one I owe for having been brought into the world bearing an old and honorable name.

> When I say an "honorable" name, in the case of my
> father, I mean a name that never was touched by any
> faintest breath of scandal of any kind. . . . There was
> no man in our county who could point a finger of
> scorn at my father and whisper that when he held a
> position of trust in the church, in the schools, in the
> affairs of the county, he had managed matters to fur-
> ther his own ends, had used funds dishonestly, or had
> not faithfully administered his office.[30]

Whether this testimony about Mark Stratton can be believed is a subject for later in-depth examination. What matters at present is Gene Stratton-Porter's assertion that the
greatest debt she owed her father was for having been brought
into the world bearing an old and honorable name. Contrary
to her declaration, the greatest debt to her father had nothing
whatsoever to do with his name, but was an ear for the well-
turned phrase. He was an engaging raconteur. Most of all,
Gene Stratton-Porter owed her father high thanks for her
storytelling ability. Nevertheless, she always talked her way
around her father's chief talent. It is remarkable that not once
did she state that she could attribute to her father her ability
to hold an audience. She evidently could visualize her father
as an entertainer, for she once referred to his daily gyrations
and elocutionary exercises as a performance. However, she
was unable to pinpoint her father's greatest gift to her, a
superb yarn-spinning ability.

As a child, Gene Stratton-Porter loved her father's stories.
She was especially fond of the one he frequently told about
the day the first train had rumbled through their valley. On
his way to watch this exciting spectacle, her father had met
up with a recluse who had not yet heard about the train, so
he had invited old Joe to join him. The story Gene Stratton-
Porter's father later told about the train builds and concludes
in his usual well-done manner:

> After we had waited perhaps an hour, there came a curious, rumbling, humming sound; this grew and swelled in volume; the big black engine came tearing down the track; the headlight was glaring in the sun. We were sitting on the embankment; but as the train neared us, old Joe leaped to his feet and started to run, but I cried to him to wait and see the train, so he stopped and stood while it roared and thundered past. As it vanished, I turned to Joe. "God, Stratton," he said earnestly, "If you hadn't been here to tell me what that thing was, I'd have shot it!"[31]

Mark Stratton possessed a deep pride in being an Englishman. He even maintained, erroneously, that he shared a birthday with an English queen whom he liked to call his twin. In light of her father's Anglican bias and his storytelling ability, one of Gene Stratton-Porter's statements about him is entirely credible: "He used to say that he would rather see a child of his the author of a book of which he could be proud, than on the throne of England, which was the strongest way he knew to express himself."[32]

At maturity, Gene Stratton-Porter bore a striking resemblance to her charismatic father. Heavy, shaggy brows were her most prominent feature. Her mother's legacy was a busy pair of hands. Even as she dictated to her secretary, Gene Stratton-Porter fingered a string of beads. At the time of Gene Stratton-Porter's death, her daughter remarked especially about the absolute quiet of her hands. Gene Stratton-Porter's hands constantly fluttered; she was a toucher. Her voice, on the other hand, is less easily described. It was changeable, sometimes reflective and deliberate and other times sounding like her father's, almost like a chant. Another nature writer, Emma Lindsay Squier, noted: "When she speaks, it is with a slow drawl, almost nasal, that changes abruptly into a soft, swift monotone when she is intensely interested in what she is saying."[33]

On meeting Gene Stratton-Porter for the first time, Squier was much surprised. Expecting a "slim, yet rugged" figure, she was unprepared for a middle-aged woman whose face had none of the wild beauty she had envisioned, and whose figure was "frankly plump."[34] Perhaps because of her mannish brows, another acquaintance has described Stratton-Porter as "a very handsome woman—not in the sense of a pretty woman," further remarking on her beautiful teeth and dark brown, silky hair. This same person, who appears to have known Gene Stratton-Porter as well as anyone ever could know this extremely private person, in referring to her frequent proud boast that she had not a nerve in her whole body, loyally commented: "May she never make the discovery that she has."[35]

Spiritually, Gene Stratton-Porter worshiped poetry, a natural vehicle for the sensitive, counting it her "greatest joy" and pitying those who lacked the inclination or the necessary equipment to share a like appreciation. She felt particularly sorry for Charles Darwin who wrote that in his later years he had almost lost his taste for art and music and could not bear to read a line of poetry. "No one thing," she averred, "will have a greater tendency to leave our souls stranded and forlorn in age, than the failure to cultivate in youth a taste for great poetry." She expressed a belief that life without the uplifting influence of poetry would inevitably lead to "mental and spiritual poverty."[36] One of her own poems was an attempt to describe a beauty she could scarcely endure.

Such a passion for poetry brings to mind Thomas Babington Macaulay's speculation that perhaps no one can become a poet without a certain unsoundness of mind, for Gene Stratton-Porter was unsound, governed by a compulsion to dissimulate, especially with respect to her family background. To examine her statements about her formative years is to pick one's way through a maze constantly stumbling into yet another one of the myths she liked to perpetuate about

Robert M. Taylor, Jr.

Gene Stratton-Porter

herself and her relatives. She was a master of the whopper, at
first assessment seemingly even a victim of self-deceit who
appears to have believed the fairy tales she liked to concoct
about her early homelife and her supposedly harmonious
family relationships. Shortcomings aside, however, this con-
summate prevaricator emerges predominantly as a perennial
child with a zest for life and a boundless expectation for what
she might accomplish. Her exuberance was best expressed by
Grant Overton: "With Gene Stratton-Porter, the quality of
enthusiasm is not strained, it droppeth as torrential rains from
the heaven of her state of mind."[37]

Someone once asked Gene Stratton-Porter how she had
opened the doors to fame and, based on her own experience,
what advice could she offer to those who aspire to worldwide
recognition. Her answer reflects her own self-image. She
mentioned two personal characteristics appropriate to a latter-
day Moses, determination and courage, and recommended a
literary style that carried behind it "a hint of a fascinating
personality."[38]

Raging Fevers

FROM long exposure to the art, a talent for storytelling came naturally to Gene Stratton-Porter. Not only her father but also his oldest brother and her paternal grandfather could spin a yarn with alacrity. This family penchant for storytelling influenced Gene Stratton-Porter more than any other. As if by an unseen hand, the direction of her life would be determined primarily by her constant, early exposure to expressive narrative.

Among the many stories in the colorful repertoire of the Strattons was one of a personal nature that Gene Stratton-Porter never tired of hearing, a tale setting forth her paternal ancestry that her father liked to deliver in a ringing manner. As she was growing up, she heard this fireside tale, the "three brothers legend," often. Perhaps because of the impressive manner in which it was customarily recited, she accepted this oral genealogy without question, unaware that it could not be verified. Her father did not know that the Stratton family history as he presented it was a hodgepodge of half fact, half fiction, strung together loosely, just as his father had not known. This story would have a profound effect upon Gene Stratton-Porter.

> All Strattons are descended from ancient titled British
> families, one Duke Robert Stratton having been a fa-
> mous warrior during the reign of William and Mary
> of Orange. . . . I was named for an ancestor Mark
> Stratton, who came from England in early day and
> settled on Stratton Island which was later corrupted
> to Staten Island; afterward he moved to northern New
> Jersey. . . . Said Stratton had three sons, named Daniel,
> David, and Thomas. Daniel, your great-grandfather,
> settled in Vernon Township, Sussex County, northern
> New Jersey, about fifty miles west of New York.[1]

It was fairly common for a pioneer such as Gene Stratton-
Porter's father—short in worldly goods, but long on pride—
to claim direct descent from Charlemagne, or even the Black
Prince. Although Gene Stratton-Porter's father lacked that
much effrontery, he certainly could not verify a relationship
to any ancient titled British families, nor to a musty duke who
had been a famous warrior. Nor could he prove descent from
the first Mark Stratton who had come to America from England in colonial days—that Mark Stratton had sired five sons,
not three. Nor, even if three of the names of these sons had
matched his Stratton three brothers legend, which they did
not, could Daniel, David, and Thomas Stratton have been the
three sons of the first Mark Stratton to America—not unless
that first Mark Stratton had been a man of high agility in his
old age and even from the confines of a pine box.[2] Also, Staten
Island, of course, does not derive from Stratton. The holes in
the ancestral legend are so apparent that an amateur genealogist could easily find his way around them—but not Gene
Stratton-Porter. She fell into a genealogical hole as a child and
would never find her way out, even with assistance. Despite
historical untruths and anachronisms, she would never question her family history as she had heard it as a child. She
would defend it, and inevitably her insistence on her father's
veracity would be challenged by an experienced genealogist.

Compared with her references to her Stratton ancestry, Gene Stratton-Porter's statements about her mother's background are scant. In all her writing she allocates only a few words to her maternal ancestry: "My mother was of Dutch extraction on her mother's side, Swiss on her father's."[3] In this, she was again misled, if only partially. Her mother Mary was of German extraction. Little is known of Mary's background, although it is known that Mary's mother, Catherine Shallenberger, signed her name with an X. In this, Gene Stratton-Porter's maternal grandmother was no different from the majority of other midwestern pioneer women of her generation. Even Catherine Shallenberger's best-educated neighbors wrote her last name variously as Shellenberger, Shellebarger, and Shellabarger. Catherine's daughter Mary, Gene Stratton-Porter's mother, may also have been illiterate, at least before her marriage. Before that time Mary Shallenberger could not spell her last name correctly. She spelled it Shelibarger.[4]

Mary Stratton's father, Jacob Shallenberger, on the other hand, could read and write. And, as Gene Stratton-Porter asserted, her maternal grandfather Jacob was of Swiss descent. His name derived from the mountain on which his ancestors had lived in Switzerland, Schallenberger or Echo Mountain. As a child, Gene Stratton-Porter was surrounded by several Shallenberger cousins, aunts, and uncles. Nevertheless, she would always gloss over the Shallenbergers. We shall never know why she would choose to ignore the ancestry of her mother in favor of a broken chain of Strattons, although the suggestion arises that, by way of contrast with the seemingly literate Strattons, she did not wish to expose the educational shortcomings of her mother's family.

Gene Stratton-Porter's father was unquestionably the descendant of an Englishman, Stratton being an old English name meaning one who comes from Stratton, a homeplace

Mark Stratton

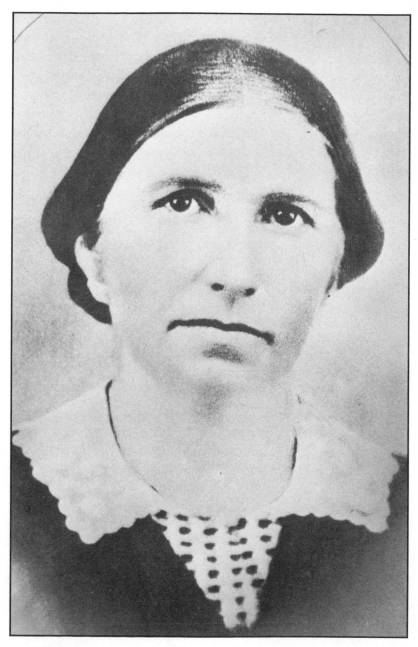

Mary Stratton

on a Roman road. More important, however, than accurately
charting her father's ancestry or refuting the genealogical yarn
he spun is examining the effect of his English puffery. The
Anglican warp of Mark Stratton shows nowhere more clearly
than in one of Gene Stratton-Porter's lapses into fantasy many
years after her father's death. Moreover, this childlike fantasy,
penned when she was over fifty, brings into sharp focus her
underlying desire to legislate, to become a lawgiver with the
weight of a Moses:

> I have wondered sometimes if a throne could be erected
> upon which was to be placed a ruler for all the world,
> a universal ruler who should deliver edicts that must
> be obeyed by every man and woman of every nation
> on earth. I have wondered if such a throne could be
> erected and if I might sit on it myself and hold the
> symbols of power in my hands, what would be the
> first things I would decree. I have carried that thought
> in my heart for years, ever since I was a little girl who
> was some day going to be the Queen of the greatest
> nation on earth at that time, the Queen of that nation
> on whose possessions the sun never set . . . who my
> father always said was his twin, because they had been
> born on the same day.[5]

Although the background of the Strattons carries no verifiable trace of royalty, their family tree was one of which any
American could be proud. And, as Mark Stratton had
insisted, there was indeed a warrior hanging on one of
their branches—not an ancient English warrior to be sure,
but a warrior just the same. As a matter of fact there were
two of them. One of them was Gene Stratton-Porter's great-
grandfather, a guard along the Atlantic coast during the
American Revolution.[6] The second Stratton warrior was one
of her great-uncles, a colonial patriot whose military valor
fairly cries to be sung. When Thomas Stratton enlisted in the
Continental army in 1775, it cost him dearly. Over the course
of the next three years he lost his hearing and otherwise per-

manently impaired his health, all because he suffered winter exposure with Washington's troops at Valley Forge.[7]

The next generation of Strattons was more peaceable. When the British stirred American waters a second time, the Strattons stayed home. During the War of 1812 Gene Stratton-Porter's paternal grandfather was raising flax in the flinty low mountains of northern New Jersey. It was there, on a small farm in Sussex County, that her father was born on 27 September 1812. When he was only three, his parents succumbed to the prevailing affliction known as Ohio fever. This affliction's chief symptom was a belief in an extremely mild climate west of the Allegheny Mountains, a belief touched off many years earlier by Thomas Jefferson. Weather observation was a hobby of Jefferson's. Later, Frenchman Constantin François Chasseboeuf, comte de Volney, had expanded on one of Jefferson's theories. In 1804, one year after Ohio had become a state, Volney had declared the climate of the basin of the Ohio and Mississippi rivers to be less cold than that of the Atlantic coast, stating that in the wintertime, throughout the basin of the Ohio, snow commonly remained only from three to eight or ten days.[8]

Whether or not Gene Stratton-Porter's grandparents actually believed there was less commotion in the atmosphere west of the Alleghenies, in the fall of 1815 they joined the general westward migration toward the Ohio valley. Their trek was difficult; its vicissitudes, many. Those months when the Strattons inched their way westward would be known as the year without a summer. Frost and ice prevailed throughout the northeastern United States even during the summer of 1816.[9] Not until late in 1817, after a lengthy sojourn with relatives in Pennsylvania, did the migrating Strattons reach their destination, a heavily timbered 160-acre tract about thirty-five miles south of Lake Erie, in Wayne County, Ohio.[10] They arrived in December, by this time surely aware that the winter climate west of the Alleghenies would be more bitter than balmy. During the long course of their icy trek to Ohio, these wayfarers were delivered of another child, the fifth in a brood that would eventually number fourteen. Eleven of these siblings would survive to adulthood, a testament not only to their sturdiness but also to their watchful upbringing.

The backwoods where the pioneering Strattons settled was unbroken wilderness, primitive beyond description. Livestock commonly perished because of wolves. Because Wayne County, Ohio, was sparsely settled, no local system of government operated here when this family first arrived. Two years later, twenty-one persons gathered at an ashery to cast their ballots in Canaan Township's first election. Gene Stratton-Porter's grandfather was elected a justice of the peace. As one of the few locals on this frontier who could read and write, Joseph Stratton also served as a schoolteacher to the neighborhood.[11]

Unlike her literate husband, Elizabeth could not even write her own name, although one source erroneously cites her as having been a woman of "unusual education," perhaps a reference to her uncommon good sense. Altogether, Gene Stratton-Porter's paternal grandmother was considered by her neighbors to be a woman of "refinement," a compliment at least partially attributable to a magnificent clock in a hand-carved case she had shepherded all the way to Ohio from New Jersey.[12] Such a clock was a symbol of luxury; many settlers had no timepiece whatsoever. An elegant clock, such as that belonging to Elizabeth Stratton, signified more than wealth; it represented good taste, even fine breeding.

Once in Ohio, Joseph Stratton affiliated with that state's most dominant sect. With more than the usual enthusiasm, he turned to Methodism. Appropriately, he eventually joined a Wayne County sect known as the "Bend" Methodists. Those who knew him well considered him a zealot, excessive in his theological pursuits.[13]

To sustain his family's physical needs, Joseph Stratton plied its members with corn, buckwheat, potatoes, beans, pork, and wild game. To sustain their spiritual needs, he plied them with the Bible. More than that, he pounded them with it. He demanded that his children memorize the Good Book in its entirety. At his command they were expected to respond with chapter and verse and to cite the location of any scripture instantly. To accomplish this mighty feat of memorization, this religious fanatic relied on corporal punishment. A dependable teaching tool, the leather strap, also taught his children to read. One of his descendants, as if still in awe of his wrath, later tempered her description of her grandfather's merciless scholastic expectations with an equivocal statement: "Although the kindest of fathers in his home he so prided himself on his impartiality toward his own children in school as to be almost Spartan in his treatment of them, and many were the hard tasks and sound thrashings that he gave them."[14] School lessons aside, it was Joseph Stratton's zealotry that left the greatest mark on his children. Anna, the oldest, was the first to emerge from her father's prickly vineyard with a predictable accomplishment. Twice in her lifetime she was able to repeat the entire Bible before a committee.

Likewise, with the exception of the books of generations, Joseph Stratton's son Mark, who would become Gene Stratton-Porter's father, early on committed the Bible to memory, a babbling feat that would both carry and bury his future reputation as a literate man. Bible memorization was not the singular achievement of the Strattons, but the hallmark of a strict religious upbringing during the nineteenth century. John Muir, the noted naturalist, confirms how it was done: "By the time I was eleven years of age I had about three fourths of the Old Testament and all of the New by heart and by sore flesh."[15] Gene Stratton-Porter's father grew to manhood to the tune of fanaticism enforced by the rod. As might be expected, steeped from infancy in the Song of Solomon, his vocabulary was rich in simile. When he married, he displayed this love for comparison by describing his bride as a "ninety-pound bit of pink porcelain, pink as a wild rose, plump as a partridge."[16]

Mary Shallenberger was nineteen and Mark Stratton twenty-three when they tied the knot forever. Because Stratton's bride was the miller's daughter and trained to industry, she was indeed a prize. It was to a mill tended by a man named Jacob Shallenberger and owned by a man named Naftzger that Joseph Stratton and his sons had customarily taken their grain to be ground, and it was there at Naftzger's Mill that the future parents of Gene Stratton-Porter had met. Jacob Shallenberger, the tidy miller who was Gene Stratton-Porter's maternal grandfather, had settled in Wayne County in 1814 when a road had been hacked to his millsite through dense forest from the town of Wooster, a few miles to the east.[17] The words were said over Mark Stratton and Mary Shallenberger on 24 December 1835.[18] Almost twenty-eight years would go by before the birth of their daughter the writer. In the meantime, the gifted storyteller who would one day become her father would show himself time and time again to be a survivor with a conniving bent.

One year after Gene Stratton-Porter's parents were married, family matters took an unexpected turn. In December 1836 her grandfather Joseph died. Suddenly, as if freed from bondage, her father laid a hasty groundwork for flight from Ohio. First, in need of a financial springboard, he bought a nearby tract of land on speculation, knowing he could turn it over shortly at a profit.[19] Then he settled his father's affairs with the utmost dispatch, parceling out his mother's meager dower and living allowance. This he did in a revealing manner. To sustain her soul, Elizabeth Stratton received her husband's Bible and a looking glass. To maintain herself and her seven minor children, she was allotted only the barest necessities. The major portion of her household goods and her husband's personal effects was consigned to public auction, pursuant to statute, and that included the family clock.[20]

This clock meant much to Elizabeth Stratton. More than a means to tell time, it was the only piece in her home that demonstrated her appreciation for fine things, her only possession with other than utilitarian value. Despite the availability in Wayne County by that time of all kinds of fancy goods—violins, Swiss linens, and even queensware, a cream-colored earthenware long since perfected by Josiah Wedgwood—Elizabeth Stratton's home was nearly bare. She even lacked such a common houseware as a frying pan. The merchants in nearby Wooster were easy enough to deal with, one proprietor advertising that produce would be taken in exchange for goods. Nevertheless, Joseph Stratton's widow had no extra produce to exchange for the local finery. Given her poor circumstances, she was certainly in no position to bid on anything at the auction of her household goods and her husband's personal property, much less a valuable clock. Yet she bid on it until she won it and paid for it by executing a promissory note.[21] Although the means by which Elizabeth Stratton eventually satisfied this promissory note are unknown, we know she never relinquished her tenacious hold on this clock. Years later, as a blind old lady, she would allow no one to wind this treasure, her most valuable possession, which, but for her persistence, might have long since been lost to her along with her sense of pride so closely associated with it.

With like equanimity, her son Mark had consigned two other important family items to this public auction. One of them sold to his brother William, the other went home with a neighbor. The items were two historical books, representing Joseph Stratton's entire library. These were the books he had brought into the wilderness, along with his Bible, from which his children had learned to read. There is no question that the Stratton children's education was deficient by reason of their father's slim teaching resources. Surviving legal documents confirm and expose their shortcomings, showing no great familiarity with spelling, often phonetic, or even capitalization, equally hesitant and inconsistent.

Short on scholastic equipment, but long on resolve, Mark Stratton was determined to leave Ohio. Evoking a gift of salesmanship, he immediately unloaded that tract of land he had earlier purchased on speculation at triple his initial investment.[22]

Ready at last to leave home in search of greener pastures, he had no reason to be concerned about his younger brothers and sisters or his mother. Although his older brother William had recently married, one of his younger brothers was single. Thus it was arranged that unencumbered Daniel Stratton, then only nineteen, would remain at home as the caretaker of newly widowed Elizabeth Stratton and her several dependents: six girls, all under fifteen, and Cyrus, only thirteen. Teenage Daniel appears to have been Joseph and Elizabeth Stratton's most conscientious offspring. He was the only son to bid on household goods to give back to his mother at the auction of his father's property.[23]

With responsibility for the well-being of his mother and her seven minor children placed squarely on the shoulders of his younger brother Daniel, Mark Stratton prepared to leave Ohio to look for farmland elsewhere, intending to return home at some future unspecified date. In the meantime he had become a father, and his wife was again expectant. This determined individual did not think twice in his preoccupied state of mind about leaving an infant and a wife who was seven months pregnant. Uppermost in Mark Stratton's mind were not the needs of his wife, his widowed mother, or anyone else, but a more important matter, a matter of the highest priority. Like his father before him, he had succumbed to the prevailing affliction. Typical of his generation, he had been smitten by the common contagion: Wabash fever.

 3

Praying Overtime

WABASH, a promising name, a venerable name. The name of a valley, the home of a river. The Wabash is a verdant valley, made green by a river that springs to life in northern Ohio. The destination of the Wabash River is 475 miles from her point of origin. She flows southwesterly, primarily through Indiana, forming the lower portion of the state's western border. When she reaches Indiana's bottom left-hand corner, her waters are drawn into an even larger river, the Ohio.

Today the lush valley fed by the Wabash and her tributaries is a national grain basket. Three hundred years ago this valley was uncultivated. Clusters of hawthorn and plum, tangled with grapevines, sprang from her riverbanks. Cacklers and loud honkers crowded the skies over her bottomlands, rich with wild hops and crab apples. Guarding this wilderness, and towering majestically over it, were giant sycamores, destined to reign for five hundred years. Long before music enhanced the charms of the sycamore along the banks of the Wabash and long before white men set foot here, this valley was the home of the Indians, whose reverence for this plentiful valley and her silvery rivers was first echoed by the French. When the beaver-trapping French rediscovered this valley, they confirmed her bounteous properties and wanted to name her life-giving river after a saint. But it was the English—the mapping, plotting English—who officially named this white shimmering river. And when they finally christened her, they laid aside their native prejudice, if only for a moment, to baptize this gleaming river in a spirit of compromise. They crowned her with a French name, "Ouabache," from the Indian word for "white," *Wah-bah-shik-ki.*[1]

Much of the territory fanning out from the bountiful Wabash River became known as the state of Indiana in 1816. Indiana was settled from her bottom up, her southern border being the Ohio River. After 1830 immigrants began to spill also into northern Indiana, this time along roads forged from the east. By 1837 only a trickle of Indians remained in the verdant Wabash valley. Most would soon be gone, victims of forced resettlement, including the infamous march to Kansas later known as the "Trail of Death."

Like southern Indiana, the lush valleys fed by the Wabash River and her tributaries in northern Indiana appeared to be the white man's promised land. Many of the migrants to this region, however, were drawn not only by the upper Wabash valley's pledge of productivity. Some were equally attracted by another element, a water transportation system that was being developed across Indiana along two of its major rivers. This artificial watercourse—the Wabash and Erie Canal— would eventually connect with other systems to carry farm produce to distant world markets.[2] Mark Stratton was one of the men who itched to investigate the farmland bordering this new canal and began his westward quest toward it in January 1838.

Ordinarily the swamps along Mark Stratton's route across northern Ohio toward Indiana would have been frozen solid. The weather had been unusually mild that winter, however, and heavy rains, instead of the usual snow, had turned his road through these swamps into a sea of mud, pocked with deep holes. All the way to Toledo, at the easternmost point of Lake Erie, he competed for a slippery toehold with drovers, pony carts, high-wheeled carriages, and horse-drawn freight wagons. Once out of Toledo, although the mud persisted, the traffic began to thin as he followed the Maumee River, a southwesterly trace that led him over the border of Ohio toward the populous town of Fort Wayne, Indiana. There he picked up the projected route of the Wabash and Erie Canal. He was now within thirty-five miles of Wabash County, Indiana, his destination. As he followed the proposed route of the canal, he occasionally met up with a few Irish, the chief source of canal construction labor from the East. Otherwise, his trek grew increasingly solitary.

When he finally reached the village of Lagro, the tiny Indiana settlement for which he had been bound, he stopped and made several inquiries. Much to his disappointment, he learned that the farmland thereabouts would not do. An earlier wagonload of settlers had been unable to camp near Lagro because of rattlesnakes. Even after moving on a few miles, they had found numerous reptiles still in residence. Finally, after killing eighteen of these potential bed partners, the men, as well as the women and children, had slept in the wagons. As Stratton later related: "Rattlesnakes had been exceedingly abundant in dens among the rocks in the bluffs of the rivers and creeks. One den was near Rattlesnake Springs, half a mile above the town of La Gro. . . . There was one also on the Salimony River, near Dora, in South La Gro."[3]

So he kept on going. After fording the Eel River, a tributary of the Wabash, he hopscotched several miles up into Kosciusko County, a wilderness dotted with numerous lakes. Although he saw many deer and turkey, even signs of bear and wolves, he tramped at one stretch for fourteen miles without seeing another person.[4] His inspection of the land to the

north soon completed, once again he vetoed an entire area.
A fever known as miasma, then believed to be caused by
noxious swamp exhalations, was taking a large toll of those
settlers in the most heavily populated sections of Kosciusko
County, particularly in its northern and central regions. Less
than two months later the most frequently used road through
Kosciusko County would be the road leading to the cemetery.[5] Although the northern and central terrain of this county
was generally level, some of it only gently rolling, Kosciusko
County had several wet prairies. These prairies were eagerly
sought by some because of their ease of cultivation, but those
with sense knew enough to avoid the miasma-inducing wet-
lands. Thus it was that Mark Stratton turned around and
headed back south to survey more carefully the border between Kosciusko and Wabash counties. It was there that he
finally found what he had in mind—a 160-acre tract, mostly
level, traversed by a small brook. This site was heavily timbered, but it had definite possibilities. The ground was comparatively dry—fewer snakes and less chance of miasma—and
the heavy stand of timber could be felled.

After he bought it, he returned to Ohio via a southern,
circuitous route, thereby avoiding the swamps. Upon his return home, he was wont to dismiss his seven-hundred-mile
journey with a touch of the blarney: "The jaunt took something more than a month, being performed on foot of course,
since (as the Irishman said) that was decidedly the 'natest and
chapest' way of getting about."[6] Three months later he loaded
his family, by this time including a second infant, into a wagon
pulled by a horse that belonged to his wife. Now he was ready.
In June 1838, with high hopes, he again headed west, back to
that promising tract of virgin soil he had purchased less than
fifteen miles north of the Wabash and Erie Canal.

Getting a foothold in upper Wabash County during the late
1830s was possible only for the hardy. More than one family
lived on pumpkin and potatoes from July through September

until their corn was fit to grind. Even those who had enough
to eat often hankered for seasoned food. Salt was dear, sixteen
dollars a barrel. Men willing to trap or hunt could barter with
fur traders for staples, but Mark Stratton was a farmer, not a
trapper and not a hunter. Although squirrel was necessarily
a staple on his table, he lacked the inclination to trap or to
hunt for big game, or even for wolves, which paid a $2 bounty,
and he did not rely on bounties or the sale of hides to augment
his meager subsistence:

> I never was a hunter; I never shot at a deer but once in
> my life, killing that, however, instantly. I once chased
> a young fawn for a long time, catching it at last when
> nearly worried down. I came upon the little creature
> suddenly, when it sprang nimbly and started to run,
> and I after it. It ran in circles, and I followed in pursuit,
> when at last it sprang against a log and stumbled and
> fell, and before the frightened little thing could recover
> itself, I seized it and held the creature fast.[7]

One day he encountered a more dangerous animal. While
showing the surrounding countryside to prospective settlers
from Ohio, including his wife's brother John, his party came
upon an old bear and her three cubs. Unarmed, yet hopeful
of gaining a useful hide or two, he ran about a mile to the
cabin of the closest neighbor. When he returned with help,
the old bear had been frightened off, and her cubs were treed.
The yarn he later spun about these bruins was one he was
fond of repeating:

> Our plan was to shoot and cripple one of the young
> fellows in the tree, and having brought him down to
> pinch and tease him to make him squeal, and thus
> cause the mother to come to his relief, so as to get her,
> too, within range and reach of the gun. That part of
> the plan, however, did not succeed. Mr. Bussard [the
> neighbor] took the first shot, because he was the owner
> of the gun; Noftsker [Joseph Noftzker] shot the second

time, because he wished to be able to tell his neighbors
when he got back to Ohio that he killed a bear; and
Hammond [another neighbor] drew trigger the third
and last time, and every shot killed a bear. Mr.
Bussard's shot killed one of the cubs dead—dead—
dead. It did not even struggle nor move a particle after
it struck the ground. Noftsker, taking the rifle, drew
up, and he, too, made a sure shot, and his game fell
lifeless to the earth. Hammond took a slow and cautious aim, and drawing trigger, down came the third
also, and he, too, was dead. None of them made any
noise, and we saw no more of the old bear. The hides
of the young cubs were quickly stripped from the dead
bodies, and the carcasses were left to rot upon the
ground, or for the poor old mother to drag away, and
we went on and finished looking at the land.[8]

Whether John Shallenberger, Mark Stratton's brother-
in-law, was impressed most by this encounter with the bears
or by Wabash River country is impossible to know. In any
event, favorably disposed, John returned to Ohio bearing such
good tidings that he was able to persuade his parents to mi-
grate to the upper Wabash valley also. Elderly Jacob Shallenberger would die after only five years in this wilderness,
although his son John survived and prospered in Wabash
County as a farmer and grain buyer.

Chief among the preoccupations of the Wabash valley
farmer, of course, was the clearing of land. By deadening—
chopping a notch around each tree, waiting a year or more,
then applying the torch—an ordinary farmer could add from
two to five acres to his plowland every year. A workhorse
like Mark Stratton could add ten. He also had an added advantage. He knew how to come up with an extra dollar when
he absolutely needed it. Having relied successfully on land
speculation to get started, he tried again during his first few
years in this wilderness to make a profitable land turnover,
and again he succeeded. Although the records fail to disclose

how he obtained it, he acquired a large parcel that lay east of his farm and then sold it late in 1843 for almost twice the going rate per acre, making this turnover at a time when he sorely needed money for salt and other staples.[9] That winter was so harsh that even turkey and deer froze to death.

Over the next five years, those who had chosen to farm in the vicinity of the Wabash and Erie Canal began to see their faith in such a location justified. Wheat prices in the upper Wabash valley doubled after 1843 because of the canal. By 1848 the town of Wabash—a few miles downstream from Lagro—boasted nine warehouses, and it was common to see wagons carrying grain lined along the sides of the road to the river, while even more wagons lined up along the surrounding streets, waiting for their chances to unload. As many as five hundred scow-like boats loaded with grain and pork were navigating the Wabash and Erie Canal in 1848. It has been estimated that during the 1840s between five hundred thousand and one million bushels of grain were shipped each season from the town of Wabash.[10]

In the meantime, as this area had begun to develop, most of Lagro's snakes had been safely lodged for all time in kingdom come. Many had been dumped one winter by the cartload, frozen and benumbed, into the canal.[11] Many had been eaten by the hogs which ran at large. Hundreds of these rattlers were burned in excess timber piles during the construction of the canal, and hundreds more had starved when the entrances to their dens were boarded up, although more than one early settler could testify that confinement was a small deterrent to those persistent reptiles who then ate each other.

After five years on the Kosciusko/Wabash County border, the vipers no longer posing a threat, Mark Stratton made arrangements to move to that area where he had first hoped to buy a farm. In 1848 he purchased a large farmstead near the settlement of Lagro in the immediate neighborhood of the canal.[12] During this period he also had acquired another parcel of real estate. He had no deed to this most recent acquisition, yet when the time came to move on he was readily able to unload all of his farmland.[13] Whether he ever tangled with an attorney to the detriment of his pocketbook over any of his early real estate transactions is now uncertain, although it is certain that thereafter he retained a healthy respect for the money a pettifogger could command, as well as a heightened appreciation for the argumentative nature of lawyers in general.

Like his first farm, Mark Stratton's second farm was densely wooded. Throughout Wabash County a heavy stand of timber was succumbing only gradually to cultivated fields. The aggravating Wabash sycamore, not yet the object of lyrical tribute, would not yield to deadening; it frequently reached 125 feet in height and from 5 to 7 feet in diameter, but produced no fruit and was considered useless as wood.

After reserving trees suitable for firewood and fence rails, the Wabash County farmer burned indiscriminately to make way for his plow—oak, beech, basswood, poplar, walnut, wild cherry—but even the farmer could not burn it all. Timber was still plentiful, and lumber found its way to town. Nothing but oak would hold brine and whiskey. The sound of coopers' hammers as they tightened barrel hoops was a familiar one in the stirring village of Lagro. Her rutted streets hummed; saddlers, blacksmiths, wagonmakers, canalboatmen, grocery dealers, more than twenty carpenters, and even a newly arrived broom maker from Pennsylvania were all busily employed. Four lawyers served Lagro Township, as well as six physicians.[14] Women and children suffering from bilious fever had their choice of ague drops every evening or a powder every other morning. Their husbands and fathers, especially the combative Irish left over from construction days on the canal, preferred a more soothing palliative for their maladies; they found it at the local tavern.

In 1850 the average age of Lagro Township's entrepreneurs and farmers was only thirty-seven, hard evidence of their vitality.[15] Mark Stratton was thirty-eight and had an even greater aversion to failure than his robust neighbors. Under his autocratic hand, his farm had begun to dispense life's necessities. He was able to barter corn for leather, butter and eggs for dry goods, and fruits and vegetables for coffee and tea. With pride in pruning, trimming, and grafting, he had begun to turn the environs of his home into a functional as well as a beautiful garden. Because of his industry, he was eventually able to afford a part-time farmhand to help with the chores.

To aid himself financially, this up-and-coming businessman was always on the lookout for a bargain in real estate, and in 1852 he made the buy of a lifetime.[16] It would be his last major real estate transaction, and with it he would be well pleased. He finagled an assignment to himself of an additional eighty acres adjoining his new farm on the east. He bought these eighty acres for only fifty dollars. It was not the best land in the world. Cut up by several streams, it would be difficult to farm. Lagro Creek, the principal northern branch of the Wabash River, ran down the middle of it. In addition, one corner of this land was useless for farming purposes because it was being used as a public cemetery. Stratton felt so good about his purchase that he allowed his church to build a frame meetinghouse next to the burial ground on one corner of this otherwise useless land and continued to allow the use of this corner as a public cemetery.

Over the years, bent on self-improvement, this ambitious farmer bought books to supplement his meager education. As he did the Bible, he committed much to memory and could recite numerous passages from these books by rote. And, over the years, no less bent on salvation, he relied on his hard-earned biblical knowledge. After passing an examination on doctrine and discipline, he was licensed in 1858 by the Methodist Episcopal Church as a local preacher.[17] This title of local preacher was probably bestowed upon him not only because he had passed an examination, but also because he had exhibited, through gifts, grace, and usefulness, special qualities. At the same time he earned yet another title, that of Wabash County Commissioner, serving in that capacity from 1858 through 1863.[18]

Not surprisingly, in keeping with his twin beliefs in hard work and the Judgment Day, this pillar of the community had chosen his wife on the basis of two important qualifications: her vitality and her Christian name. At the time of his marriage, he had concluded his Solomon-like description of his bride as "never ill a day in her life, and bearing the loveliest name ever given a woman—Mary."[19] And, as a wife, Mary Stratton had put her vitality to work in the way most valuable to a pioneer farmer, as a bearer of future farmers. A typical farm family in Lagro Township in the mid-nineteenth century had eight or more children. In this respect Mary Stratton was more than typical for she bore twelve children. However, by the time her last child was on the way in 1863, none of her children had fulfilled her husband's high expectations, nor would they ever do so.

In 1857 his eldest had married a young man of the neighborhood who was the son of a boisterous Democrat. When Catherine Stratton married the son of Riley Marshall, she became the aunt of Thomas R. Marshall, who would later become governor of Indiana and vice president under Woodrow Wilson. Mark Stratton could not know that, however, nor would he have cared. The Marshalls were Democrats, and Democrats were anathema to a hidebound Republican like Mark Stratton.

By 1863 his second daughter, Anastasia, a schoolteacher, was preparing to marry a lawyer, an argumentative calling that might jeopardize anyone's safe crossing. His third daughter, Mary Ann, had hired herself out as a domestic. His fourth and fifth daughters had died of childhood diseases. Samira and Louisa Jane had long rested in that public cemetery on one corner of his farm.

Every true farmer intends, of course, that his first son should also become a farmer. Jerome, Mark Stratton's first son and perhaps his greatest disappointment, not only wanted to become a lawyer instead of a farmer, but also liked the taste of whiskey. By 1863 none of Mark Stratton's prayers for his second son had been answered, for like Jerome, fifteen-year-old Irvin also wanted to become a lawyer. Moreover, the only other thing Irvin ever seemed to think about was horses. Yet, when his last child was on the way, this eternal expectant still had hopes for his children yet at home—Florence, twelve; Leander, ten; Lemon, seven; and Ada, five. Mark Stratton especially had high hopes for Leander. Finally, in Leander, he had a son who said he wanted to become a farmer, a son who loved the soil.

His twelfth child was unexpected, conceived when he and his wife were convinced that her childbearing days were over. On 17 August 1863, when Geneva—later known as Gene—made her entrance, Mark Stratton was fifty, his wife forty-seven. They gave her the middle name of Grace, perhaps in the hope that by the grace of God she would be the last one, which she was. She was a quiet baby, seemingly content, and her father expected to rear her the same way he had reared her brothers and sisters, with his voice alone. Mark Stratton could not know that in Gene he had a child with a strength and a drive to surpass his own. He did not suspect that, in order to bring up his last child, he would have to pray overtime.

The Hum of Life

BY the time the twelfth and final blessing had
been added to their household, the pioneer
struggles of the Strattons had eased considerably. Twenty-five years had gone by since their
immigration to the Wabash valley, and the forests had faded away. In keeping with Mark
Stratton's most-used word, "tidy," his farm presented a neat
appearance. A public highway now bisected his acreage, yet
not a weed grew in any fence corner on either side of the road.
Bridges spanned the creeks that ran the length of his land, and
oak rail fences contained his bountiful fields. His wife's industry was equally in evidence. Close by the house a large
vegetable garden flourished behind a screen of cinnamon
pinks and hollyhocks.

A shining double carriage with side lamps and patent
leather trimmings occupied space in the big red barn, also
home to a pair of long-tailed matched grays. Nearby, a two-
story house sat solidly on two-feet-square hewed hardwood
beams. Inside, dainty paper graced the parlor walls, and baskets of flowers danced between bands of cream and green
velvet. The parlor furniture, red cherry and black walnut, was
covered with shiny black haircloth. In back of the parlor, off

to one side of the kitchen, an ample pantry overflowed with
barrels of sugar, flour, and cornmeal. Two fireplaces in this
farmhouse held backlogs big enough to burn for days, and
throughout all of the rooms except the kitchen, soft paddings
of wheat straw underlay bright carpets.

Out behind this comfortable dwelling stood a neat
woodshed, although the most inviting picture there was the
orchard in springtime, its fallen blossoms a big pale pink
blanket with a border of deeper pink. In the corners of this
orchard bloomed privet, catalpa, and sweet lilac. Among the
many flowers surrounding her childhood home, there was
one that the youngest Stratton was fondest of recalling. She
remembered especially the intoxicating scent of the petals of
a sweetbrier that spread its wide branches near a corner of the
family's back porch. This fragrant rose was also her mother's
favorite. Proud of the overall appearance of her home and its
grounds, she considered it a privilege to have been born on
such a well cared for farm: "No other farm was ever quite so
lovely as the one on which I was born after this father and
mother had spent twenty-five years beautifying it."[1]

One of her earliest distinct memories concerned a bird. She
was much perplexed one morning to find a woodpecker lying
still in the grass. It had been shot by one of her brothers as it
raided the fruit in the orchard. Determined to revive this
creature, she first spread its wings and tossed it into the air.
That failing, she launched it from a second-story window,
but still it would not fly. Next she pried open its beak and
stuffed it with green gooseberries. It was not until she asked
her father what she could do to help the woodpecker fly that
she heard, for the first time, the word *dead*. And when she
heard it, immediately she sensed its import—not because of
her father's explanation, however lucid that might have been,
but because of her own unsuccessful resuscitative efforts.
Much distressed, she tendered her father a business proposi-
tion: "If you will make the boys stop shooting woodpeckers,
I will not eat another cherry. The birds may have all of mine."[2]

She said he agreed to this, but her mother declared that such a sacrifice was unnecessary. Mary Stratton commanded that the bird shooting stop, stating that there were enough cherries in the orchard for everyone in the family, as well as enough for the birds.

When Gene was only a toddler, her mother contracted typhoid fever, a disease from which she never fully recovered. This unstable physical condition may have been caused by an occasional sequel to typhoid fever known as typhoid spine, a stiff back accompanied by physical weakness and severe pains in the spine. Gene later had little use for any clinical explanation, however, preferring to attribute the vacillating state of her mother's health to sheer exhaustion, brought on by long years of pioneer drudgery.

When her mother took to her bed and her older sisters took over, Gene must have sensed that she was underfoot in the house because she took to the out-of-doors. Allowed to wander the farm unsupervised, she roamed at will, napping in fence corners while her father worked the fields nearby with his hired help and her brothers. She later described these pre-school years: "By the day I trotted from one object which attracted me to another, singing a little song of made-up phrases about everything I saw while I waded catching fish, chasing butterflies over clover fields, or following a bird with a hair in its beak."[3] Her daughter, Jeannette Porter Meehan, tells that she was given to understand that her mother "ran wild all day, and no questions were asked so long as she appeared on time for meals."[4]

Gene's closest family relationship at this time was with her teenage brother Leander, whom she affectionately called Laddie, and whom she later wrote that she adored. No less strong than Gene's love for Laddie was his love for her. An ideal older brother, he was thoughtful and kind.

On the other hand, her adolescent brother Lemon, three years younger than Laddie, was considerably different. Although he looked angelic, Lemon was inclined to devil-

ment. A little towhead, his mother sometimes called
him "weiskopf." Lemon was undoubtedly the namesake of
the Reverend Orange Lemon, the presiding elder who had
appointed Mark Stratton a local preacher. The name of this
divine, however, did not always fit. There were many times
when it must have seemed to the Strattons that they should
have named their son Demon instead of Lemon for he was
more than ornery. Once, when he talked Gene into swinging on a sapling, she flew completely over the top of it and
landed in the pigpen. Another time, he put a noose around
his little sister's neck and pushed her off a barrel, having
first explained to her that she should tell him when she was
finished hanging, then he would replace the barrel. She was
rescued in the nick of time by her father, who by chance
was working close by in the barnyard. Lemon's fiendish
ideas met with more resistance from Ada who, at nearly
Lemon's age, was old enough to take care of herself. Sometimes, buffered by the presence of Ada, Gene played "Indian"
with her sister and her devilish brother. She also liked to
go with them down to the nearby creek where all of them,
especially Lemon, took great delight in pushing into the
water the big black snakes that sunned themselves on the logs
lining the creek.

Ordinarily, however, because of her mother's illness and
the industry of the others in her family, the smallest Stratton
played by herself. For companionship as she roamed the farm,
she liked to cradle a doll made from an ear of corn and
wrapped in the wide leaves of a catalpa. An unusually energetic and alert child, she explored her surroundings with intense curiosity. And as she wandered, she looked up, as
children do, not down, and thus it is no wonder that her
attention soon came to be fixed on birdlife. Heavy concen-
trations of birds—especially wild pigeons, which frequently
darkened the sky in droves—were exceedingly common during the nineteenth century, a familiar sight to any farm child.
Young Gene Stratton had more than the average child's spon-

taneous interest in the study of living things, however, and she liked to sit for long periods in a forked branch of a catalpa in the dooryard, watching the larks that undulated overhead in scattered flocks and the swallows that darted back and forth under the eaves of the barn. Up among the clouds she sometimes glimpsed the red-tailed hawk, a bird she would always envy because its freedom was even greater than her own: "I envied these birds their power to soar in the face of the wind, to ride with the stiff gale of a beating storm, or to hang motionless as if frozen in air, according to their will, as I envied nothing else on earth."[5]

One day, while wandering the fields alone, she pushed through the tall grass of a meadow to its far side, on her way to play in a nearby brook. When she got there, she made an unexpected discovery. There, in a towering oak tree overhanging the brook, hung a bird nest bigger than a bushel basket. Observing it quietly for a few minutes, she soon learned that this huge nest was the home of a pair of red-tailed hawks. Immediately, she began to worry. She had heard her father state in no uncertain terms that the red-tailed hawk was a predator to be eliminated. Thus she told no one she had discovered a hawk nest, but instead returned to this site every day, to consign telltale rabbit and chicken skeletons to the current of the brook where they were quickly carried downstream.

Early one morning, while inspecting a robin's nest in the orchard, she heard the crack of a rifle. Looking up, she saw a large bird spinning to earth. She found it in the milk yard—a chicken hawk—one wing held out stiffly, its tip bleeding and broken. Standing over this injured bird, prepared to club it with his rifle, was her father. Automatically, she lunged. Her father whirled, the butt of his weapon narrowly missing her head.

"Are you mad?" he shouted. "I barely missed braining you!"

"I'd rather you did hit me than to have you strike a
bird when its eyes are like that! Oh, Father, please
don't kill him! He never can fly again. Give him to me!
Do please give him to me!"

"Keep back! He will tear your face!"

"He won't! This bird knows me. He knows I would
not hurt him. Oh, do please give him to me!"[6]

Like others of his kind, this hawk was nearly two feet in
length, with long curved talons. Nevertheless, with no fear,
Gene laid her small hands on this bird to protect it. Her father
fixed his piercing gaze on her in defeat: "God knows I do not
understand you. Keep the bird, if you think you can!" and
with that he stomped away. With the aid of her mother, who
gave her a white powder to treat its injured wing, the hawk
recovered and, much to the wonderment of her father, within
a month began to follow Gene like a puppy and would eat
from her fingers.[7]

This display of sympathy for a wild bird was nothing compared with what happened next, a behavioral manifestation
so peculiar that her father was moved to consult the family
doctor. He could not believe it when his youngest said that
she could detect sounds that were to him, and to others in
the family, inaudible. Much to Gene's pleasure, on her daily
perambulations over the farm she had begun to sense a force
usually undetectable by mankind—an irregular outdoor
rhythm, an audible current. As a child, she did not know she
was experiencing anything out of the ordinary. She felt this
rhythm, more than heard it. Yet she heard it too. She liked
to play with this invisible force, much as other children play
with tangible objects. Often she climbed to the second story
of the barn and there, on a beam, as on the keys of a piano,
beat out the rhythm of force and sound that she felt and heard
around her.[8] These special rhythms that she sensed as a child
were reinforced by various other sounds on the farm. When
sent to gather chips for the fireplace, she said she heard music
as her brothers cut great ricks of wood.

Because of this behavior, Mark Stratton knew that his youngest was different from his first eleven children. Lacking precedent, he consulted the family doctor. The doctor, who knew the family well, gave Mark Stratton an apt explanation why Gene preferred the out-of-doors, inasmuch as she was being reared there almost exclusively. However, he could not medically explain her unusual extrasensory notions, nor did he know how to effect a cure for such strange deportment.

Perplexed and concerned, Mark Stratton was left to devise his own solution. An experienced parent, he must have known he could not divest his child of her peculiar belief in natural rhythms, nor could he change what seemed to be an overly protective attitude toward birdlife. Thus he did what must have seemed to him the next best thing. As might be expected, he called upon religion to respond to this child of nature. He gave her a special gift, a gift from the Creator. Formally, as if he were presenting the keys to God's kingdom, he endowed his daughter with all of the birds that made their homes on his land as her own personal property. Yet, even as he was elaborating on his wondrous gift, she scarcely heard him:

> Even while he was talking to me I was making a flash-ing mental inventory of *my property*, for now I owned the hummingbirds, dressed in green satin with ruby jewels on their throats; the plucky little brown wren that sang by the hour to his mate from the top of the pump, even in a hard rain; the green warbler, nesting in . . . wild sweetbrier beside the back porch; and the song sparrow in the ground cedar beside the fence. The bluebirds, with their breasts of earth's brown and their backs of Heaven's deepest blue; the robin, the rain song of which my father loved more than the notes of any other bird, belonged to me. The flaming car-dinal and his Quaker mate, keeping house on a flat limb within ten feet of our front door, were mine; and every bird of the black silk throng that lived in the top branches of four big evergreens in front of our home was mine. The oriole, spilling notes of molten sweet-

ness, as it shot like a ray of detached sunshine to its
nest in the chestnut tree across the road was mine.[9]

With her father's sanctified gift of all the birds on his farm,
Gene's morning rounds to inspect their nests quickly became
ritualized. Selecting sixty-four of them for daily observation,
she chased away cats, red squirrels, and snakes. Tiptoeing
carefully among the nests, first she observed what a mother
bird chose to feed her young. Then, stuffing half her breakfast
in her apron pocket, she scoured the farm for more food:
insects for her wrens; grubs and worms for her red-winged
blackbirds; caterpillars for her tanagers; and bugs for her robins in summer, berries in the fall. When she needed grain,
she robbed the bins in the barn.

One particular bluejay, a type of bird curious by nature,
began to follow her on her daily rounds. Delighted, she plied
him with food. Before long she had earned his constant companionship. She named him Hezekiah and taught him to roll
cherries across the floor on command. Then her oldest brothers, Jerome and Irvin, gave her another pet, a bantam rooster.
She named this one Bobbie and taught him to crow on cue
for "Amen!" when she imitated church services out in the
orchard.

This almost total preoccupation with birdlife necessarily
came to a seasonable end when her personal properties flew
south for the winter. Still, insofar as the youngest Stratton
was concerned, wintertime on the farm had its compensa-
tions. When the snow was crunchy, she liked to play on a hill
next to the orchard, coasting across the frozen cowslip bed
on a meat board. And wintertime meant family togetherness.
When the sun began to set behind the big woods every night
before five o'clock, as the youngest she always had the seat of
honor on her father's lap after dinner:

> Every winter night of my memory, up to the time that
> I was big enough to go to school and to take my place

at the table with my slate and pencil, I went to sleep in my father's lap. When I was ready for bed, I would unbutton his vest, curl up on his breast and pull his coat around me, between him and the book or paper he was reading. And except when he had to turn a leaf or a sheet, my feet were in the care of his big, strong right hand, held there, . . . chafed lovingly, given little tender grips and touches, to reassure me of his love and care. My left arm used to creep up around his neck, and play with his hair and in his beard, and stroke his cheek in response, and it never bothered him.[10]

Snuggled against her father's chest, she loved to listen as he read aloud with emphasis and gusto. One of his electrifying deliveries—the tale of John Maynard who steered his burning boat while he slowly roasted at the wheel—always caused her to sit up straight. Another story she liked to hear was from Sir Thomas Noon Talfourd's tragedy, *Ion* (1835), that of Clemanthe and her lover's immortal answer to the question, "Shall we meet again?" According to her, "I am convinced my father could equal a great actor in reciting that, for he believed in and loved that answer, and his heart thrilled to its depths when he repeated it."[11]

As the one in the family with the most imagination, Gene thrived on her father's recitations. With the natural receptivity of a child to meter, she liked to entertain her family in turn by dramatizing children's rhymes, acting and chanting with all the inflection she could muster. Soon she began to compose her own stories and poems:

I cannot remember the time when I was not tugging at my mother's apron, begging her to "set down" things which I thought were stories and poems. I was literally pushed and driven, so that I found an outlet by slipping away alone, to recite these efforts from improvised platforms on the fences, trees, and in the barn loft, or by delivering impromptu orations on al-

most every feature of our daily life. In this, I found
unspeakable delight.[12]

Her customary platform was in the orchard, atop two wide
boards slipped between the rails of a fence corner. Designed
to shelter a brooding turkey hen, these boards boosted her to
a view of the meadow below, the adjoining wood pasture,
and the fields across the lane. From this elevation, in imitation
of her father, she recited poetry. To the best of her ability, she
delivered selections from such works as "Ode on a Grecian
Urn," "The Prisoner of Chillon," and "Genevieve" before
she was six years old.

Many years later several of her acquaintances would complain that they could not understand a new book of poetry,
The American Rhythm, written by a mystic named Mary
Austin. As a small child Austin had a profound reverence for
the out-of-doors. She said that she talked to God under a
walnut tree when she was five years old. Unlike her friends,
Gene Stratton-Porter had no such difficulty understanding:
"It was about the life we lead in this great land of ours—the
song of the axe stroke, the sweep of the scythe, the hum of
life where it strikes in measured rhythm that I have heard all
of my life."[13]

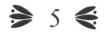

Softly, and with Whispers

IN spite of a strict religious upbringing, or perhaps because of it, as an adult Gene Stratton-Porter did not attend church on a regular basis, nor did she espouse the doctrine of any particular religious denomination. Although she was a Christian, she made it clear that she conformed to no special creed: "Such a thing as a Methodist, Presbyterian, Episcopalian, or Catholic,—Jesus and the men He chose to follow Him never heard of any of them."[1] Her church was the out-of-doors: "I am a member of no church save the Big Cathedral of the Woods, where God furnishes music and sermons of His own making."[2] In an explanation of her beliefs, she speculated:

> He may be the good in each one of us. He may be the Invisible Hand that evolves and governs the Universe. He may be a great personality sitting on a far throne, ruling the world inexorably. Whatever He is, He is truly the spirit of worship that is born in the heart of every living creature when it begins to palpitate as a separate entity.[3]

Generally, in describing her early religious training, she preferred to write about what little humor had been connected

with her constant exposure to the Word. This casual, somewhat irreverent approach comes through best in her novel
Laddie, an autobiographical work published in 1913. In this
book she depicts her brother Lemon, thinly disguised as a
boy named Leon, as the savior from what would otherwise
have been an interminable church service. Directed to memorize scripture for Sunday worship hour recitation, Leon
chooses Bible verses with certain church members in mind.
Then, the following Sunday morning, in front of the congregation, he lets his sallies fly.

To a man known as stiff-necked Johnny, Leon directs: "Lift
not up your horn on high: speak not with a stiff neck." To a
man who likes to sleep through Sunday worship, Leon in-
tones: "Give not sleep to thine eyes nor slumber to thine
eyelids." Another biblical verse is even more provoking: "I
was almost in all evil in the midst of the congregation and
assembly." Near the conclusion of his recitation Leon bright-
ens considerably as he announces: "When my father and my
mother forsake me, then the Lord will take me up." Leon's
final statement confirms his optimism: "The Lord is on my
side, I will not fear; what can man do unto me?" With that,
he bows and walks to his seat. Leon's father deals with this
awkward situation in the only possible way: "Let us kneel in
prayer."[4]

His soulful prayer stirs the congregation to tears. Those
crying the loudest are those who have given the most offense.
Leon, white as can be, apologizes, and his father—although
he is tone deaf, unable to carry a tune—leads the congregation
in singing "Sweeping through the Gates." Like thunder, the
congregation rolls into the chorus. Leon's mother begins to
rock on her toes "like a wood robin on a twig at twilight,"
crying "Glory!" at the end of each chorus. Even stiff-necked
Johnny, at the conclusion of the benediction, is moved to shake
hands all around.[5] Such lively occasions as this one described

in *Laddie* must have been few and far between, however. Ordinarily, at least according to her daughter, Gene sat through
Sunday services "wondering in her own mind if God was not
outside rather than inside."[6]

Needless to say, worship in the Stratton home was not a
matter shelved for Sunday. Although she did not intend her
words to be disparaging, Gene Stratton-Porter once wrote
that her father's religion was "oiled, regulated and in working
order from early Monday on to Saturday night."[7] She was
fond of elevating his title of local preacher to that of "ordained
minister of the Northern Indiana Methodist Conference."[8]
Yet he was never ordained. Although he had received the
honorary designation of local preacher from his church, his
name was not listed in the Methodist Annual Conference
minutes at any time.[9] But he might as well have been ordained
for he had the ringing delivery of a born-again evangelist. His
emphasis when he pronounced the Methodist benediction was
special. His enunciation penetrated to the bone: "Now unto
Him, Who is *able* to keep *you* from falling."[10]

Just as impressive were Mark Stratton's day-in, day-out
pronouncements and demonstrations with respect to secular
matters. Like an auctioneer, he conducted even the most me-
nial tasks around the farm with cadence and much flair, a
most effective teaching method. It was to the beat of this
constant vocal drum that the youngest Stratton received a
practical education. From her father she learned everything a
farm child would need to know, and more. He taught her not
only what varieties of fruit to set in an orchard, but why, and
how to graft them. He taught her how to bore a post hole
and set a tree, how to sharpen a shovel, how grain should be
cut and measured, how sheep should be sheared, how to wash
and dry wool, how to ready wool for market, and how to
select geese. She learned how to butcher, how to make sauerkraut, how to gather maple syrup and boil it down and work

it up, how to make a fiddle from a cornstalk, how to doctor livestock, and how to thaw out a newborn lamb. As a result of her father's instruction she also knew how to use a drawing knife on a fine piece of wood and how to fix or build almost anything.

Gene's first teacher from a scholastic standpoint was her brother Irvin. That is, Irvin was the first person who tried to teach her. First he had to catch her, and then he had to hold her, which was no small feat. Utterly lacking his father's flair for spellbinding verbiage, Irvin never managed to hold Gene's attention long enough to teach her anything, although he tried to the summer she turned six. Home from Wabash College, Irvin was idle, recuperating from the kick of a horse. Choosing a frustrating way to entertain himself, he tried to teach his youngest sister her ABCs. Totally uninterested, she slipped away at every opportunity unless he held her firmly. One day, annoyed at her constant inattentiveness, he tightened his grasp. Immediately she flared: "You Mister Irvin Stratton! You know you are not allowed to give me such raps in the stomach!"[11] On being enrolled shortly thereafter in the Lagro Township school, she protested even more vigorously, at first refusing to go. Not even Laddie could persuade her. Ada, already the most tactful member of the family, half tugged, half coaxed her down the road.

Before one month at school had gone by, Gene had reason to believe her regular teacher was worse than Irvin. When the following lesson appeared on the blackboard one day, "Little birds in their nests agree," Gene snapped to attention. Birds!! At last she had the chance to talk about a subject she liked and understood. "Oh, but they *don't* agree!" she explained to the teacher, "They fight like everything! They pull feathers and peck at each other's eyes until they are all bloody!"[12]

Punished for this outburst, thereafter she was an indifferent student. Yet her lessons did not end when classes were dismissed for the day. Every night, while school was in session, her father required his children to sit with their slates at the dining room table and prepare their lessons for the following day. Then, after he had inspected their work, he lined his charges in a row, picked up a McGuffey reader, and, from the biggest to the least, drilled all of them until they could spell and define every word in it. Surprisingly, in view of her dislike of school, Gene accepted this nightly regimentation and her abrupt promotion from the comfort of her father's lap to the front row of his drill team quite readily, merely remarking: "When we became so expert at this that it became tiresome he branched out into geography and readers for broader culturing."[13]

Lessons concluded, the family commonly adjourned to the hearth. There also, no idleness was permitted. While their father read aloud, family members cracked nuts or cut alder stalks into spiles to draw sap off the maples. One never-ending fireside task was the shelling of corn, bushels of it, into wash-tubs: small ears for popping, field corn to be ground at the mill, white ears for riving and using in batter, and yellow ears for mush and corn bread. In season, they peeled fruit and lined it in compact rows on the drying racks in the kitchen above their mother's stove, and, because there were many days when Mary Stratton was unwell, Gene was told her tasks were not "work," but, in her father's words, "helping mother."[14]

Complicating the need of Gene Stratton-Porter's mother for all the help she could muster was her fastidious nature. Highly particular, Mary Stratton maintained a clean, orderly home. Gene recalled one instance when she defied her mother's need for order and miraculously escaped a reprimand. One day a nest of swifts tumbled down a chimney, scattering ashes in every direction. While her mother fumed about the mess, Gene wired this bird nest back together, climbed to the roof, and replaced the nest in the chimney. She must have known she was pushing her luck. Soon after, when a family of wrens set up housekeeping in a knothole over the kitchen door, she was careful to clean up their droppings. This time her mother declared that the knothole would be nailed shut, or else. It might seem as if Mary Stratton cared more for cleanliness than she did for birds. Not so. Any woman who felt poorly half the time and yet permitted the presence of a pet rooster in her kitchen had to have been something of a rara avis. In the wintertime Mary Stratton relegated Hezekiah, Gene's pet bluejay, to the back porch, although she allowed Bobbie, the rooster, full run of the kitchen.

Gene Stratton-Porter's mother appears to have been an exceptionally amiable woman. Given her day-to-day chores as a nineteenth-century farm woman, her apparent good nature could reasonably be cause for wonder. She had learned to cook over an open fireplace and bake with the aid of a tin reflector. Her new woodburning stove was an improvement, although it did not begin to compensate for long hours at a churn, or for drawing water from a pump to feed and bathe a large household. Nothing could make up for having to station a child at the dining room table to swish away swarms of flies, or for the inconvenience of standing out next to the cistern in the woodhouse laundering by hand, especially in the wintertime. Despite all the drudgery, despite having lost two children, and despite the vacillating state of her own health, Mary Stratton appears to have been a happy woman, content with domestic pursuits and well equipped to cope with whatever life had in store for her. She lived by a biblical injunction: whatsoever her hand found to do, she did it with all her might.

Because her mother compounded her own medicinal remedies, from time to time Gene was sent to the woods for roots and herbs. She was happy here, where she could give her imagination free rein, decorating stumps with flowers and moss and pretending that toadstools were fairy footstools. These herb-gathering expeditions were not always pleasant.

Once, a crazy Irishman who roamed these woods at large had chased her father with an ax. Later describing this lunatic in *Laddie*, she wrote with horror about daft Paddy Ryan with his matted hair, clad in flying rags, who had been seen in their big woods eating snakes. As a child, Gene trembled at even a glimpse of this mortal goblin through the trees, yet the delightful pull of the woods was stronger than her fear. Many were the quiet hours she spent there alone, dawdling and gathering roots and herbs for her mother. Her overall recollection was one of early childhood delight in an arboreal realm, a "perfect" experience that repaid her many times over for flights in "headlong terror" back to the safety of the house and her mother.[15]

When she was able, Gene's mother used various herbs and home remedies to nurse the neighborhood sick. Charitable to a fault, Mary Stratton aided even the shiftless and welcomed them to her table. Because of her training as a miller's daughter, she knew how to set a fine table, and her dinner invitations were highly sought after. She was above all a contented home-maker, happy with farm life. Her most-used phrase, "What a pity," could end either of two ways: "What a pity little children in the city cannot have milk from cows that eat clover," or, "What a pity butter and eggs are often stale before they reach the city."[16]

One day when Gene was watering and feeding the chickens, she watched as her mother removed newly hatched chicks from under a brooding hen. As Mary Stratton lifted the hen to see if she had recovered all of them, a tiny piece of shell flew up on an egg.

> "There!" said her mother, "That is the beginning. The little chicken has broken the shell with its bill; now it will soon be out."
> "Oh, mother," Gene begged, "do please let me take it. Let me hold it in my hand when it comes out!"

Suddenly, however, an old rooster nearby screamed a shrill warning, and every hen in the barnyard scurried to cover her brood.

"That settles it!" exclaimed her mother, carefully replacing the egg under the hen, "That chicken will not move again for half an hour, and I can not possibly spare that much time."[17]

Gene marveled at this wisdom, at a mother who knew that an unhatched chicken which has not seen the light of day will lie dormant at the danger signal of a cock. According to Gene, her mother had many gifts, "the crowning one, flower magic in her fingers," a seemingly effortless ability to make any seed sprout, even the tiniest ones she sometimes found in rice and coffee. Gene's memory of her mother never failed to bring back a familiar scent, a perfume distilled from hyacinths, homemade by her mother by adding clusters of these spring flowers to bowls lined with fresh unsalted butter, then cutting the few drops of oil thus extracted with alcohol.[18]

Gene was able to describe her mother very briefly, with only one word, "capable."[19] She could not, however, characterize her father so succinctly. In an attempt to describe him, she once wrote a laudatory essay of five thousand words. In it, as was her custom, she said nothing about any of her father's shortcomings, but devoted her entire essay to an explanation of why she felt her father was entitled to nothing but her grateful praise:

> Dimly, from the time I was a little thing, I realized that it was because my father's shoulders were square, and his head was high, and his eyes were on the stars, and his hands were strong and capable, that we had this big white home and the patent-leather carriage and the gray team; that Mother stepped out in her billowing silks of gray and brown and black, and her dainty little bead-and-flower-trimmed bonnets, and her pretty, shiny shoes, and the flashing pin of

goldstone at her throat, and the ring of gold from California on her finger.

Very early I figured out for myself that the men who shuffled along the road with humped shoulders, . . . their eyes on the path before them, were going to log cabins in the woods, to blear-eyed children and fault-finding wives, to bare tables meagerly set.[20]

One aspect of her father's nature seemed to tower above all others: "He had a streak of genius in his make-up: the genius of large appreciation. Over inspired biblical passages, over great books, over sunlit landscapes, over a white violet abloom in deep shade, over a heroic deed of man, I have seen his brow light up, his eyes shine."[21]

One hint that her father had a darker side appears in an autobiographical short story in which she describes him as possessed of a volcanic temper. His eruptions must have been almost deafening. Sometimes his wrath was directed toward his neighbors, as when their dog came over and sucked eggs. Sometimes it was directed elsewhere, as when the old gray mare balked with the last load of hay, just as a big storm was coming. More often than not, however, Mark Stratton's crashing thunder appears to have been directed at his children, and, much like their mother's chickens, when the Stratton offspring heard their father's apoplectic "Jupiter Ammons!" every last one of them scurried for cover.[22]

Similar fireworks were also likely when the Strattons received a letter from Ohio. Daniel, Mark's youngest brother, was an argumentative Democrat whose opinionated letters riled the elder Stratton to the boiling point. It was always Mark's practice to pen a heated reply immediately. Before launching such a missive, however, he liked to read it before his assembled family as only he could, with bombs bursting in air.

Such a gift for forceful expression was then a decided asset. During the 1870s the popularity of oratory was at a high-water mark, and a flair for resonant oratory was a ticket to high regard. The more grandiloquent and persuasive a man, the more upstanding his reputation, and Mark Stratton's reputation always would hinge on the forceful qualities of his voice box. Because of his wife's objections, however, he was not always permitted to stretch this grand voice box to its utmost indoors. Ordinarily, therefore, he exercised it out on the back eighty while leaning against a plow. During the noon hour, as his hands rested, Mark Stratton ventilated his love for his sonority by quoting history—not just any history, but English history, the more rolling and resounding the phrases the better. He was especially dazzled by Edward Gibbon, Thomas Macaulay, and David Hume. Incredibly, he even loved to spout a work on the forms of water by an English agnostic, perhaps because its paradoxical author, John Tyndall, was also a hymn singer. Small wonder Mark Stratton worshiped England. The descendant of an Englishman, he had been born in a state that was once one of the thirteen original colonies. Small wonder, too, that his youngest child was susceptible to her father's Anglican exuberance. Daily in the fields, she was always within range of his noon-hour outpourings. One of her childhood games derived directly from this constant exposure to all things English. When she tagged along with her father in Lagro, she liked to play "Colonial Dame" in Faunce's carpenter shop, aided by Joseph Faunce who reached into his father's barrel and tossed her long, spiraled shavings to hang over her ears.

Gene Stratton-Porter's father bore the average colonialist's reverence for everything English with one exception—governmental control—which he willingly conceded to the United States. In this, he was possessively patriotic. He always said: "My country, my state, my county," often prefacing his remarks about his nativity and his residence with the long-winded theory that, "if each man who lived in the state of Indiana would culture himself to the furthest extent to which he could push his opportunities, would carry his family and his neighborhood with him on this march for better living conditions and fuller mental and spiritual life, the example would spread to all states, and soon our land would truly be the 'land of the free and the home of the brave.' "[23] His is an interesting theory, although that does not mean it would be palatable every hour of every day. One day he got his comeuppance when, on his wife's return from a Fourth of July outing, he anxiously inquired about the speech she had heard: "Mother, did you hear a grand and glorious effort?"

"Oh, yes!" snapped Mary, "The speaker waved the bloody shirt until he fringed it from hem to neckband, and he didn't leave the American eagle even one tail feather to steer with."[24] Along with his intense love of country, his genius for rhetoric, and his educational skills, Mark Stratton possessed one other verifiable sterling quality. It seems that there did exist one particular time when he knew how to be almost silent. Gene said her father would always, as he approached a bird nest, "walk softly and whisper."[25]

❧ 6 ❧

Her Father's Daughter

EARLY in 1872, when Gene was only eight, tragedy began to knock repeatedly at her family's door. Over the next several years, the agonies wrought by these unending woes would exact a heavy toll not only from herself but also from her entire family. These difficulties set in motion new patterns for daily living with which the Strattons could scarcely cope.

It all began with a fatality. In February 1872 one of the Strattons' oldest daughters died as a result of injuries received in an accident. Mary Ann, the former domestic, had eventually married the son of one of Lagro Township's most prosperous farmers, a union now turned to dust.[1] Gene seems to have been little affected by this first death in her immediate family. Such was not the case, however, when tragedy struck a second time.

Five months after the death of Mary Ann, on a muggy summer evening, death called again. Late in the afternoon, when even the prospect of sunset afforded no respite from the suffocating heat, Laddie hitched up a wagon and drove into Lagro. While there, in company with several other young men, he sought relief from the stifling heat by taking a dip in the cool waters of the Wabash River. Although neither he nor his companions were strong swimmers, when challenged by one of his acquaintances to swim this broad expanse, Laddie started across accompanied by two others, Wallace Curnutt and William Wilson. About halfway over, Laddie gave out. Curnutt, closest to him, swam to his aid, but Laddie strangled him and both boys went under, locked together. When they bobbed to the surface, crying for help, Wilson responded immediately. Alarmed, however, by the sight of a frantic struggle, Wilson feared to touch either of them, and both Laddie and Curnutt sank for the last time.[2]

Laddie—kind, even-tempered, dependable—the brother Gene most adored, drowned on 6 July 1872, six weeks short of her ninth birthday. When his body was carried home, she ran into the house clutching one of his boots in each hand, screaming for the only person who could possibly comfort her, her mother. Yet she would not, could not, be comforted. This loss left her with an emptiness that would continue to haunt her throughout her life. The Strattons were not alone in their grief. The loss of their son and brother echoed throughout Wabash County. Flowery obituaries were then the custom rather than the exception, although the tribute to Laddie in a local newspaper leans more to facts than embroidery, expressing a genuine regret at the loss of a young life so full of promise.

After the drowning, Mark Stratton, then sixty and no longer able to farm with vigor, was faced with a dilemma. Laddie, besides being his most reliable hand, had also been his intended heir to the farm. Jerome, his oldest, did not want the farm; he was practicing law. Irvin did not want it either; he had recently completed two years of college and was then weighing his options, trying to decide whether to read for the law also. In the meantime Irvin was teaching in the Wabash County school system, where his thorough methods had begun to draw favorable local attention. As for Lemon, it

Gene Stratton-Porter, age ten

was out of the question to groom him as a potential heir
to the farm. Lemon, then sixteen, was undisciplined and
irresponsible.

After wrestling for six months about what he should do
with the farm, Mark Stratton advertised it for sale in a local
weekly newspaper early in 1873.[3] It was a halfhearted move,
made in the dead of January. He must have known, with
twenty inches of snow blanketing the ground, that no buyer
would miraculously appear and become excited over the prospect of a well-producing orchard and waving fields of grain.[4]
Three weeks later he withdrew the advertisement.

In addition to trying to decide what to do about the farm—
and worrying about the rapidly deteriorating health of his
wife—Mark Stratton was also preoccupied at that time with
another matter. During the last year his fellow churchmen
had erected a substantial brick edifice on that corner of land
he had allowed them to use over the past twenty years.[5]
He was expected to deed over the ground on which this
new church stood—a small plot, 63 x 70 feet. Finally, on
17 March 1873, three months after this church was dedicated, he made out the deed. At the same time, however, he
retained possession of the cemetery next to the church because
that had proved to be very profitable to him. True to his
hustling instincts, he had platted this graveyard three years
earlier and had been selling burial lots from it ever since at
$10 each.

Other than his extra income from cemetery lots, Mark
Stratton had little to crow about financially the year following
Laddie's death. The increasingly sorry state of the Wabash
and Erie Canal contributed to his fiscal miseries. Victim of
high maintenance and repair costs, as well as drought and
other disasters, the canal had begun to fall into disuse, sup-
planted statewide by a more reliable system, the railroad.
Indeed, the only viable argument for the continued maintenance of the Wabash and Erie Canal stemmed from its

depressing influence on railway freight charges during the summer.[6] With rails now available to a wide segment of Indiana's pork and grain farmers, no longer did the Wabash County farmer enjoy any special privileges by virtue of his close proximity to the Wabash and Erie Canal.

As if all of these economic and personal woes were not enough, in the summer of 1873 Wabash County's corn crop was destroyed by worms.[7] By September of that year, the Wabash County farmer was in dire straits. He was not alone. The failure of Philadelphia banking house Jay Cooke and Company, which began in the fall of 1873, marked the beginning of one of the worst financial panics in American history. When this nationwide depression began to grip the banks of the Wabash, farm prices plummeted. This financial panic was the final blow. Faced with what appeared to be certain ruin if he stayed on the farm, Mark Stratton decided to retire and move to town. Simultaneously, in his usual sharp manner, he figured out a way to live off whatever fat remained in his land. It took him nearly a year to come up with a suitable plan, but when he finally got it worked out, he was all set. First, he found a dependable sharecropper—a fellow Methodist—willing to live on his land and work it. Then he arranged to move his wife and four children yet at home into the house of his daughter Anastasia, who lived in the nearby town of Wabash. Anastasia, a virtual copy of her capable mother, was well equipped to cope with her mother's serious illness and was married to a prominent local attorney who could well afford to take on six extra boarders. To everyone in the family except Gene, the prospect of residing with Anastasia must have been like looking forward to old home week. Irvin was already a boarder with Anastasia and her husband, Alvah Taylor. A few months earlier, Irvin had been appointed Wabash County superintendent of schools and, in his spare time, had begun to read for the law with Alvah Taylor.[8]

All of this prospective renewal of family togetherness meant absolutely nothing to the youngest Stratton. Unable to accept the coming move to town, she resisted with all her might. She had already been robbed of Laddie and also lately of her mother's attention, and now she had been told by her father that on moving day she must give up all of her birds. When the day arrived to abandon the farm, she refused to budge. Not until her father yielded to a certain demand did she capitulate. Overall triumphant, but still antagonistic, Gene boarded the carriage for Wabash with a most precious boodle—nine pet birds, none smaller than a grosbeak.

From the standpoint of a conscientious parent, the town of Wabash, population four thousand, was unquestionably a desirable place to finish bringing up a family. The Wabash County schools, under Irvin's new direction, had begun to employ a learning system better than most. Irvin emphasized clear communication, focusing on letter writing and composition, yet he was also a stickler for instilling more than English grammar. Irvin firmly believed that the mastery of higher mathematics would strengthen the mind.[9] If the course of instruction he propounded was beneficial, it was also difficult. Only five students managed to graduate from Wabash High School the year Irvin took it over.[10]

Its sound school system was not the only advantage to be had in this community. Typical of a small midwestern town, Wabash was a highly desirable place to live from a puritanical Prostestant point of view. Here zealous churchgoers, reinforced by a fearless press, governed the local collective conscience. Woe betide anyone who refused to wear the red ribbon of temperance or otherwise deviated from the norm. If, by some chance, the pulpit failed to point out a local indiscretion, and the folly of it, the weekly newspaper quickly took up the slack. The *Wabash Plain Dealer* liked to flay those whom it perceived as wayward. Paternity suits automatically made its front page. Nor was this newspaper enamored only with dastardly deeds. As one resident could attest, it was literally impossible to have a bad case of piles without the *Plain Dealer* observing that your screams could be heard three squares away.[11]

Despite its community watchdogs, Wabash appeared to be a forward moving community. The year the Strattons moved to town, it was enjoying a second boom. Two railroads had replaced the dying Wabash and Erie Canal. One of the largest customers for these new freight rails was a local mill that bought flaxseed by the thousands of bushels and annually shipped 360 tons of oil cake. Hard on the heels of this oil mill, competing for boxcar space, was a hub, spoke, and bending factory that monthly turned out seventy-five thousand spokes. Strung out along the canal, still the gathering point for the town's industry, sprawled several other manufacturing concerns—a planing mill, two furniture factories, and a buggy and carriage works—all of which were at nearly full employment, as yet affected only slightly by the national depression. Add to this the flour and woolen mills, the foundry, the cigar factory, the tannery, the brickyard, the lumber wagon establishment, and the local slaughterhouse—which yearly handled tens of thousands of hogs—and the picture begins to emerge of a town in the midst of prosperity.[12]

Downtown, business was no less brisk. As the county seat, Wabash had attracted enough entrepreneurs to satisfy the most exacting customer. Any household item not readily found elsewhere could be purchased at the local catchall, the drugstore. There, on shelves behind the penny horehound, were varnishes and paints, wallpaper and borders, specifics and blood purifiers, spectacles and trusses, supports and shoulder braces, and—for medical purposes only—fine wines and liquors.[13] Characteristic of the generation, the citizens of Wabash had a surefire remedy for life's ills—a positive outlook. Buttressed by favorable past experience and grounded in the rigid standards hawked by the town's clergy and the fourth estate, these shakers and movers were enviably positive that tomorrow would be better than yesterday, enviably confident of their ability to handle any difficulty, whether personal or communal.

Only a handful of residents regarded their community in a less favorable light. Few bothered to complain of the hogs still roaming freely through town, and even fewer objected to sharing the sidewalk with a horse occasionally.[14] Most were accustomed to the local odors, predominantly foul. A powerful stench emanated from the slaughterhouse to mingle with that from alleys piled high with manure.[15] Compared with its advantages, the annoyances confronting Wabash seemed minute, even insignificant. One such annoyance was the courthouse, its once white exterior now beginning to darken, victim of the soft coal that fueled the town's industries. Another drawback, also directly attributable to the town's industries, was not so easily overlooked, yet this matter was also generally accepted as an inevitable part of the cost of doing business. Simply stated, after its shops and factories had closed for the day, the good citizens of the town of Wabash were required to disappear indoors, required that is, unless they were intrepid. Those same clicking rails that so efficiently carried the spokes of Wabash to distant markets also carried a less desirable product, often an unsavory product, known as the American billy, one of the thousands of tramps who had begun to ride the rails after the Civil War. The town trustee would lodge them, if he could catch them, but he was opposed to feeding them, and nightly they roamed the streets hungry. There was no way to avoid the possibility of being accosted by a billy in Wabash after sundown. Lacking gaslights, its streets were dark.[16]

In short, Wabash was no place for a carefree woodland sprite. It was a place for people watching, not bird-watching, and it was confining. Yet it was here that Gene Stratton found herself incarcerated in the winter of 1874-75, on a street two blocks north of a canal and its industrial row and only a block and a half from the rumbles of the Toledo, Wabash and Western Railroad. It was this dusty main thoroughfare, a bustling street full of horse-drawn rigs and drays, that would be her home, in the loosest sense of the word, until she was twenty-one.

Nearly asphyxiated by her new environment, trapped between the railroad tracks and the industries lining the Wabash and Erie Canal, the youngest new resident of Wabash found only one outlet that sparked her interest. She immersed herself in caring for her birds. Religiously she scraped perches, boiled bathtubs, and changed sand, all the while yearning for the woods she was forced to leave behind.

At the same time, her mother's health rapidly declined. On 3 February 1875, less than four months after moving to town, Mary Stratton died. She had carried with her into the Wabash valley from her home in Ohio two cuttings of a timeless tree given her by a man who brought such a tree from the white sands of Palestine. When her husband had moved her to the heart of Wabash County, she had transplanted one of these trees to her dooryard, the other to her husband's cemetery. To this burial ground with its ageless cedar of Lebanon her family now returned her and laid her to rest near Mary Ann, Samira, Louisa Jane, and Laddie.

During her illness, Mary Stratton had sustained at least a semblance of united family life in the crowded Taylor household. In her absence, the congestion called for immediate relief. Thus Mark Stratton moved into a rented house down the street. He took along Florence, Ada, and Gene, at the same time executing another wily maneuver: he left troublesome Lemon behind with the Taylors.

Lemon, however, was not his only problem. His youngest child was not manageable either. Finally, in desperation, Gene's father sent her back to the farm for a few days. While there, she had the good fortune to capture a large colorful moth, the cecropia. The next morning, anxious to show her lucky catch to Ada and Florence, she borrowed a stone jar from the tenant farmer's wife and placed the moth inside on a bed of peony petals. Then she tied her sunbonnet over the top of the jar and stationed herself at the front gate, hailing each passing team with lifted hand, as she had seen others do. At last a bony farmer with a fat wife and a fat baby said she might ride to town. With quaking heart she handed up the jar and climbed in. On learning the contents of the jar, the farmer's wife stuck her elbow into her husband's ribs and said, "How's that for the queerest spec'men ye ever see?" He answered: "I never saw nothin' like it before." Then she said: "Aw pshaw! I didn't mean in the jar!"[17] Then they both laughed. Certain her sisters would appreciate her treasure, Gene paid little attention to the fun-making comments of her hosts.

That night she placed the moth on the curtains in the parlor, covered the sill with flowers and leaves, and went to bed happy. She awoke to the shrieks of her sisters that their best lace curtains had been ruined. When she went into the parlor her cecropia was gone: "My disappointment was so deep and far-reaching it made me ill; then they scolded me, and said I had half killed myself carrying that heavy jar in the hot sunshine, although the pain from which I suffered was neither in my arms nor sunburned face."[18]

Months of like misunderstandings followed, coupled with the strains of beginning adolescence. Formerly only stubborn, Gene fast became rebellious and defiant, incensed at being uprooted from the farm and now robbed of her mother. Later, although she was eleven years old at the time, Gene Stratton-Porter recalled nothing of her mother's passing beyond a hushed room and the specter of a pale face. Yet her mother's death marked a crucial turning point in her life.

Thereafter, although she was unable to articulate her feelings about the death of her mother, she had no difficulty expressing an opinion about the next hurdle she was expected to negotiate. It was school, which she was expected to attend eight months a year, a session more than twice as long as she had previously had to endure while living in the country.

She soon earned a reputation for intractability among her teachers. Those earnest ladies, quick to blame her recalcitrance on an under-average mentality or an inherently bad disposition, apparently never suspected her true composition. Gene Stratton-Porter would always think of herself as considerably different from other individuals, and she would always blame her hostility toward a standard education on her teachers, not on her own unique personal circumstances:

> In the whole of my school life I never had one teacher who made the slightest effort to discover what I cared for personally, what I had been born to do, or who made any attempt to help me in any direction I evinced an inclination to develop. I was to be pushed into the groove in which all other pupils ran.[19]

Aside from a lack of rapport with her teachers, she was also uncomfortable with her schoolmates. She said it was because they poked fun at her apparel. Her outer trappings had made little difference on the farm, although in Wabash she felt she was being judged by her peers on the basis of her clothing. She may have been overreacting about her clothing. Possibly she was a ragamuffin only in her own sight. A former classmate has described her on one of her first days at school as a perfect example of rugged health clad in a gay plaid dress and a white bib apron.[20] Nevertheless, whatever it was that Gene wore to school, she was unhappy with it because she felt it made her look like the stereotype of the farmer's daughter, as if her dresses came in only two shades, clean and faded.

And her hair! Her bright brown hair hung in heavy braids, unadorned by ribbons. How she wanted some violet-edged ribbon!

Her description of her circumstances after her mother's death tells us emphatically how much she felt she had been misled about the benefits of being a farmer's daughter. More than that, her words shed considerable light on the attitudes she was forming about money and affluence:

> After mother was gone, and it was time to go to the city and enter school, I faced a condition. I was as good-looking as any of my schoolmates. I had a world of practical, first-hand information concerning the workings of nature and of human nature. But very early I came to a revelation galling for a girl: Land might make one healthy; it might make one capable; but it would *not* bring to one as much ready money as a bank, or a store, or the practice of the medical or legal professions brought. Most of the girls in my classes could have finer shoes, and prettier dresses and hair ribbons than I had.[21]

One day, on her way home from school, she was stopped by a woman who gave her \$4.75 which the woman owed Mr. Stratton for cherries: "Be sure to run straight home, and don't lose it." "Oh, I will," Gene assured her, neglecting to add that she could be contrary. She walked ten blocks out of her way just because she wanted to know "how it felt to walk the streets with that much money."[22]

By the time she was twelve, Gene had begun to sound like her father's daughter, a country girl with a hankering for self-improvement. Having been schooled in the advantages of the country, however, she had more than a few nagging doubts about the niceties of city life. What was it her mother had always said? "What a pity children in the city . . . ," but her mother had known nothing but a rural way of life. She had been born on a farm, lived her entire active life on a farm, and died without ever having had to debate the advantages of country versus city living.

Gene Stratton had met an impasse:

> I had been trained from the day of my birth I must not ask for things. I must be content with what was provided for me. And I was *not* content. I wanted dresses such as Edith Elliot wore, and hair ribbons like Madge Busick's. I wanted a carriage like the McCray [McCrea] girls' and trips to Florida like the Gillen girls'.[23]

Hers was an unalleviated self-consciousness and a desire for what money could buy that would not pass with the end of her grammar school days, nor would it ever pass. On the subject of wearing apparel, she would remain a permanent adolescent. When she later volunteered her opinion on suitable school attire, she recommended without hesitation a stiff dress code designed to eliminate discrimination, suggesting "uniforms, or at least rigid dress restrictions, for public schools, grade or high, and colleges."[24]

At the time she entered Wabash High School, her greatest source of enjoyment continued to come from her pet birds. She retained an interest in their habits and cared for a large bevy of them every day after school. Moreover, she was still a carefree sprite in another way, with an impish resemblance to her brother Lemon. When provoked, she knew how to retaliate. One day when she and a like-minded acquaintance named Anna were snubbed by one of the senior girls, they decided to take revenge. During commencement ceremonies, they sent this stuck-up senior, who was seated onstage, a straggly bunch of stringy, dead flowers accompanied by the following note: "Will you please make me happy by accepting these flowers, not for their intrinsic value or beauty, but as a token of sincere admiration for your loveliness. (signed) Admirer." Their prank took an unexpected turn. The note came loose from the flowers, and the girl who was the object of

Gene Stratton-Porter, age sixteen

their devilment began an eager, smiling search for the face in the audience who had favored her with such a compliment.[25]

Gene's closest friend at this time appears to have been her sister Ada. The two had not been close as children, perhaps because of six years difference in their ages. But after the death of their mother, Gene had grown to depend on her older sister. Jeannette Porter Meehan wrote that they were an ornery pair, with a like sense of humor, always primed to dissolve into giggles at the slightest provocation.

In Wabash if a young person wanted to have a good time, he or she automatically followed the lead of a coterie of girls known throughout Wabash County as the "Big Five."[26] This exclusive clique engineered the county's most raved-about sleigh rides, musicales, and taffy pulls. Two of these girls were the daughters of James McCrea, president of the Citizen's Bank and also a prominent clothing merchant. Walking advertisements for their father's wares, Flora and Edith McCrea were commonly seen prancing around in pale polonaise over white swiss, or satin and cashmere. Ada got along with the "Big Five" all right, as a member of one of their Greek letter organizations. As did Lemon. Every New Year's, along with several other gay young blades, Lemon got himself all dressed up in swallowtails and toothpick shoes and paid his annual respects to the "Big Five" at their open houses.[27] If Gene ever had anything to do with this prestigious clique, she never mentioned it.

Outside of participating in social activities engineered by the "Big Five," a girl starting high school had little to do in Wabash. It was now safe to walk the streets, electricity having been installed to light the town, and there did exist a theater downtown that regularly featured comedy troupes and the like, although Gene was forbidden to go there. But then, neither would the "Big Five" have been allowed to patronize this theater because no troupe of any respectability booked there. Haas's opera house was like a hogpen. The odor of

horse manure drifting up from its basement caused one resident to complain that this hall smelled like an emigrant car.
Under its seats, rats held high carnival.[28]

With no entertainment available to her outside of the "Big
Five"—other than, of course, the weekly oyster supper or ice
cream social in the basement of the Methodist Church—
Gene's days in high school began miserably. She later com-
plained that she "never had any spending money" and that
the theater and dances were forbidden.[29] Of course the theater
was forbidden. No parent in his or her right mind would have
allowed a child to visit that rattrap. As for dancing, it is easy
to understand why Mark Stratton disapproved of such a
seemingly sinful shenanigan. A justification, however, for his
reluctance to part with any spending money on his daughter's
behalf is not as readily apparent.

It is a mistake to assume that poverty was part of the reason
for Gene's distress. By 1880, when she entered high school,
the depression was over. At that time, the financial circumstances of the Strattons were no worse than those of the average middle-class family. Far from being hard up, Mark
Stratton had a full larder because of his farm. In addition, he
had a steady income from this farm, still rented on half shares.
Furthermore, he continued to have a somewhat erratic, but
dependable, income courtesy of the grim reaper. He was continuing to sell cemetery lots. On the other hand, it is just as
much of a mistake to assume that Gene's demands on her
father's pocketbook were reasonable.

The truth regarding her financial situation at this time lies
somewhere between her own unreasonable expectations and
her father's stinginess. Although Gene did not seem to realize
that her demands for fine Yankee notions were out of line
with her father's means, she did know, however, that he was
excessively frugal. Later, she would camouflage his stinginess,
just as she tried to hide his other less desirable characteristics.
She liked to robe her family in a more genteel garment, like

poverty. Not only would she fail to accuse her father of being parsimonious but, to the contrary, she would later paint a portrait of him as a magnanimous benefactor. It is nearly impossible to count the number of times she refers to his donation to his fellow Methodists of land for church purposes. Verily, verily, Mark Stratton was a sharp businessman, but my! was he tight with a dollar. And merrily, merrily, Gene Stratton was a fun-loving teenager who expected too much from her father, even if he had been a generous man, which he was not.

With stiff resolution, she set out when she was seventeen to exact some joy from life in a way that required no money. The first step she made in her own behalf was to suggest to her sister Florence that perhaps Florence might give music lessons to the children of a local dressmaker. In exchange, this seamstress could supply Gene with better dresses. Florence, a generous person, readily agreed. By 1880 a family that bartered for clothing in this way was either poor or overly thrifty. By that time a woman of ordinary means, not only a rich woman, could get measured in a tailoring house, select her goods, and expect a big box to be delivered the next week with everything machined to fit, down to the latest tucks and frills. The dressmaker came only to homes of the less fortunate or the pinchpenny; nevertheless, Gene was pleased to have her. What a pleasure to be able finally to tell the other girls how she had hitched up her marguerite, a bustle arrangement pitchforked up into heaps behind. As she finally began to look better than many of her classmates, she also began to feel better, again thanks to Florence, who gave Gene banjo, violin, and piano lessons. Doggedly, Gene exacted of herself four hours of practice every day, soon developing a taste for Franz Schubert, Felix Mendelssohn, Carl Maria von Weber, Richard Wagner, Wolfgang Amadeus Mozart, and Franz Liszt. With this insulation, Gene later wrote, "I did not feel the gap so wide between me and the girls whom I passed on the streets and met in school and on social occasions who could not have done the same thing to have saved them."[30]

While trying to become an accomplished musician, Gene demonstrated again in another way that persistent ingenuity by which she had acquired a better wardrobe. This maneuver required utmost diplomacy. Tenderly she put her hands on her father's shoulders and asked in the politest way she knew, for she did not want to upset him, if there were some way she could take painting lessons. A Mrs. Grant was teaching the other girls how to paint on canvas, satin, and china.

Considering her question briefly, her father asked whether this Mrs. Grant had a family. When Gene named five Grant children, the question of how to pay for painting lessons was readily solved. They became a Saturday reality, paid for with potatoes and apples from the rented family farm. Gene counted these lessons one of the greatest joys to date in her hollow existence:

> Perhaps the greatest joy I had known in life up to that period came when I opened a package that Mrs. Grant laid before me and found that it contained a small china palette, a beautiful thing, a tiny, flat double-edged knife for mixing paint, a big brush of camel's hair called a "blender," smaller brushes of fine badger hair, and a tiny bottle of turpentine.[31]

Her first assignment from Mrs. Grant, to her grateful surprise, was to paint a wild rose from a pencil sketch. For two hours she sat absorbed, practicing, before she transferred her painting to a piece of satin. When finished, she knew her mother would have said she had reproduced real, live sweetbrier roses. When she took her artwork home, her father picked it up and held it to the light. Turning it around, his sharp black eyes appraised it quickly. It *looked* fragrant. "But isn't this a rather remarkable performance for a beginner?" he asked.[32]

It was a rare compliment. Mark Stratton was not in the habit of praising the efforts of any of his children. Prior to Gene's birth, he had had reason to be disappointed in all of them. Since her birth, contrary to his high expectations, Laddie had died and the older girls had not turned out well. Mary Ann was dead. Catherine, the one who had married a Democrat, was now living in Wabash—fittingly—on Hell Street, and the most that had ever been said about her husband was that he was an active Odd Fellow. It was beginning to look as if Florence would become an old maid, and to what must have been Mark Stratton's further disappointment, Irvin was no longer the Wabash County superintendent of schools but was now practicing law with Jerome in a nearby city. As for Lemon, Mark Stratton had completely given up on Lemon. Anastasia was still taking care of Lemon. It was yet too soon for Mark Stratton to tell about Ada, but not too soon to judge his youngest child. She still was rebellious and held peculiar notions about rhythm. She also hated school, but she was a devoted student in those particular areas that suited her interest.

One reason Gene hated school was because she could not comprehend mathematics. She failed it consistently. Another reason she detested school had to do with the way she handled criticism. When her schoolmates teased her, she generally bristled. And of course, the more they picked on her, the more she reacted. One day she returned home in tears. One of the girls had made an unkind remark about her father. Rumor had it that he planned to remarry, the implication being that if he did not plan to wed, then perhaps he *should.* The account of this incident in Jeannette Porter Meehan's biography of her mother neglects to state the basis for this rumor, although it could have originated only because Mark Stratton had made an unprecedented move. He had taken on a nonpaying boarder, a young widow named Sarah Duncan. When the gossip at school about their father became so prev-

alent that even Ada became uncomfortable, Florence was dispatched to talk to him about it. One night, as she accompanied
Mark Stratton to prayer meeting, Florence gathered her courage and asked him if he planned to remarry. He denied it: "I
don't know who would start such a report. I am not thinking
of anything of the kind. I know how my children feel on that
subject, and I cannot afford to risk losing their love."[33]

Gene's reading materials also affected her attitudes at this
time. Although her access to books was still limited, she no
longer read only historical and religious titles as she had on
the farm. Titillating dime novels were then the vogue, but
Beadle's Half Dime Library with its outlaws' retreat would have
fallen outside her father's framework of uplifting literature.
Thus, for the printed stimulation of her imagination, Gene
was confined to the classics—mostly English. From the titles
she listed among her favorites, it is known she preferred fiction
to fact, devouring *The Vicar of Wakefield*, *Jane Eyre*, and numerous works by Charles Dickens, William Thackeray, and
George Eliot. It shall never be known how two fictional works
by Frenchmen came to rest on the Stratton shelves—*Le Comte
de Monte-Cristo* by Alexandre Dumas père and Xavier Boni-
face Saintine's *Picciola*. It was the latter book that particularly
took Gene's fancy, and it is no wonder that she found it ab-
sorbing. *Picciola* is the story of a person much like herself, a
prisoner incarcerated against his will, deprived of all which
had previously brought joy into his life. This man's sole interest in life had been reduced to a tiny sprout of green among
the cobblestones outside his barred window, possibly sprung
from a seed dropped by a passing bird. Moreover, this prisoner was no ordinary individual. Like Gene, convinced that
she was a descendant of the Duke of Stratton, he was an
aristocrat—an Italian count.

During her second year in high school, in revolt and total
exasperation at her given assignment, Gene prepared a colorful, inspired review of *Picciola*. She had been instructed to

deliver a recitation on "Mathematical Law" and had agonized over it: "I do not know why such a beastly subject ever was assigned a sophomore."[34] What she did know was how flowers bloomed and seeded and how birds lived and reproduced. No one had yet recognized her potential or appeared to understand what she knew best or thought about most.

When the day of reckoning for delivery of her mathematics paper arrived, she took her place apprehensively before the weekly assembly and began instead to recite her review of *Picciola*. Shortly after she began, however, the principal asked her to stop while he went to fetch the superintendent. When he returned with this higher authority in tow, to Gene's relief they each took a seat and she was told to begin again. Suddenly she realized her paper was better than she had hoped, and she began to read with greater confidence: "My father never lifted his head higher when he tried to tell an audience his conception of the uttermost glory of God, than I lifted mine."[35]

At one point the room was in laughter; the next moment the boys turned their heads and the girls who had forgotten their handkerchiefs cried into their aprons. Her final page delivered, she swept the hall with one long look. Of that radiant moment, she wrote: "I realized that I had something in my heart, something in my brain that, through the help of my father, would bring to me lovelier dresses and fancier shoes, and a finer method of conveyance than any of the other girls had or would possess."[36] Yet her fantasy stretched beyond material gain to even loftier heights. From her youthful perspective she had an even greater vision, that

> I might be able to bring to others beauty that I had learned for myself; I might teach to others what I had been taught of persistence, patience, and sane, economical marching straight ahead, with my head high, as my father's always had been, toward any goal I sought. I would reach my goal through the satisfaction

of a something in my soul that would make things
possible to me through my own effort.[37]

She imagined herself like unto Pallas Athena, the goddess
of battle with a double name. As Pallas, in one hand she would
carry the aegis, or storm shield, of her father. As Athena, a
virgin who reigned in all gentleness and purity, she would
instruct men in all that gives beauty to human life.

Much encouraged by the overwhelming reception of her
review of *Picciola*, she began to neglect her schoolwork in favor
of putting her newfound talent to work. Worried that her
father might deem her writing foolish, she found it necessary
to be devious. She wrote hiding behind her books at school
and hiding in her room at home. Soon, under the guise of
working on mathematics, she compiled three volumes of
poetry.

Gene Stratton-Porter never named the person to whom she
carried these fledgling efforts, although she obviously showed
her work to a local pedant. The remarks of her first critic
were devastating. She was told that one must be born a poet,
that certain rules for the measurement of verse must be followed, and that no one could write poetry without exhaustive
and special education. Depressed and squelched, she used two
of her first efforts for kindling and otherwise destroyed the
third. She lived to regret this wholesale destruction, explain-
ing: "There is something in the first abandon of creative
power, guided by the optimism, the hope, the faith of youth,
that cannot be recaptured."[38] In one place, she uses a vague
plural to describe her first critic, blaming "some friends."[39]
In yet another place, she uses the singular, regretting having
shown her poetry to the "wrong person."[40] The latter is more
likely, for once while writing of a different matter she averred:
"It was to my father I carried the first line that I ever wrote."[41]
Thereafter, she wrote, "life became with me a matter of
suppression."[42]

❧ 7 ❧

A Catalyst

ALTHOUGH she was rapidly approaching adulthood, Gene Stratton did not have an opportunity to expand her horizons beyond the confines of Wabash County until after her sophomore year in high school. Then, about a month before her eighteenth birthday, she took a short trip and glimpsed what lay beyond her narrow boundaries. Chaperoned by Florence and Ada, she visited a lakeside resort about seventy miles north of Wabash for the purpose of attending a two-week summer chautauqua.

The chautauqua, the famous adult education movement, derived its name from Chautauqua Lake in western New York, the place of its beginnings. Originally organized as a camp meeting for religious workers, by the early 1880s this movement had evolved into a means by which persons with limited access to higher education, such as Gene Stratton, could be illumined, perhaps even overnight. This high aim reflected the religious-democratic faith of the era in the popularization of knowledge. To make this instant education as attractive as possible, promoters of these gatherings relied heavily on a double drawing card—"first class entertainment" coupled with old-time religion—a winning combination that drew the rural element as well as the revival-minded in droves. One early observer described a typical chautauqua tent assembly as a cross between a county fair and a camp meeting. In general, the chautauqua's promoters liked to regard themselves as missionaries of culture among country folk.[1]

By 1881, when Gene Stratton attended her first chautauqua, these assemblies had sprung up in countless towns and hamlets across the nation. The particular session that she attended was an outgrowth of an earlier interdenominational Sunday School Congress that had promoted institute and public lectures as well as a Grand Excursion Day and, of course, a Temperance Day. Subsequently, this chautauqua had become known as Island Park Assembly because of its location, a heavily wooded twenty-acre island in the middle of a large lake.[2] Those who enjoyed the out-of-doors could not have asked for a more stimulating setting. Sylvan Lake, near the village of Rome City, Indiana, had long been a favored summer retreat because of its wholesome diversions and picturesque natural setting. When the humidity climbed and the pavements began to blister, city dwellers who could afford it closed their blinds and fled in the direction of Sylvan Lake's cool breezes. Such excursions were not expensive, at least at the annual chautauqua assembly. Entry to Island Park was twenty-five cents a day.

Its natural setting notwithstanding, this wooded island had all of the amenities. Numerous bridges, boardinghouses, and docks had been constructed there over the years for the use of annual assembly goers by the Grand Rapids and Indiana Railway Company, holders of the lease on Island Park. When assembly attendance had begun to swell, the Railway Company had further erected on these park grounds a tabernacle, illuminated with calcium lights, that could seat three thousand. Because of its religious emphasis, Island Park Assembly was governed in a strict and orderly fashion. Ticket transfer to other than the original holder constituted grounds for fraud. When the night bells rang at 10 o'clock, lodgers retired to their rooms for the night, and the grounds were closed until 5:30 the next morning. Intoxicating beverages were not permitted. None but the moral were welcome here.

The session Gene attended that July with her sisters offered Bible instruction as well as other lectures. It is possibly no coincidence that one reason she was permitted to attend was because one of the lecturers was a former Wabash County minister. Prominently displayed on the grounds of this assembly was a plaster of paris cast of the topography of Palestine. As the main entertainment, students from Central Tennessee College sang and lectured in the interests of the Freedmen's Aid Society. Four of these harmonizing prose-lytizers had been slaves. One of the singers at this assembly captivated assembly goers with his tales of years in wretched bondage. The shouting tenor, Mr. Washington, had been a three-time runaway. It may be that it was here, at her first chautauqua, that Gene first learned of Harriet Tubman, the Moses of black men and women.

Other stirring diversions at Island Park that year included a barge decorated with Chinese and Japanese lanterns, which paraded nightly on Sylvan Lake. By way of a daytime attraction, for only five cents visitors could ride a passenger ferry fashioned from the hull of a side-wheeler steamer from the island to the mainland, or to Triplett's point on the mainland south. Those who had more than five cents could take advantage of the local rowboat concession, one more enticement to the crowds who flocked here every summer to play and to reaffirm their faith and broaden their cultural horizons.

Under these highly stimulating conditions, Gene again tasted the exhilaration of freedom from direct parental supervision that she had known as a small child. More important, she sampled her first protracted exposure to woods and water after an arid seven-year separation, although her thirst to explore the environs of Sylvan Lake more fully would have to wait until her next visit to Island Park. Although she did not write about her first chautauqua, she could only have been transfixed by this new world of professional entertainment, as well as revived by her old world of fresh air and sparkling water. As if drawn by a magnet, she would return year after year to this lakeside chautauqua. It would become her front door to the world. She would hear a Professor Bailey apprise his audience of world problems by means of a large celestial globe. She would be in the startled audience when one Captain Boynton prepared a meal in and on the water—went fishing, caught, cleaned, and cooked his fish dinner without any assistance but his bathing suit—a positive demonstration of how nature could take care of her own. Sylvan Lake, surrounded by an inviting expanse of green, was well suited to Gene Stratton's inclinations because it was a natural bird habitat. No less significant, the thrust of the chautauqua, with its emphasis on clean living and culture for the uneducated masses, was well suited to be her catalyst.

After returning home from her first visit to Island Park Assembly, Gene Stratton's next year passed uneventfully. Occasionally she visited the home of her brother Irvin in Fort Wayne, although she avoided the home, also in Fort Wayne, of her brother Jerome. She was fond of one of Jerome's daughters, Cosette, and possibly even fond of Jerome. The main reason she avoided him was because he liked to drink. Politically prominent Thomas R. Marshall, one of her shirttail relatives, relates one story in his memoirs about her brother Jerome's heated affair with the demon rum that is irresistible. According to Marshall, following a legal disagreement with a certain judge, Jerome stumbled into this judge's courtroom one day, brandishing a revolver, and threatened the judge's life. Whereupon the judge, seemingly an intrepid soul, calmly arose from the bench, jerked away Jerome's revolver, and kicked him down the stairs. However, Jerome, a fearless scamp and cunning as well, was not about to be denied. Bent on revenge, he returned to this courtroom a few days later with a different weapon, a butcher knife, with which he proposed to open the judge from end to end. Whereupon His Honor, being a man of enormous abdominal proportions, fled for his life clutching his breadbasket.[3]

Shortly after Gene turned nineteen, what then remained of her shrunken family circle began to break up completely. At that time her sister Anastasia was terminally ill and had been in and out of a cancer clinic in Aurora, Illinois, for over a year. Lemon, after receiving two years of college at the behest of Anastasia's husband Alvah Taylor, had been teaching school in the city of Wabash, although he was thinking about leaving shortly for employment in Ohio. The first person to break away was Florence. In October 1882 Florence married a well-to-do widower whom she had met earlier at Island Park Assembly.

After Florence had departed for what would become her new home in Bronson, Michigan, there was comparative quiet for the next five months. Then, late in March 1883, Anastasia—again undergoing special medical treatment in Illinois—took a turn for the worst.[4] When Anastasia's death seemed imminent, Florence was summoned home from Michigan. As neighbors and friends gathered to await the inevitable sad news from Illinois, tension in the family began to grow.

After a few days of receiving no word about Anastasia's condition, Mark Stratton sought relief from the mounting strain. In the interest of hearing what his fellow Protestants were saying about Higher Matters, he attended a local Presbyterian Synod. One day, while thus absorbed, he chanced to hear the moderator begin a fine sermon. In the middle of it, however, the moderator had a lapse of memory. He needed a particular quotation from the Bible. When he called on his fellow Presbyterians for help, however, they were embarrassingly silent. In desperation, the moderator then asked whether anyone else in the audience could tell him where the biblical reference he sought could be found, in order that he might proceed. Again, no response. After what seemed to him a reasonable length of time, Mark Stratton volunteered from the audience the exact chapter and verse. That evening, because of this display of erudition, he enjoyed a glorious repast downtown, dining with the moderator. On his return home, impressed because he had dined at the elaborate Tremont Hotel with the moderator, Gene was so proud of him she threw her arms around his neck and cried: "Oh, Father, you were the smartest man there!"[5]

Instantly, the light faded from his brow. She had misunderstood him completely. Seldom did he have the opportunity to discuss the scriptures with another student of the Bible. His had been a grand day, a day to be forever remembered. Disentangling Gene from around his neck, he turned away, saying: "Child! Child! If I have produced any such impression, I have told my story very badly."[6]

Later that week the Strattons decided that they would move back down the street into the Taylor household once Anastasia passed away. That way Alvah Taylor, who was still boarding Lemon, would have help from Ada and Gene with household chores and his two children. Informed of the impending move back to the Taylors, the youngest Stratton retaliated in a way calculated to wound her father irrevocably. She quit school. What a hellish week! Saturday night, word was received that Anastasia had breathed her last. The fireworks started after the funeral.

Years later, Gene Stratton-Porter said little about what had actually happened that week. Most of what she did relate was untrue. Implying that her reasons for leaving school were praiseworthy, she said she had missed the last several weeks unavoidably because she was needed at home. She said she left high school to care for an older sister in her last illness, although it is well documented that this sister died 160 miles removed from Wabash in a clinic where she had resided for many weeks. What Gene Stratton-Porter did not say was that she was already failing school when she chose to quit. She also failed to state that there was a personal reason for her rebellion. Only a short time earlier, because of her failing grades, Gene had been forced by her father to give up her pet birds and put their cages in storage. Although her father's wrath must have been great, it was matched by the firmness of Gene's resolve.

About five months later, now living in the Taylor home, the Strattons experienced another earthquake. The difficulty this time stemmed from Gene's overreaction when the last sibling besides herself and Lemon threatened to fly the family coop. When Ada married a local man named Frank Wilson, she expressed the natural desire to move into a home of her own. Ada might as well have declared she was leaving for parts unknown. Gene gave her older sister two alternatives. Ada and Frank could either stay in the Taylor household, or they could expect to be joined by Gene and Mark Stratton in any move out of it. Gene was not about to be the only female remaining under the Taylor roof, with sole responsibility for the housework. Mark Stratton concurred, perhaps uncomfortable at the thought of trying to get along without the buffering presence of Ada. In response to her younger sister's alternatives, Ada—always easily intimidated—went nowhere.

The upshot of all this family togetherness was predictable: pandemonium. Gene, her father, Lemon, Ada and her groom, and the widower Alvah Taylor and his two children were all under one roof. One month after Ada's marriage, Lemon bolted. He picked a poor way to exit. In October 1883 he eloped with a local girl named Alice Lowery, who had been raised by her aunt. Afterward, Lemon and Alice moved immediately into a home owned by this aunt.[7]

Although no one knows exactly what was the matter with Alice, or her aunt, there must have been something. As Ada tactfully put it several years later: "This marriage was not pleasing to our family."[8] Evidently not. This marriage spelled the end of Lemon insofar as keeping in touch with his family was concerned. He became a floater, jumping from place to place, from job to job, even from wife to wife. Not until thirty-three years later, on his deathbed, would Lemon be welcomed back into the Stratton fold, and then only by Gene, who appears to have been the family member with the largest capacity for forgiveness.

Two months after Lemon left home, one of the rooms in Alvah Taylor's mini-hotel was converted to a convalescent center for its most temperamental resident. Gene had caught her foot on an iron grating in a downtown sidewalk and suffered a fall that knocked her unconscious, cracked her skull, and sent her to bed for several weeks. To add to the trauma, her doctors found it necessary to shave her head to treat her scalp.

Ada said the entire family would have "shipwrecked upon the shoals" that winter had it not been for the level-headedness of Mark Stratton.[9] As usual, Ada was being too modest. Had it not been for Ada, who took care of the household as well as her disabled sister, the ship would have foundered. To add to the confusion, Florence came home from Michigan in January to show off her new baby. Ultimately, it was Alvah Taylor who put an end to the mob gathering in his household. In May 1884, a year after he had been invaded, Alvah married a widow in the neighborhood. No longer needed or wanted, all of his Stratton in-laws moved out, back to their former residence down the street.

That summer Gene made plans to attend the next chautauqua at Island Park Assembly on Sylvan Lake. She had been invited to stay at a cottage belonging to friends of her father, the Reverend and Mrs. Wilkinson, whose daughter Cora was about her own age. Once at the lake, the two girls spent long lazy hours fishing and exploring from a rowboat.

Sylvan Lake offered endless opportunities for investigation. Considerable in size, it was irregular in outline, with numerous points, narrows, and islands, and ranged in length to an extreme of three and one-half miles. It was an artificial lake, created many years earlier when a deep river had been dammed, pulling into its backwaters several nearby smaller bodies of water. Wide and tangled forests rimmed its shoreline. Puddle ducks and divers and blue herons dotted its inlets. Ashore, there were berries to pick and abundant wildflowers.

Because of her access to the Wilkinsons' boat, Gene was less restricted than she had been at Island Park Assembly on her first visit, and her meanderings around the lake proved relaxing and restorative. This therapeutic diversion was good for her because she was still recovering from her fall. But this was a resort, and there were many here whose interests ran counter to her own and who did not share her enthusiasm for the out-of-doors.

One day, on the assembly grounds, when she extended a straw full of plump berries to another woman in friendship, she met with scornful rejection. To a parlor denizen she had made a grievous error. A lady had no business picking berries. It was here that she first felt the stirrings that later caused her to write: "On account of my inclinations, education and rearing, I felt in a degree equipped to be their Moses."[10]

As usual, the chautauqua session that particular year was parochial. The highlight of this 1884 assembly was its main speaker, the Reverend DeWitt Talmage. Talmage could be counted on to preach against card playing, sports, theatergoing, Mormonism, and the sizzling fate of those who frequented watering places. From all parts of Indiana, Ohio, and Michigan, thousands converged on Sylvan Lake to hear his message.

Gene Stratton-Porter, age twenty. This photo was taken for her fiancé.

Florence, who was tenting at the lake with her husband, said that Gene's personal appearance among the heavy throng that summer was striking. Her hair, said Florence, had grown since being cut by her doctors at the time of her fall seven months earlier, and she wore it "piled high on her head; her keen grey eyes and heavy brows gave her a very different look from any one else."[11] In a photograph taken at that time she looked somewhat old-fashioned. At her throat she wore a bunch of black-eyed susans, gathered on her excursions into the surrounding wilds. The reason she wore the flowers, as she later related, was to hide the hollow of her throat: "My father thought the dress a trifle low at the throat, so the opening was closed with a bunch of flowers, in the interest of modesty."[12]

Still recovering from her fall, she walked the assembly grounds that summer with the aid of a cane. One day as she limped around the park, her unusual appearance caught the eye of a man named Charles Dorwin Porter, who was attending Island Park Assembly with a party of his cousins.[13] Fearing a serious breach of etiquette, Charles Porter dared not approach Gene directly, a problem readily solved by his cousin, Will Finch. Will approached Florence's husband, who by coincidence was acquainted with Finch's family. Thus availed of Gene's name and address via the ingenuity of his cousin, Charles Porter dallied for two months after the close of Island Park, and then, on 18 September 1884, he wrote her a letter. In it he identified himself as a druggist with a store in Geneva, Indiana, not far from Wabash. He also mentioned his interest in a drugstore in Fort Wayne. His was a polite letter, asking Gene for a reply in the event she felt he had not overstepped the bounds of propriety.

Gene did not receive Charles Porter's letter immediately because she did not return to Wabash from Sylvan Lake until a month after his letter had been delivered. After Island Park Assembly had closed in July, she had stayed on at the

Wilkinson cottage through September, and then had gone straight to Irvin's, with Cora in tow, to spend another couple of weeks. No longer compelled to get ready for school in the fall, she was in no hurry to return to Wabash. When she finally did return in mid-October after a three-month absence, she found Charles Porter's letter waiting.

Victorian etiquette demanded that she be cautious about answering a letter from a total stranger. Never having been a stickler for any kind of rules, however, Gene was not bothered one whit by receiving a letter from someone she did not know. She answered it right away. Hers was a cheerful reply, optimistic about eventual complete recovery from her fall. It was also candid about her family, even to the point of introducing one of her brothers—surely Jerome—as "all bad." In her letter, she also briefly outlined her modest family circumstances, depicted her father as an Englishman, and told Charles Porter that, if pleased with her response, she would like to hear from him again.[14]

$\gg$ 8 $\ll$

Enter Mr. Porter

IT is impossible to know exactly what happened to
Gene Stratton the year she met Charles because the
story she later concocted to fit this time slot was considerably less than truthful. Still, her melodramatic tale
is worth reviewing despite its many fallacies because it
contains at least one nugget of truth.

In 1884 the presidential election pitted James G. Blaine,
Republican, against Grover Cleveland, Democrat. Along
about July, the temperature in the Stratton household suddenly shot up by several degrees—not because the furnace had
been stoked accidentally that summer, but because Mark
Stratton was in a white heat. The Republican party had been
in the White House for twenty-eight years, and, naturally, he
would have felt that it was its God-given right to stay there.
And, by the same token, naturally he would have supported
the Republican nominee. James G. Blaine could have been a
madman, which he was not, and still Mark Stratton would
have supported him because of his party affiliation. After all,
as any good Republican then realized, Blaine's qualifications
were above reproach. The fact that this honorable Republican
was unable to clear himself of charges of political corruption
was clear evidence that he was being victimized. And just

because a man's monetary scruples were elastic did not necessarily mean that he was unfit to lead the country. Beyond this, Blaine was an unusually well-qualified presidential candidate for another reason. He had a royal nickname, "The Plumed Knight," bestowed by an orator, no less.

And so it was, according to Gene, that her father set out to spread James G. Blaine's first-rate qualifications as far as his voice box could carry, which was no small distance. It seems that Mark Stratton worked his neighborhood prior to the presidential election with as much fire as if he had been spreading the gospel. Every night, however, Gene said he came home "worried sick," stating that one unfortunate phrase in the mouth of a Republican would surely elect a Democrat. Of course that is exactly what came to pass. On election eve in New York, a Republican clergyman named Samuel D. Burchard made an offensive speech that characterized the Democratic party as partial to "rum, Romanism, and rebellion." Whether Blaine was defeated the next day by Burchard's offensive remarks or by the rain in many rural districts is yet a matter for debate. Whatever reasons account for the outcome of this election, they cannot match by way of human interest the public spectacle that Gene said occurred in Wabash that gray day after the Republican party went down to defeat. She said her family's small frame house was surrounded by a "howling mob," by neighbors who had listened to her father crow about James G. Blaine once too often. She also said her family was forced to shut up the house while a parade of Democrats, bent on sweet revenge, rode "up and down the sidewalk, up the front walk, and with long-handled brooms, swept the house from the upper story to the lower." Like water, these triumphant neighbors flowed into, upon, and over flower beds and the lawn.[1]

While this makes a good story, it is nothing more than that. There were no broom sweepers; there was no lawn watering; and her father did not spend several weeks prior to the election

Charles Dorwin Porter

exercising his voice box, at least not in Wabash. He could not
have because he was not there. Six weeks prior to this national
election, he had gone first to Irvin's in Fort Wayne for a short
visit and then on to Daniel's in Ohio. Gene was not in Wabash
prior to the election either. Except for two weeks in Fort
Wayne with Irvin, she had spent the entire three months after
Island Park Assembly with the Wilkinsons. She had returned
to Wabash in mid-October, when her father was still out of
town visiting Daniel. She and her father had not crossed paths
since early July.[2]

However, to find the nugget we must continue her story.
Gene said further that, informed of a Republican defeat, her
father was inconsolable:

> That day he sat with his head bowed and his heart
> almost broken; then we waited in fear and trembling
> to learn what the awful Democrats were going to do.
> I have not the faintest notion today as to exactly what
> I expected they would do. It was to be some big, black
> menacing thing that was to blast the entire country.[3]

She describes herself as being caught up in her father's fearful
preachments for several months after the election, and she
tells us that Mark Stratton continued to lambaste the Cleveland administration after the election as if Judgment Day
would be the day after tomorrow. Then, when the expected
Democrat doom failed to materialize and the Wabash Post
Office, under this administration, became the best the city
had ever known, Gene finally came to the "dumbfounding
realization" that her father's opinions were not necessarily
gospel: "It marked the first period in which I quit being gullible and began to think for myself."[4] Not really. She tended
to be an independent thinker from the very beginning. A new
and efficient post office had not triggered any latent ability to
think for herself. Nor was this a time in her life when she
"quit being gullible." She had not been completely cured of

partisan politics and never would be; she would always have Republican sentiments. Moreover, she would never lose her Anglophilia; she would always believe in the superiority of all things English.

Thus, though Gene had long thought independently and would long remain gullible to some extent, this was the first time she was able to look at her father objectively. While this realization may have been partially responsible for the transformation she experienced at this time (the nugget of truth in her story), other factors also contributed to her newfound emancipated state of mind. She felt good about herself for the first time in ages when something came along that raised her expectations and injected some joy into her life. All of her melodrama to the contrary, it is obvious that Gene Stratton declared herself capable of thinking for herself when she first attracted favorable attention from an eligible bachelor named Charles Dorwin Porter.

Porter wrote her often during the long winter months of 1884, gradually revealing himself as a self-made businessman, accountable and beholden to no one. A member of the Masonic Order and the Sons of Veterans, he had been brought up a Presbyterian. Divested of his associations and convictions, he appeared to have come from a locally prominent family, and what Gene learned of his manners from his correspondence conformed to her sense of refinement. Although his roots were Irish, not English, nevertheless his background was similar to hers. Both had been reared in small agricultural communities, and as adolescents both had lost a parent.

Charles Porter had grown up a short distance east of Wabash in rural Adams County abutting the Ohio line. His grandfather, Dr. Alexander Porter, had been a pioneer physician in the county. There, too, his father, Dr. John Pomeroy Porter, also practiced medicine until he joined the Union forces during the early days of the Civil War as a first assistant surgeon with a regiment that saw active duty. Captured in

Kentucky and paroled the next day, he was allowed to return home once on a furlough to visit his wife and three children. At that time, Charles, the oldest, was only thirteen. One year later, having earlier been exchanged and returned to his regiment, John Pomeroy Porter was shot and killed by guerrillas near Lexington, Missouri.[5]

Although Charles Porter's mother was entitled to a pension based on her husband's military service, after the war the wheels of the federal bureaucracy turned slowly, especially in Elizabeth Porter's case. Her application for financial assistance was not approved until after Charles had reached the age of sixteen. That meant she was ineligible for any federal funds on his behalf. However, being underprivileged was no handicap to Charles, who quickly proved himself a self-starter. At the age of eighteen he had already established himself in the drug trade, first in Fort Wayne, then in Decatur. In 1872 he opened the first drugstore in the Adams County hamlet of Geneva.[6]

As the community of Geneva expanded, Charles Porter grew with it. Possessed of an almost uncanny knack for making money, he prospered early. An ambitious man, fully mindful of his financial genius, he carried himself with a confidence that complemented his brisk stride. Charles Porter's shrewd way with a dollar was not lost on the residents of Geneva. When the village incorporated in 1874, the locals elected him town treasurer. By the time he began corresponding with Gene Stratton ten years later, Charles Porter's reputation in Adams County was that of an entrepreneur who merited the tip of a hat, as well as that of an eligible bachelor.

Charles's marital availability was the subject of much merriment among his many friends because of his long-standing posture of indifference to marriage. Despite his pose, however, late in 1884 Charles Porter had clearly begun to contemplate the altar. When he had first solicited Gene's friendship, in September 1884, his mother was ill. Four weeks later she died. When Charles Porter began writing to Gene Stratton in earnest several days later, he was thirty-four years old, had just lost his mother, and was ready to marry.

Yet the young woman on whom Charles Porter suddenly began to focus his attention was no mother substitute with domestic inclinations. In the privacy of her room, Gene Stratton did not dream of a future home and hearth surrounded by smiling cherubs. There were other things on her mind. She liked to remember that day when she had stood before the assembly and held her classmates spellbound. Her thoughts strayed often to what might lie ahead for her personally, to what might be required to become a woman of accomplishment. She apparently felt one clue might be in the lives of those successful individuals of her father's generation, and she had begun to put together a scrapbook filled with biographical sketches of prominent persons. It was an unusual compilation for a young woman. The scrapbook Gene Stratton pored over as a young adult is filled not with the usual personal mementos and dried flowers, but with articles that set forth the exploits and accomplishments of such giants as John Jacob Astor and Commodore George Dewey.[7]

Charles Porter should have known that the girl with whom he had begun to correspond was ambitious because of her remarks in her letters about Cora Wilkinson, a quiet, contented girl. Cora's main fault, as Gene perceived it, was her self-satisfaction: "She won't *progress*."[8] Likewise, Gene should have known that she was beginning to tangle with a man who would tolerate no nonsense. When Charles sent her his photograph, she appraised it in her usual forthright manner, replying in her next letter that his chin looked so cross she wondered if he would bite. Overall, however, her letters to Charles Porter were light and tantalizing. What man, especially a druggist, would not respond to her prescription on how they should be read? "'This epistolary effusion is to be taken at one dose—the patient to be placed in a reclining chair, pillow under the head, slippered feet at an angle of 23 1/2, best Havana and palm leaf."[9]

Ten months after they began to exchange letters, they arranged to meet. They first gauged each other's personal mettle at a retreat familiar to both, Island Park Assembly, a gathering marked as much by joyful reunions as by the peal of the old bell inviting classes and spectacular entertainments. The atmosphere at that chautauqua assembly was more broadening than usual, with a mounted exhibition on the grounds of a mastodon recently unearthed nearby, as well as a museum brought over from Jerusalem. Sylvan Lake was dotted that July with boating pleasure-seekers. Excursions by steamer went out daily up the lake to Spring Beach, so named from the numerous springs of sparkling water gushing forth from the rocky bottom at this elevated point. Love, or at least its symptoms, was contagious in such a fair setting. One observer recalled that the white water lily scarcely raised its head above the water that summer before it was plucked to adorn some fair lady. [10]

Gene was not entirely smitten, however, by what appeared to be romantic overtures toward her by Charles Porter. On meeting him, she was disturbed. She saw something in him that gave her pause. Because of this, she decided to address him formally as "Mr. Porter."

On her return to Wabash, any lingering thoughts she may have had about getting better acquainted with Charles Porter quickly disappeared in the face of what had happened at home in her absence. Without her consent or knowledge, all of her belongings—her scrapbook and her personal notes, her clothing, everything—had been moved several blocks to a new residence purchased by Ada and Frank. Her father was gone. He had left for Ohio, ostensibly to be out from underfoot when Ada's first baby arrived in September. It is just as likely, however, that he had left home for another reason: to escape Gene's probable reactions. For in her absence that summer, he had committed the unforgivable. He had loaned Ada's husband several hundred dollars.[11]

Mark Stratton had no reason to think of his loan to Frank Wilson in terms of further depriving Gene of any money. This loan to Frank was merely a kind of insurance policy. Mark Stratton was then in his seventies, perhaps on the verge of forgetfulness, but acutely aware that he wanted to spend his final years in comparative comfort. His loan to Frank and Ada had enabled them to buy a house, and Mark Stratton expected to live in that house with the Wilsons for the rest of his days with no strings attached—no strings except, of course, Frank's repayment of the loan along with 8 percent annual interest. Gene was bound to have been irked. Her privacy had been invaded when her personal belongings had been moved in her absence to Ada's. Moreover, even though there seemed to be enough money to carry Frank Wilson, whenever Gene asked for money the family well was always dry. In addition, she was exceedingly tired of boarding round. For ten years she had shuttled back and forth among her relatives.

She was still smarting over all this after her return from the lake when Charles began to pester her. In his letters he repeatedly asked why she chose to address him as "Mr. Porter." Possibly he thought it was because he was thirteen years her senior, not quite old enough to be her father, but at least old enough to command a certain respect. If that is what Charles thought, then he was in for a surprise. Her reason for addressing him thus had nothing to do with his age, and nothing to do with respect. Boldly, in a candid letter, she explained that she preferred to address him as "Mr. Porter" because of the awe she felt in the presence of his "cold blue eyes."[12] Having dropped one bomb, she let go another one, outlining in her letter what she perceived to be the pitfalls of matrimony.

Obviously, after his overtures at the lake, she felt Charles Porter had matrimony in mind, for she openly mused in her letter to him about its consequences, pondering much on the difference between "engaged love" and "married love." Although she denied being either "a carper or a howler for woman's rights," she did state that cheerfulness was absolutely too much to expect of any married woman daily burdened with household chores, finally concluding that matrimony was potentially satisfactory for men only.[13]

That did it. Charles was hooked. Any woman who said she favored matrimony for men only was safe to chase. He called on her in Wabash soon after, taking the weekend train. During this first visit, Irvin met Charles and gave his stamp of approval, although the reactions of Mark Stratton and Ada were less enthusiastic. If Mark Stratton ever voiced approval of Charles Porter, he was very quiet about it. Inasmuch as Mark Stratton did not know how to be quiet, we can be certain that he found fault with Gene's suitor, as did Ada. Ada had met Charles at the lake three months earlier. Contrary to her usually agreeable manner, Ada was not enthusiastic about her sister's beau. Possibly Charles Porter was too sophisticated for Ada. As for Irvin, Gene had reason to be pleased with his acceptance of Charles because, of her three surviving brothers, she was fondest of Irvin. Her brother Jerome, because of his drinking habits, was certainly no prize, and the personality of banished Lemon, ever the joker, was not calculated to inspire sisterly trust and confidence. Irvin, on the other hand, although very much the pedant, was mature and stable. Besides this, he and Gene shared an important bond, a fond memory of their drowned brother Laddie. Within the past year, Irvin had named his first son in Laddie's memory. Thus when Irvin offered to let his little sister meet Charles on weekends at his home in Fort Wayne, she accepted his invitation readily. At Irvin's, she could put any disapproval by her father and Ada out of her mind, at least temporarily.

Charles Porter must have represented to Gene Stratton the antithesis of her life up to that time, and a desirable catch besides. Charles was a man of affairs, and he liked to travel. Surely a girl from the country could learn a great deal from such a man. Also, he came from a respectable family; his brother Miles was a physician; and his sister had married a missionary. When his widowed mother had remarried, she had chosen a Presbyterian minister. By way of further personal endorsement, Charles Porter was Republican in politics and a member of the Republican Central Committee of Adams County for the past five years, although, unlike her father, Charles's politics did not seem to be overheated.

Moreover, Charles Porter's financial condition was sound. In fact, he seemed to be well off, and his wife could expect to be well cared for. He owned an eighty-acre farm in Adams County and was negotiating to acquire an adjacent one hundred acres. In addition, of course, there was his interest in that Fort Wayne drugstore, as well as the larger store in the village of Geneva that carried an inventory worth $6,000. Only recently, in order to allow more time for what he hoped would be an even more lucrative venture, Charles had taken on a partner in the drug business.

Charles Porter's ultimate goal was to become a banker. Recognizing the need for a bank in the community of Geneva, he had installed a large vault-like safe in the rear of his drugstore to accommodate those whose businesses required them to handle large sums of money. Gene could only have been overjoyed with what marriage to a prospective banker might mean for her own future financial security. Charles Porter was tailor-made for a girl with money problems. Commingled, however, with her thoughts about the compatibility and financial comfort of life with Charles Porter were her thoughts about the possible negative aspects of marriage to anyone. As evidenced by her letters, she felt that the daily chores expected of a married woman could constitute an onerous burden. She was resisting marriage, both inwardly and outwardly. At the same time, she must have been betting that, once married, she could change or overlook whatever bothered her. In October 1885 she and Charles became engaged, only three months after they had personally met.

The wedding was set for late spring. In March Charles purchased a two-story frame house on Main Street in Decatur, near the Adams County courthouse. He had lived in this house as a youth. The old Porter homestead, however, had not been built for comfort, its old-time windows small and many paned, its rooms cramped and dark. Flush with the sidewalk, a boardwalk at its front, the house fronted an un-paved street. One entered by a double door at its center that opened into a narrow hall, low-ceilinged and with a narrow stairway, leaving a small space that led to the rear and the kitchen. There was nothing of a backyard, nor any room for trees, flowers, or shrubs. When he bought the property, Charles was under the impression Gene would be happy there. At his suggestion that the house could be enlarged, she told him it would be all right as it stood. After they were married, however, she would appear to change her mind about this house. Before his marriage, Charles had no idea how difficult it would always be to satisfy his wife's desire for the ideal house.

Two weeks before the wedding, Florence came home to help with the plans. Without Florence it would have been a simple ceremony with no frills. Mark Stratton said he could not afford to pay for a wedding. So Florence agreed to pay for it, in exchange for her father's promissory note. Mark Stratton signed the note, although he later refused to pay it. A few years later, upon his death, Florence would collect in full from her father's estate the amount she had advanced for her youngest sister's wedding.[14]

The nuptials were scheduled for 21 April 1886 at Ada's. They took place in an evening ceremony attended only by family and a few of Charles's friends. Befitting the occasion, the bride was the center of attention. Her wedding gown was beautiful. So like a sweetbrier rose, it surely would have pleased her mother. Pink silk, paneled with pink taffeta and brocaded with tiny rosebuds and soft green leaves, the gown was complemented by a delicate fan, also sprinkled with tiny rosebuds and true blue forget-me-nots. Gene's going-away dress was in regal high fashion—peacock blue, with matching wrap, crowned by a velvet hat, its emphasis a large curled ostrich plume.[15]

And so it was that, after the ceremony, equipped with little more than a new dress, a young woman with a mind full of mixed notions about the benefits of matrimony went straight to a dingy house in a city full of strangers with a man about whom she had serious reservations, a man whom she would continue to address as "Mr. Porter," even after her marriage.

❧ 9 ❧

Simmering Like a Teakettle

FORTHCOMING difficulties aside, Gene's marriage to Charles Porter was the best thing that could have happened to her. Charles appears to have loved her, and she needed that. Under his wing, she began to blossom.

A photograph of her taken soon after their marriage projects nothing but poise. Gone is the old-fashioned, submissive look that had attracted Charles in the first place. In its stead is the confident expression of a sophisticated woman who looks as if she could be a duchess. This new self-assurance, coupled with her mercurial emotional makeup, was an explosive combination, eventually bound to rock even the most stable marriage.

Gene Stratton-Porter once described her fiery temperament as "boiling and bubbling like a yeast jar in July."[1] It was a keen self-appraisal, for, indeed, she could bubble with enthusiasm, particularly about birdlife, and she could also boil with anger, especially when she felt imposed upon. And, like a yeast jar, one would not suspect she was in any degree heated under the lid because she usually looked cool enough on the surface. Moreover, when subjected to a simmering heat, she was slow to reach the boiling point. Here the similarity ends, however, for when a yeast jar begins to boil over, it is generally silent. Gene Stratton-Porter's temperament was more like a boiling teakettle than a yeast jar. Once she had begun to steam, there could be no mistake about the urgency of her whistle.

During the first few years of her marriage, Gene Stratton-Porter was much like a teakettle on simmer. She had not yet begun to whistle, even though she was unhappy living in Decatur, a county seat that closely resembled Wabash in size and general atmosphere. One of Charles Porter's reasons for choosing to reside in the hub of Decatur was logical. This city was convenient to both of his drugstores. His store in Fort Wayne was twenty-one miles northwest of Decatur. His store in the village of Geneva was south of Decatur, about eighteen miles away. By situating his wife in the middle of his weekly travel track, he would be able to spend more time with her.

Charles Porter's other reason for choosing to reside in Decatur was not quite so logical. As a matter of fact, it was rooted in a false assumption. Jeannette Porter Meehan tells us that her father felt the social opportunities in a community as large as Decatur would redound to her mother's benefit. If that in fact is what Charles did think, then his wife's distaste for city living had wholly failed to register, because Decatur offered her no more than Wabash. Except for Ada, she had been virtually friendless in Wabash. She would likewise be friendless in Decatur. Even if she had joined a local social circle, chances are she would have been a misfit because of her inability to subordinate her own interests to those of most organized groups, social or otherwise, in any city. The rank and file of Decatur's formidable Women's Christian Temperance Union would most likely have welcomed her membership. The effectiveness of such small-town groups depended on women with the social leverage of the new Mrs. Charles

Porter. The last thing *she* wanted, however, was to join a group of females with axes to grind. She made that clear in a letter to her niece Cosette shortly after her marriage in which she elaborated on the joys of homemaking versus club membership and further expressed her utter contempt for clubwomen in general.[2]

When first married, Gene Stratton-Porter vowed to become a homebody. It stands to reason she would want to try her hand at domesticity because, for the first time since she had left the farm, she was no longer "boarding round." Now she had a house where she could do as she pleased, a house that belonged not to her father, nor to the Taylors, nor to Ada, but a house of her very own.

She should have known that this homebody notion would wear out in a hurry. The old Porter homestead was not fixable in terms of comfort, and housework had never been her idea of a good time anyway. Even if she had been enjoying herself at home, Charles was seldom there long enough to appreciate her efforts. For years he had spent his work weeks zipping between his drugstores by rail. After he married, his habits remained the same. Sometimes he became so absorbed in the conduct of his affairs that he missed the evening train and failed to come home. When that happened, Gene wrote him a letter. That she felt neglected can be seen from a letter written shortly after her marriage in which she wavers between expressing her loneliness and berating herself for being bothered by such a trifle.[3] To pass the long, lonely days she began to spend several hours a day in the kitchen. Her idea of ambrosia was a staple she had learned to eat on the farm—dock, dandelion greens, and horseradish leaves, boiled with a ham bone. Charles, unaccustomed to such fare, humorously referred to these greens as "fodder."[4]

A few weeks after they were married, Charles Porter effected a major change in his life-style. He disposed of his interest in his Fort Wayne drugstore, thereby reducing his

Gene Stratton-Porter as she appeared soon after her marriage

travel time in order to spend more time at home. Then he gave his bride a late honeymoon, leasing a cottage on Sylvan Lake at Rome City for the chautauqua season. Island Park was bursting at the seams that year. It is easy to see why both of them might have been less than enthusiastic about that particular assembly session. Thirteen thousand pairs of feet descended on the park grounds that July and tromped all over the greenery, all irresistibly drawn by a popular spectacle, the plain-speaking Reverend Sam Jones, who abused the English language almost as much as he abused his audience, with epithets of "hog" and "beast."[5] Aside from what had become Bible-thumping exhibitions such as this, however, the Porters enjoyed Sylvan Lake for its own sake during their early married years. They would continue to vacation here summer after summer, later staying at Triplett's Hotel, a large rambling frame structure facing the beach south of Island Park.

After her delayed honeymoon at the lake, Gene began to get bored and restless. Then, in September, Irvin announced his intention to give up his Fort Wayne law practice and move west. He planned to follow Jerome, who had already left for Kansas. By 1886 homestead entries had reached a maximum in Kansas. The Great Plains was cattle country; the cowboy was king. All Irvin had to do was get himself a horse, which he had been wanting to do for years anyway, buy a small herd, turn it out to graze, watch it fatten and multiply, and practice law on the side. As for Jerome, he had taken the temperance pledge and renounced the devil in his soul. He honestly meant to walk the straight and narrow. Otherwise, he would not have chosen to reestablish a law practice in Kansas, which was bone dry.

When Irvin began to prepare for his move, Gene, too, was smitten by western fever, although not especially by Kansas. Perhaps she knew the plains women were apt to spend their days gathering buffalo chips. She had a more attractive destination in mind, a place where recently there had been a gold

Gene Stratton-Porter

rush, the Black Hills of Dakota. She was soon sidetracked, however, by an even more compelling prospect, one that would take the steam out of her whistle for several years to come: motherhood. Less than eight weeks after beginning to badger Charles about moving to Dakota, Gene discovered she was expecting.·

At first this knowledge filled her with anxiety. As her delivery time neared, however, her fears gradually subsided in favor of joyful anticipation. She was expecting a boy, and she had a name already in mind. She planned to name him Mark. Whether she was disappointed in the sex of what would be her only child we shall never know. The baby was born 27 August 1887, and they named her after Charles's sister Jeannette.

With the delight and busy responsibility of a baby, Gene Stratton-Porter was temporarily content. Her independent nature asserted itself only infrequently, in brief sputters, as in one flare-up shortly after Jeannette's birth. Charles continued to work long hours, and married life had become increasingly lonely. Gene was miserable that winter, as was most of the upper Midwest, marooned indoors for days on end by a great blizzard. With difficulty, the following spring she managed to persuade Charles that she and the baby should leave Decatur and move to the village of Geneva, where Charles would then be within walking distance of his business. Jeannette Porter Meehan says she was later given to understand that her father agreed reluctantly, which is probably true. Charles would continue to hang on to their home in Decatur for five more years, possibly hoping that in time his wife would come to appreciate the desirability of living in the county seat.

In the spring of 1888, Charles Porter bought his wife a little yellow cottage on a fenced double lot within a few blocks of his Geneva drugstore. It even had a chicken house and an orchard.[6] Although she grumbled at its small dimensions, once settled Gene was happier here than she had been in

Decatur. Besides not having to wait for Charles to come home on the train, she was now a short distance from something quite familiar. By virtue of her move to Geneva, she was now in Wabash Township of Adams County, close once more to the Wabash River, only forty miles upstream from the place of her beginnings.

Once more, she began to accumulate a family of pet birds. Her first was a green linnet. Soon she found him a mate. Their first brood consisted of six sturdy youngsters; the second, five; and the third, four. Such a large bevy called for a special home—six feet high, four feet long, and three feet wide, under a green roof. To Gene, these babies were a picture: "When the birds of this cage were asleep in a row, filling the highest perch, with their heads tucked under their wings, and their feathers fluffed in cold weather, they looked exactly like gaudy swan's down powder puffs."[7]

From the last brood she had one bird with a slight handicap. He could fly and hop around nearly as well as his brothers and sisters, although he had one leg out of joint. This gave him an awkward gait. More than once Charles urged that this crippled bird be put "out of its misery." Much to Gene's pleasure, however, this special bird exceeded all the others in size and was a fine singer, imitating indigo finch, song sparrow, and robin nearly to perfection. One day when she was absent from home, this special bird disappeared. She was told that a woman, whose name she could never discover, had called at the house begging to be sold a singer and that Gene's favorite bird had been given away. She was heartbroken: "My best beloved bird was easily caught and given to her, which was a small heartbreak from which I never have recovered."[8] It does not require a detective to determine who gave her singer away—or did away with it. Charles was the only other adult living there.

As in this instance, nearly all of Gene Stratton-Porter's comments about her early married years are veiled. Moreover, they are sparse. As such, they are highly conspicuous, and from these indirect references emerges a dismal picture. Obviously, during the early years of her marriage, she felt as if she were under contract as a domestic: "I did not write, but I continued violin, painting and embroidery lessons, and did all the cooking and housework with the exception of the washing and ironing. I had agreed to love a man, and to keep his house neat and clean."[9]

Moreover, her financial expectations had not come to pass. Although Charles Porter was a hard-working individual, he was also a saver and an investor who could not justify to himself spending any money over and above their actual needs. Once again, Gene found herself in a familiar rut, both emotionally and financially, as can be seen from another of her rare remarks about the early years of marriage: "In my own home for the first time I had the handling of money myself, but with the old stipulations. It was to pay for food, for the washing, for clothing; with a little left over for music lessons, a course in fine needlework. There was nothing wildly hilarious about any of this."[10]

For recreation she continued to rely on her steadily growing bird collection. On his return from Mexico, the husband of Charles's sister brought her a black-headed evening grosbeak. Then Florence sent her a parrot named Major. Major had been trained to whistle with a flute. He also performed with the piano and the violin. Next Gene rescued two nesting orioles. It was inevitable, given her love for music, that she would eventually notice the similarity between the song of these orioles and the familiar refrain from Friedrich Adolf Ferdinand von Flotow's opera *Martha*. She concluded that her orioles liked to practice the spinning song, "I can wash, sir, I can spin, sir, I can sew and mend, and babies tend," and she felt these birds sang this couplet much as would a trained singer, in a "sharp, worried, busy tone."[11]

All of Gene's birds seemed to be doing extraordinarily well as she tried to teach them to accompany her on a musical instrument. Eventually she felt ready to have her bevy per-

Gene Stratton-Porter charcoal sketch of Mark Stratton and his granddaughter Jeannette

form before an audience: "I grew vainglorious and wrote to my father to come and be convinced."[12] Then one day Jeannette caught her apron on a nail, tearing a long slit across it. When Gene sat down at her sewing machine to mend her daughter's apron, she was in for an awakening. Every one of her birds, with the exception of the parrot, could accompany the sewing machine quite as well as they had ever accompanied the violin or the piano.

Soon after she had invited him to a bird concert, her father, then still living with Ada and Frank in Wabash, became seriously ill. High blood pressure had finally begun to get the best of him, perhaps partly because Ada's husband had never repaid that house loan, nor even kept up the interest. On 10 January 1890 he died after suffering a stroke. Mark Stratton may have planned to become the first man in history to take his material possessions with him, for his estate would not be settled for eighteen years. He died without a will, his only legal preparation being a deed executed eight weeks before his death to the Hopewell Cemetery Society for that graveyard next to his old church—not conveyed gratis, as Gene liked to imply, but in his usual sharp manner, for $150.[13]

As an old man, her father had always worn a cardinal red handkerchief in his vest pocket, symbol of the red ribbon of temperance. Thus it was on the day he died. Gene, ever loyal to only the best memories of her father, had only one comment at the time of his death: "It was so like him to have that scrap of vivid colour in his pocket."[14] This brief remark does not do justice to the ambivalence she felt at her loss. In a letter to Cosette shortly afterwards, she apologizes for her inability to write about her father's demise. The words would not come.[15]

After the funeral, her personality began to undergo a marked change. Week by week she grew increasingly anxious. Totally unprepared for this growing disquietude, she began casting about desperately for a way to deal with it. She could not seem to find the right spot in her heart for her father's memory. Many months went by, uneventful except for a building personal torment: "In those days I was experiencing constant struggle to find an outlet for the tumult in my being. . . . Because I dearly loved music I thought that might be my medium."[16]

Daily she worked to perfect her skills on the piano and the violin. Music, however, was not enough to dispel the constant unrest set in motion by her father's death. Finally, three years after his passing, she apparently made an effort to come to terms with her restless spirit by another means. Overwhelming circumstantial evidence suggests that Gene Stratton-Porter tried to purge her emotions by writing a book. In 1893 a fictional work by an unknown writer appears that has all the characteristics of a Stratton-Porter novel. Her "fingerprints" are all over this anonymous publication.

Students of Indiana literature have long considered it gospel that Gene Stratton-Porter first broke into print in the year 1900. This date is supplied by Gene Stratton-Porter herself in several separate accounts of when her first article was accepted by a publisher. It now appears, however, that her first work, a short book, was actually published seven years earlier. The reason Gene Stratton-Porter would have suppressed the fact that she published as early as 1893 becomes clear when one reads the book in question. It is a transparently autobiographical work, with a strong negative aspect.

The title of this anonymously written work is *The Strike at Shane's*. It was submitted as a writing contest entry for a prize offered by the American Humane Education Society of Boston, Massachusetts. In 1892 this society announced the offer of three $200 prizes to anyone who could write a story with as much appeal as *Black Beauty*, one of its earlier publications that had met with high success.

The rules of this humane society's writing contest were much in the anonymous writer's favor. All manuscripts were

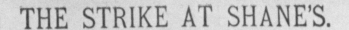

THE STRIKE AT SHANE'S.

GOLD MINE SERIES No. 2.

Sequel to "BLACK BEAUTY."

A PRIZE STORY OF INDIANA.

WRITTEN FOR, AND REVISED, COPYRIGHTED
AND PUBLISHED BY THE

"AMERICAN HUMANE EDUCATION SOCIETY."

For prices, etc., write GEO. T. ANGELL, President,
19 MILK STREET, BOSTON.

Title page of The Strike at Shane's

required to be submitted under a pseudonym. If a contest entry was eventually adjudged a winner by the society's editorial committee, then and only then would the true name of the author be revealed. Although *The Strike at Shane's* was selected as a winning entry, it was published anonymously, and the name of its author was never revealed. On the title page of this book appears the notation: "Written for, and revised, copyrighted, and published by the American Humane Education Society." *The Strike at Shane's* was published a few months later than the first three winning entries. That may mean that the manuscript was first rejected, then later revived by George Angell, president of the American Humane Education Society and a prodigious writer. Angell may have felt *The Strike at Shane's* was worth salvaging and published it after he had reworked it. Angell died in 1909 without revealing who had originally written this book, and the identity of its original author cannot now be conclusively determined. Nevertheless, given its story line, its characterizations, a grammatical error found also in an early Stratton-Porter letter, as well as a certain peculiar phrase found also in one of her early works, it is not difficult to attribute *The Strike at Shane's* to Gene Stratton-Porter. Nor is it difficult to understand why she would have suppressed any knowledge of this autobiographical work and denied having written it, had it been uncovered during her lifetime. Her authorship of *The Strike at Shane's* was Gene Stratton-Porter's best-kept secret, the one she carried to her grave, the secret she was contemplating the day she died as she read a poem of deep personal significance to her secretary: "God is much the safest place to hide a secret—or your face."

The Strike at Shane's is set on a farm during the late 1800s. Its main character is a carbon copy of Gene Stratton-Porter's father, a pioneer who has farmed for twenty-five years in an Indiana agricultural valley. Strongly contrary, however, to the favorable way Stratton-Porter always depicted her father, farmer Shane is described as greedy and ill-tempered: "A hard man to deal with, and always aimed to make a dollar where other people made a dime. . . . Avarice held full sway over his mind, and there was no room in his nature for kindness. Everything on the place felt the effects of his ill-temper—even his family did not always escape."[17]

This greedy, bad-tempered farmer and one of his sons, a boy much like Lemon Stratton, habitually shoot the birds that raid the cherry orchard. Shane the farmer is especially cruel not only to these birds, but also to his wife's horse, an old nag named Dobbin who had carried Shane and his wife into this valley but who has now outlived his usefulness.

Two other characters in this story have an equally familiar ring. They are farmer Shane's wife, Mary, who, like Mary Stratton, is ill and overworked, and his young daughter Edith: "Invariably kind and gentle in their ways, they were loved by everything on the farm, and their righteous indignation would sometimes get the better of their judgment, and they would speak their minds about the cruelties practised by father and son."[18] Minor characters include an Irishman and a girl friend of Edith Shane's named Cora, reminiscent of Cora Wilkinson.

The story is simple. One day the birds and animals who have been mistreated on the Shane farm hold a secret meeting. They meet at a site much like that place on her father's farm where Gene sent telltale hawk evidence downstream: under a large oak tree down in a pasture beside a brook. At this convention of abused creatures, a quail speaks for all of the birds about the merciless guns of Shane and his son. A cow contends that Shane's ornery son beats her when he comes to milk her and likes to tie her tail to her leg so she cannot switch flies. The most maligned animal testifying at this meeting is a bay horse named Dick, who complains of being tied to a strong post for hours on end in checkrein, head up. In hopes of remedying their situation, these birds and animals decide

to go on strike. After an overenthusiastic hawk—who wants
to kill all of the chickens—is driven away by a crow and a
kingbird, the remainder of these birds and animals take strong
action. They stage a sit-down.

The cow starves herself so she can no longer give milk.
The hen hides her eggs. The blackbird enlists his friends to
deposit worms on Shane's corn crop. Dick feigns lameness.
Farmer Shane, incensed, tries to drive him anyway with a
whip, pulling on the reins until Dick's mouth begins to bleed.
Whereupon Dick deliberately fails to negotiate a curve, and
the horse cart overturns, throwing Shane to the ground unconscious and leaving him incapacitated for the next two
months with a broken leg. Afterward, from his sickbed, although he fails to understand it, farmer Shane learns that
worms have devoured his corn crop. Meanwhile, he neglects
to appreciate the beauties of his trusting wife and the tender
ministrations of his daughter. Eventually—overwhelmed
by the paralyzing effects of his animals' strike—cruel, ill-
tempered, avaricious farmer Shane is persuaded by a neighbor
and his loving daughter Edith to mend his errant ways. That
brings an end to the strike, and everyone lives happily ever
after.

At about the same time *The Strike at Shane's* was published,
Gene Stratton-Porter made an uncharacteristic about-face in
two respects, which suggests she had suddenly acquired a
newfound sense and appreciation of freedom. First she gave
the wild birds in her home their freedom, reducing her bird
family to Major the parrot and a few canaries. Then, completely reversing her avowed contempt for clubwomen, she
started a club. She organized a literary society, the Wednesday
Club. As might be expected, Gene Stratton-Porter was no
ordinary organizer. She never did anything by halves. Like
her mother, whatsoever her hand found to do, she did it with
all her might. This Wednesday Club had a constitution and a
strong set of bylaws, and it was not for the typical joiner. Any

local woman who was willing to donate Wednesday afternoons, plus several hours per week, to the study of American and English literature could apply for membership to Mrs. Charles Porter. At the same time this club was being organized, a lively literary review column that carried no byline suddenly appeared in the *Geneva Herald*, the local newspaper. This regular column was well written, with much flair. One of the books that found favor with the anonymous local reviewer was, of course, *The Strike at Shane's*.[19]

Gene Stratton-Porter's main interest at this time was her newly organized literary club. When it was her turn to deliver a book review before the village literati, she chose to interpret *Leaves of Grass*, by Walt Whitman.[20] That Gene Stratton-Porter even knew about Whitman is surprising. Whitman was popular primarily in Europe; his poetry had not yet caught the full attention of America, certainly not the ear of a villager.

One might expect that, attuned as a child to the oratory of her father and later steeped in the popular culture afforded by the chautauqua, Gene Stratton-Porter would have chosen for her book review a more popular or traditional poet—perhaps Henry Wadsworth Longfellow, or even Alfred, Lord Tennyson or Ralph Waldo Emerson. But the throb of Whitman's offbeat verse appealed to Gene Stratton-Porter because it was like her own sense of meter, irregular and unique. Moreover, she felt close to Whitman in another way. She identified with his family background, seemingly much like her own. In her book review she noted Whitman's "Dutch and English sturdiness" and his common school education. Twice she mentioned how he had "boarded round," and she stressed his feasts on nature. He affected her greatly. Later, she would write that, because of him, she marched the open road, combing the grasses, ever loving the earth and sky.[21]

Leaves of Grass has been called a "multiple-symbol of fertility, universality, and cyclical life," expressing an all-encompassing rhythmical renewal of life, permanent and infinite.[22] It was Whitman with his large appreciation of nature's handiwork, an appreciation even larger than that of her father, who finally baptized Gene Stratton-Porter. It was Whitman who began to steer Gene Stratton-Porter toward finding her own spiritual base. Her struggle to free herself from her father's influence would become easier. She pronounced *Leaves of Grass* "a great book—greater than many—time may prove it the equal of any ever written."[23] Her concluding words before the Wednesday Club were glowing with appreciation:

> If you believe in God; if you love the green grass, flowers, and trees; if you know what the leaves whisper and the waters murmur and the birds sing; if you love God's creation above man's manufacturing—read the book. If in your heart there is the throb of universal love and pity; if your hand has lain on the bare body of man and it has not frightened you, read the book. You will be better for it.[24]

Meanwhile, Charles Porter had also been enjoying a large measure of fulfillment. His outlook for the future had never been rosier. Thanks to the oil industry, Adams County was booming. Oil had been discovered near Geneva shortly after the Porters were married, although few persons had then paid much attention to it as gas was not found in paying quantities. By 1892, however, black gold fever had begun to rise in Adams County. The population of Geneva peaked at three thousand that year, with the influx of oilmen from New York, West Virginia, Ohio, and Pennsylvania. Land prices skyrocketed. Those fortunate enough to own acreage leased their farms and received royalties at the rate of several hundred dollars per month. The sounds of gas engines and rattling rod lines riddled the air throughout Adams County.

Along with the black gold, of course, had come tank factories, barber shops, more saloons, bathhouses, and other houses besides oil supply houses, all of which had meant an increase in bank deposits. When oil money began to flow in quantity in Adams County, Charles Porter came out in the open as a full-fledged banker. In 1892 he started the Geneva Bank, with himself as president and cashier. It was a comparatively small-scale banking operation, lacking a state charter, though legal. Because of this bank and his farm, on which sixty oil wells would eventually be drilled, Charles Porter had more than a little extra money in 1893. In the fall he used some of it to treat his wife to a holiday. Leaving six-year-old Jeannette in the care of Florence in Michigan, the Porters took in the World's Columbian Exposition in Chicago.

This exposition was a watering place with all of the potential of Lourdes. Water was its central element. The grounds were accessible only by gondola; other conveyances were prohibited. This assemblage of formal pools, canals, and lagoons had been designed for the Columbian Exposition by Frederick Law Olmsted, creator of New York's Central Park. The effect of Olmsted's "water, water everywhere" in Chicago's Jackson Park on the shores of Lake Michigan defies measurement. Olmsted's creation set off a chain reaction in the hearts of the nearly twenty-six million Americans who viewed the monumental architecture reflected in this waterscape with glassy-eyed approval. Exposition goers left the grounds unaware that the architecture of the two hundred plus buildings they had so admired in this shimmering setting would eventually prove to be a cavernous calamity. Thousands upon thousands began to imitate Chicago by constructing drafty courthouses, museums, and libraries marked by gargantuan columns, echoing halls, and marble stairways to nowhere.

Like an epidemic, the mammoth architecture of the World's Columbian Exposition infected all those who experienced it, including the housewife who yearned for a larger home. Gene Stratton-Porter came away from the Columbian Exposition with big ideas. She was particularly impressed by the huge Forestry Building. Rustic in design, with twenty-four double outside doors, it was the only building at the exposition in which no nails had been used in interior construction. One of the Forestry Building's most attractive features was the porch, or colonnade, that surrounded it. The supporting columns of this colonnade were tree trunks, each twenty-five feet high and the finest specimen of timber that could be furnished by a particular foreign country or state or territory of the United States. This Forestry Building appealed to Gene Stratton-Porter immensely, and she wanted a home with a similar appearance.

Financially speaking, however, it was a poor time to be thinking of building a house, not only for the Porters, but also for Americans in general. The closing of the Columbian Exposition in late October 1893 found the United States in the worst business depression of the nineteenth century. Nevertheless, the following spring Charles Porter agreed to build for his wife what would become and remain for their lifetimes the most pretentious dwelling in the Geneva area. At the same time he also made plans to erect a new two-story farmhouse for his tenant farmer.

Early in March 1894, when it was yet too early to break ground for either of these construction projects, Charles decided to take a vacation. He wanted to go to California, to the annual midwinter fair. Gene, however, preoccupied with her literary club as well as work with an architect on the style of new house she had in mind—Queen Anne rustic—was too busy to go along. So Charles went to California without her, for two weeks, accompanied by his brother Miles. In mid-April, about a month after he returned, workmen commenced construction on the new Porter dwelling. It required nearly a year to complete the house to specifications, and, when finally finished in the spring of 1895, the unusually fine home was the subject of much local envy.

On the extra lot next to their small yellow cottage, the Porters had erected a massive two-story house of Wisconsin red cedar logs. The upper story and the roof were shingled with redwood. Like the Forestry Building in Chicago, this

Limberlost Cabin

Wildflower Woods

wooden dwelling had a colonnaded porch. Inside, the entrance hall, library, and dining room were paneled in quarter-
sawed golden oak ordered from an out-of-town mill. Other
rooms downstairs included the kitchen, a bath, two bedrooms, a music room, and small conservatory filled with
masses of tulips, hyacinths, and daffodils. A unique window
arrangement allowed wild birds to enter and exit this greenhouse freely. A special cupboard graced the dining room for
one of Gene Stratton-Porter's passions: blue willow Dutch
dishes. She had hired artists to paint frescoes in two rooms
downstairs. Upstairs, there were four extra bedrooms. None
of the rooms in this house measured less than fourteen feet;
three of these rooms were eighteen by twenty-two feet. Heat
came from seven natural gas fireplaces, and huge windows let
the sunshine in every corner. The floors were hardwood, laid
diagonally, and the furniture was no less impressive, much of
it solid mahogany.

Overall, the decor was most unusual. Owl carvings were
prominent throughout, even on the Porters' walnut bed. The
outside of this mansion, which Gene called a cabin, was enhanced by a windlass well in the side yard. Even the barn
behind the cabin, also of cedar logs, had a chimney and windows because the hired boy lived there. About the cabin grew
fruit trees, vines, and wild Virginia creepers. In her garden
were buttercups, pinks, tiger lilies, hollyhocks, sunflowers,
and every other old-fashioned flower her mother had known.
There were mulberry and alder bushes, wild honeysuckle,
sweetbrier and goldenrod, all planted to attract and feed birds
and insects.

However, the mistress of this expensive new house with its
lovely grounds was not completely satisfied: "The first house
that I was on the job in building was paid for by the man of
the family, and naturally what happened inside the house was
not an individual emanation; it was a compromise."[25] Her
teakettle would soon begin to whistle.

"Shades of the Pottawattomies"

ONE summer night about five months after the Porters had moved into their new residence, Gene was awakened shortly before midnight by cries of "Fire!" Racing to her windows, she could see a tremendous blaze only a few blocks away in the direction of the downtown business district. Charles was out of town on a buying trip. Quickly, she put on a pair of slippers, fastened a skirt over her nightgown, grabbed a sweater, and ran out of the cabin toward the roaring fire.

An all-consuming fire had long been predicted by local sages because of Geneva's numerous rickety frame buildings and lack of a fire department. Buckets were the town's only defense, and a poor one at that, as many of the town's wells and cisterns were dry that summer. The fire had begun at the rear of a grocery, in a storeroom that held a large quantity of excelsior, boxes, and other flammables. Within five minutes the blaze had reached an adjoining building. By the time Gene reached the scene, it was apparent that at least thirty businesses were doomed, including Charles Porter's drugstore.

She pitched in immediately where help was most needed. Fallen embers made short work of her slippers, and her feet began to bleed. Nevertheless, she had the time of her life. It was worth it, even her burned feet, because she was in for some unexpected fun, a brief exchange with a harried hotel employee, the later recollection of which would invariably send her into stitches. When the steps of the Shamrock Hotel caught fire, she told the excited hotel cook to use water out of the reservoirs of his stoves to extinguish the blaze so as not to interfere with men at the pump. Much to her surprise, however, a few minutes later she discovered this distracted cook pouring a crock of milk over the steps. When she asked him whyever in the world he was using milk to put out the fire, in all earnestness he replied: "The water in the tanks is boiling hot, so it wouldn't do. I got the milk out of the refrigerator, and it's ice cold."[1]

She was so useful to the men directing the fire that a reporter for the local newspaper recommended her a few days later as an energetic fire chief whenever the village got around to forming a fire department. The local newspaper also commented on the looting that followed the conflagration. In keeping with the prevailing sure sense of cause and effect, these acts of theft were then attributed not to any socioeconomic frustrations of the looters, but solely to their character: "There are thieves and thieves, but the lowest thief of all, twin brother to an imp in hell in principle, are those disgrace to humanity, the sneaking scoundrels who went about the streets Wednesday morning."[2]

As a result of the fire, nearly all of Geneva's business district was destroyed. All of these buildings were underinsured. Many had no fire coverage whatsoever. Despite their devastating losses, however, the town's proprietors were generally optimistic. Businessman Jim York allegedly said he had lost everything except one nightshirt and his reputation, yet he had no intention of going into the hands of a receiver, unless he could find one of feminine gender.[3]

After the fire Charles proposed to make a quick recovery. Rather than being discouraged over his loss, Charles deemed this time especially right for a new undertaking. Charles Porter not only began to rebuild his drugstore ten days after being burned out, but he also announced his intention to build two brick business rooms for banking purposes next to the Shamrock Hotel. As soon as they had been completed, he was ready for business. On 25 September 1895 Charles Porter and other subscribers, mostly from the Geneva area, formally organized the Geneva Bank. This bank was capitalized at $45,000 and chartered by the state of Indiana; its largest single stockholder was Charles Porter, who pledged one-third of its capital stock.

When Charles committed $15,000 to the Geneva Bank he put himself out on a long limb financially. Tied up in the midst of a depression with a stock commitment to his new bank, along with an expensive new dwelling and a new farmhouse, Charles Porter had committed all of his assets. It would be a long time before he would have enough of a financial cushion to spend money freely. It was beginning to look as if Charles would never be a spender, that he would always be a saver and an investor. Thirty-two years old and faced with long-term austerity, Gene Stratton-Porter's speculations about her future resulted in the decision of a lifetime:

> I do not know what would have happened to me had I chanced upon a life of affluence. What did happen was that I was squarely confronted with a "sink or swim" proposition. I was not by nature or teaching a sinker, so I lifted my chin and pulled for the shore. . . . Learning to swim because you will drown if you do not is a rather messy performance—slow, but it is dead sure. You will either sink or you will swim. I swam—slowly, to be sure, but I never once went entirely under. I took up my pen.[4]

Wisely, she decided to write about what she knew best. She began by submitting an article about wild birdlife to an outdoor magazine. This first article was rejected for lack of illustrations. She refused to use the illustrations available from mail-order houses, of dead birds stuffed with excelsior, stating: "I was horrified." However, "editors insisted upon illustration."[5]

A solution to this problem presented itself when Charles and Jeannette gave her a small camera for Christmas. She tried it first on Major the parrot, developing the negatives herself with the aid of chemicals from Charles's drugstore. The results were much better than she hoped. Before the dim, streaky print of Major had finished its first bath, she was running through the cabin, shrieking with excitement. She had found a medium to illustrate her work, photography: "I knew that with patient work I could master the camera; how to make friends with the birds I understood better than I did any other one thing on earth. . . . All I had to do was find a nest, and then repeat my childish methods. The birds had not changed; neither had I."[6]

Convinced that she could eventually photograph birdlife well enough to illustrate anything she might write, she still lacked one more ingredient for success—a quiet place where she could observe wild birdlife undetected. What she now needed most was access to a spot attractive to many varieties of birds, a site that had not been plowed or otherwise disturbed and that afforded good cover for observational purposes. Such a place did exist less than a mile from her own front door, although none but the brave or the foolhardy ventured there because it was a great dismal swamp. Known locally as the Limberlost, its gloomy depths stretched southwest of Geneva for miles. The Limberlost had taken its name from an athletic young man nicknamed "Limber Jim," who had wandered in circles for three days while hunting there. There was no interior access to this vast wild morass, only corduroy roads around its border, made by felling and sinking trees in the muck.

The dark obstacles in the Limberlost would have been enough to discourage the most ardent nature lover. Full of insects and disagreeable crawlers, the swamp, with its fetid, dank odors, drew swarms of mosquitoes. Bat colonies hid in its hollow trees. Its high stiff grass and tangled underbrush were nearly impenetrable. Poisonous snakes lurked near its murky pools. Lacking anywhere else to go, however, Gene Stratton-Porter began to go bird-watching in the Limberlost when weather permitted. Much to her delight, once she had penetrated its oozy depths she was so attracted by its myriad forms of birdlife that she was able to overcome any fear she might have had of the Limberlost's many dangers. Just as she had put aside her fright of snake-eating Paddy Ryan as a child, she chose to put aside the swamp's terrors in order to concentrate better on its treasures.

Bumblebees and hummingbirds vied for the honey of cascading trumpets and creepers. Millions of bees beat around the plum and red haw. Carpeting this swamp were thousands of delicate wildflowers, their fragrances attracting silky butterflies and dusky moths. In this no-man's-land Gene Stratton-Porter found what she was looking for. Feasting on insects and gorging on mandrake, like diners in a restaurant, were seemingly endless varieties of wild birds: chip-churring scarlet tanagers, whistling cedar waxwings, mewing catbirds, hopping yellowhammers, jolly goldfinches, zigzagging snipes, and old familiar redwing blackbirds. Fat, long-billed woodcocks probed in the mud, then rose with loud cries straight in the air to perform high-flying acrobatics. Also, in the clearest pools, like statues, blue herons stood motionless, and from the cattails came the persistent *whichity, whichity, which* of yellowthroats. In the trills of the white-throated sparrow Gene was certain she recognized Carmen's song from the first act of Georges Bizet's opera. The little song sparrow

Charles Dorwin Porter fishing in Sylvan Lake

Photograph of Jeannette Porter Meehan taken by her mother. Inscription on back of photograph reads, "Her hands filled with anemones and spring beauties."

seemed to her to imitate Guiseppe Verdi's "Di Provenza Il Mar" from *La Traviata*, and the Nashville warbler, as it flitted among the swamp's tallest trees, seemed to her to sing the opening notes of Gioacchino Antonio Rossini's *Il Carnevale di Venezia*, "We are beggars, struck with blindness, living on a rich man's kindness."[7]

Charles was livid when he learned that his wife had been traipsing about the local swamp. In an effort to curb his anger, Gene rashly promised to stay out of the swamp, a promise she could not keep. When he realized that he could not keep Gene out of the Limberlost, Charles quickly came up with an alternative. He introduced her to wild birdlife elsewhere, on the banks of the Wabash River. One of his business acquaintances, a man named Hawbaker, owned a large farm bordering the Wabash. On weekends Charles began taking his family to Hawbaker's, where they could all go fishing.

Charles loved to fish. Gene once said it cleared his mind of eternal columns of figures: "He is content to fish all day and go home empty-handed; and quite as eager to go the next time as if he had caught a full stringer, and had his picture taken."[8]

His angling preparations were usually elaborate. He liked to work an hour before he was quite fixed. First, he baited a strong hook on a stout line attached to a cane pole and set it for suckers. Then he fixed another, somewhat similar, and set it on the bottom for catfish. Next he wired an enormous hook to a clothesline. He baited the hook with a wad of worms and meat and threw it into the center of the deepest pool, tying the line to a stake on the bank—all for a patriarchal turtle that had eluded him for years. Then he readied a small lancewood casting rod and spent the remainder of the day casting with live minnows sixty, eighty, or one hundred feet from the end of a rowboat.

With all these painstaking arrangements and Jeannette and Gene fishing besides, one might have expected at least one catch to brag about. But the river was no longer crowded with fish. A dozen good bass in a season would have been a good catch. Still, they all enjoyed the beauty of the river. The Porters felt their family outings along the Wabash were especially beneficial to Jeannette: "She wades to her waist sailing birch canoes, manned by fierce Indian dollies, and hunts rare pebbles and shells. She lunches like a farmer and sleeps the sleep of the untroubled. What more would you for childhood?"[9]

Once she had been introduced to the riverbank at Hawbaker's, Gene Stratton-Porter became a familiar sight there. When Jeannette was out of school, she took her along. Like the swamp, the wooded riverbank at Hawbaker's teemed with birdlife: spotted sandpipers, wood thrushes, wrens, black-billed cuckoos, cardinals, phoebes, drumming woodpeckers, pugnacious kingfishers, nuthatches, grackles, and tufted titmice. Gene Stratton-Porter loved to spend time at the river. She especially loved it there in the morning, when the air was tinged with the dampness and mystery of night and the birds were in full song:

> Hope is so high in the morning. You are going to succeed where you failed yesterday. You are going to advance so far beyond anything already achieved. God is good to give to men a world . . . ringing with music and . . . you resolve to be good as well. So you add your voice, and travel the long road in the morning with a light heart.[10]

Between 1896 and 1900, Gene Stratton-Porter studied the birdlife of the upper Wabash valley with intensity, recording her observations afield with great care, answering to her own satisfaction several questions about their physiology and regular habits. She noted that her feathered friends were unaffected by scent. They would go anywhere and eat anything: "It is nothing to find them raking the river bank for worms at the very mouth of a sewer discharge."[11] Most impressive, however, was their keen sight, especially that of the lark:

> The lark, poised out of the range of our vision, flings his ringing melody down to the tired old world, but he never loses focus on one little spot of meadow where his mate is brooding. To prove this you have only to hear his notes while he is invisible and then approach his nest, and in a flash he is to earth trying mightily to interest you in a spot many rods away.[12]

She felt there was no way to compute the range of some of the most farsighted birds.

She learned that flight was not altogether a matter of instinct: "Many young birds are nervous and timid and have to be taught, and, as a last resort, fairly hustled and driven from the nest."[13] Warblers, flycatchers, and thrushes seemed to her to learn to fly with relative ease—not so a few members of the sparrow family, buntings, finches, and grosbeaks, as well as some of the birds of extreme heights, who commonly clung to the nest in fear while their teachers repeatedly coaxed, illustrated, and encouraged.

Although some birds, once they had left the nest, seemed to become self-supporting almost immediately, she noted that robins, larks, blackbirds, crows, and many others, especially sparrows, had to be shown again and again how to forage. The bathing lesson was also sometimes a hard one: "In case a young crow refuses to enter the water and bathe properly it is immediately set upon by its band and picked to death."[14] One of her lengthiest observations concerned the crow:

> They form in companies, and under the leadership of the oldest and wisest have a daily drill almost military in its precision. Each young bird is taught to know every member of its own company and not to attempt attaching itself to any other. They are taught to mass in flying, and to scatter and hide at a danger signal.[15]

She watched young crows repeatedly drilled in these lessons until the bleary, blue eyes of the babies changed into the wise, dark, watchful eyes of the elders. Any young crow too stubborn or slow to learn was immediately set upon and killed by his elders.

Because of the high elevation at which most birds nest, Gene grew adept at rigging her photographic equipment from trees with the aid of a wagonload of ropes and tall ladders. She used different lures to attract birds to the camera, such as beefsteak wired to limbs and bushes. Her usual practice was to hide near a nest or another likely spot, carefully set her camera, and then wait with Indian-like patience—sometimes for hours—before pulling the long string to the shutter when a subject came into view. Never idle, she used these quiet hours to advantage, beginning the study of wildflowers, moths, and butterflies. Habitually she dressed in clothing the color of foliage, to make herself inconspicuous.

To perfect her photographic techniques, she experimented, using the bathroom in the cabin as a darkroom. Her developing tools were simple. She washed her negatives and prints in the sink and dried them on turkey platters. Frustrated by inadequate equipment, she sold some jewelry to pay for a larger camera. She had this camera made to order and used it in all possible locations. It had three feet of bellows and used eight-by-ten-inch plates and three different combinations of lenses.

With this new camera, no after-enlargements of negatives were required, thus avoiding much work and also loss of detail. She felt it altogether better to use a large camera than a small one, despite the added expense: "The birds seem to regard a large camera more in the nature of a building and evince less timidity and make up with it sooner."[16] Gene felt that the birds mistook a small camera for an animal intruder. Although her new larger camera certainly meant harder work, it also meant usable pictures in one operation and three

Gene Stratton-Porter charcoal sketch of her daughter Jeannette at age twelve

times the chance of including the subject on the plate. By trial and error she eventually developed her own workable technique: "Given a subject afield, nine times out of ten, if its movements do not compel you to snap, shifting leaves and lights will, so use fastest plates, snap, weaken your normal developer fully one-half and coax for detail."[17]

Dividing her attention between field trips along the Wabash River, forays into the Limberlost, and occasional longer excursions elsewhere, Gene Stratton-Porter also seemed to find the time to perform well as a housewife and mother: "I kept a cabin of fourteen rooms, and kept it immaculate. I made most of my daughter's clothes, I kept a conservatory in which there bloomed from three to six hundred bulbs every winter, tended a house of canaries and linnets, and cooked and washed dishes besides three times a day."[18] Not quite. Such a full-time undertaking coupled with her passion for fieldwork could only have been accomplished by a woman who was motorized. With respect, however, to the immaculate condition of her cabin, her remarks are truthful enough, for she was meticulously organized. One acquaintance described her as a "perfect housekeeper"—perfect, that is, if one could overlook a wounded bird perched anywhere, cocoons pinned someplace else, newly emerged moths flying through the cabin to feed on the flowers in the conservatory, and boxes of caterpillars scattered over the furniture.[19]

Without a doubt Gene Stratton-Porter tended a house filled with canaries and linnets, and, as far as Jeannette was concerned, if her mother was guilty of anything, it was overindulgence. One person has described Jeannette's room as a fairyland, beautifully furnished, housing more dolls than one could count. As for cooking and washing dishes three times a day, however, Gene Stratton-Porter's remarks were exaggerated. As a matter of fact, her kitchen might as well have been boarded up. Her cast-iron range was seldom available for cooking because it was usually covered with something of greater importance, either to herself or to Jeannette: at one time, guinea pigs. The Porters, especially Charles, who eventually became accustomed to eating monotonous meals downtown, ate many meals out. Eating out was not the only change in his routine. If a moth laid eggs on the seat of his favorite chair, Charles just sat someplace else until they hatched.

Quite naturally, at an early age Jeannette began to show several signs of becoming very much interested in matters similar to those that most engrossed her mother. By the age of eight, she possessed a fruit can full of baby garter snakes, six mice, a bucket of turtles, and a gift from a friend of her father who lived in Florida: a pair of tiny alligators. Jeannette was as comfortable as her mother among the creatures of the wild, and on one occasion, when she was a small child, her trusting state of mind in the woods saved her from possible disaster. One summer, while visiting Florence, Jeannette had what could have been a fatal experience, but thanks to her mother's frequent demonstrations that no wild creature would willingly cause anyone any harm, Jeannette had the presence of mind to hold perfectly still while a fat massasauga rattler crept between her feet.

The damage that could be done to her daughter by indoor critters was one Gene Stratton-Porter assiduously avoided. She refused to let Jeannette play with the other children of the village. By Jeannette's own admission: "I was not allowed to play much with the children of the town, so that when I was home Mother spent considerable time with me."[20] Together they tended a small vegetable garden. In the fall they liked to go berrying. Now and then Jeannette was released to the care of the wife of Charles's tenant farmer, who lived about a mile west of town.

As his wife became increasingly busy with fieldwork, Charles Porter began to take a more active interest in his daughter. Although he was later described as "grouchy" in the presence of other children, Charles Porter was obviously interested in the development of his own child.[21] He taught her to shoot a rifle, to fish, to row a boat, and to ride a horse, so that she could freely roam his tenant farm. Nevertheless, Jeannette led an isolated life, insulated by her parents from those in the village her own age.

Much as she secreted Jeannette from public view, Gene Stratton-Porter also attempted to screen her own activities. It was impossible, however, for her to study and photograph out-of-doors without subjecting herself to idle speculation. She was already the target of local gossip because of what was perceived as her uppity personal standards. She almost wished she could be invisible: "Being so afraid of failure and the inevitable ridicule in a community where I was already severely criticised on account of my ideas of housekeeping, dress, and social customs, I purposely kept everything I did as quiet as possible."[22]

Nearly five years of self-imposed exile and solitary field-work elapsed before Gene Stratton-Porter's self-apprenticeship as a writer and photographer paid off. Then, early in 1900, she submitted an article of protest to an outdoor magazine about the use of birds and their feathers as hat trim. Her protest was based on a personal experience. They had thought her mad at the milliner's one day when she bought a hat, asked to borrow their scissors, and cut the birds off and to pieces. As she left the shop, she overheard two men standing out front.

> "Well, Judge, what do you think of it?"
> "I don't like it! It is a shame! It is a crime! It is worse this fall than I ever saw it before. This [millinery] window represents 500 dead birds."[23]

This incident was the basis for Gene Stratton-Porter's first published article. Entitled "A New Experience in Millinery," the article appeared in February 1900 in *Recreation*, a magazine known nationally for its active campaign against the slaughter of birds for millinery purposes.

About four months later, Gene Stratton-Porter exercised a certain prerogative, unaware that someday it would be used as another piece of cumulative evidence regarding her lifelong supersensitivity and tendency to dissimulate. When the census taker called at her home, she gave him some misinformation. She told him that Charles was only eight years older than herself, instead of thirteen. This falsehood could be dismissed as a slip of the census taker's pen were it not for another error. She also said she had been born in August 1863, yet she listed thirty as her age in June 1900, instead of thirty-six, her actual age. The census taker, who apparently had enough sense not to argue with a lady about her age, lopped off six years and wrote down thirty.

Over the next several months, a column written by Gene Stratton-Porter titled "Camera Notes" appeared in *Recreation* magazine. She was paid in photographic equipment for these columns. A tiff with *Recreation*'s editor moved her to *Outing* magazine, where she continued to write about wild birdlife. Meanwhile, the *American Annual of Photography* published thirteen of her photographs along with an article about her viewpoint as a field-worker.

One of Gene Stratton-Porter's most enlightening early articles describes an autumn jaunt to Indian River in northern Michigan. She had talked about the advertised beauties of this spot ever since she began taking pictures and writing for publication. After much cajoling, she persuaded Charles to take her. They decided to go by way of Lake Michigan.

As she was packing for their trip, an invitation came from friends, whom Charles did not want to offend, first to stop over at Mackinac Island. This minor delay in getting to Indian River was a sore point with Gene, but once under way, she put it out of her mind. The excursion up Lake Michigan was a delight: "From the minute I stepped on deck, the *Illinois* was mine. The captain took me into partnership, the pilot shared his box, the first mate lifted the ropes and let me and the cameras have full sway."[24]

Also on board, eyeing Gene with annoyance all day, was a portly bejeweled matron who persisted in making herself conspicuous. Seated beside her at dinner that night, Gene watched as the woman attempted to serve herself planked whitefish from a platter. She speared it with her fork, but it was hard. She sawed at it with her knife, but it would not cut. In desperation, the woman then turned the platter on edge, to slip the fish onto her plate, but it rolled away among the table decorations. When the waiter retrieved the fish and returned it to the platter, and the woman realized she had been trying to cut the end of the board on which the fish had been cooked, she nearly fainted and seemed to lose her appetite: "Whereat I was glad, for I had heard her say earlier in the day that people who carried one camera were nuisance enough, but people who carried three should have a keeper to detain them at home."[25]

After a short stop in Petoskey, they went on to Mackinac where Charles's friends met them at the dock and carried them to a palatial hotel. Fountains sprayed, flowers bloomed, and cut glass and silver shone. The meals were banquets, and the guests were arrayed in diamonds.

> It soon developed that we had been delayed on our way
> to Indian River in order that I might assist my hostess
> at a reception of her dear 400 friends. Shades of the
> Pottawattomies! To think that people who might go
> to the woods and waters and live with Nature, would
> outdo winter's fatigues in a summer rout of ball and
> reception, three to six social engagements in a day, and
> call it resting.[26]

The awful day of the reception arrived. Two hours ahead of time Gene was put into the hands of a hairdresser: "I barely escaped with my life."[27] Hair ironed, crimped, pinned, waved, and knotted, she was then turned over to a dressing maid. Gene had taken on a few pounds, and her party frock would not meet by an inch. There was nothing to do but reef her sails until it would. With a string of fiery opals and a pearl fan, she looked similar to the remainder of the crowd. As a matter of fact, when her hostess came to get her, Gene looked so much better than she had fancied she would that her relief was comical. For two hours Gene stood and was presented to persons she had never seen before and hoped never to see again. She hated every minute of it. As soon as possible she made her escape, muttering to herself in garbled Whitman:

> I found myself repeating, "I think I could live with the animals, they are so placid and self contained. I stand and look at them and long and long. They do not sweat and whine about their condition; they do not lie awake in the dark and weep about their sins; they do not make me sick discussing their duty to a God; not one is dissatisfied; not one is demented with the mania of owning things; not one is respectable or unhappy over the whole world."[28]

The Porters left Mackinac Island the next morning on the first boat, bound for a nearby fishing village, a peaceful spot where Gene said she might have the glory of sunshine, the whisper of the leaves, the murmur of waters, and the calm of night.

They fished the winding Indian River for several days. There was charm in the shadowy depths of the surrounding northern forest, in the swiftly running water and the clear cool air, fragrant with pine resin. Forests of spruce, cedar, pine, and birch locked branches across the narrow river. In a few places the river narrowed until they dodged low limbs as their boat swept past. Along the steep banks, atop drying rushes thrown up by a channel dredge, were scores of coiled snakes, sport for those campers who peppered away at them with revolvers from the safety of boats. Several primitive log cabins, with stumps for foundations, stretched along this waterway, their exteriors covered with guns and rods, fish heads, and animal skins.

There was one glad, golden day on Indian River, rich with experience and pleasure. Gene Stratton-Porter once referred to it as a "perfect day, all my own, the best outing day of my life." That was the day the big one tried to get away. It was also the day she scored a stunning victory for womanhood.

They had been fishing all day and were ready to quit when Charles decided to pull up at Muskrat Landing, where he announced he was going to stop long enough to land a thirty-pound muskellunge that had been seen there the day before. As they docked, Gene turned to see if her trolling line was free of weeds, and there, trailing after it, were three nice bass. She cried to Charles for help.

"Pull that minnow out," he ordered as he handed her a casting rod baited with a live frog. "Lower that from among them and don't try to take their pictures!"

With Charles scooping bass and supplying fresh frogs she soon had all three. They moved on, then, to a corduroy dock a mile or two above a nearby village. Unwilling to quit until *he* had made a good catch, Charles settled down to some serious fishing at one of the widest spots in the river. Gene relaxed in the boat, idly watching an argument between a kingfisher and a raven over a rock bass someone had thrown on the bank.

Before long, restless to be up and doing, she took up her little lancewood rod and began making lazy casts thirty and forty feet up the river, letting the current carry the bait past the boat and down the river the length of the line, then reeling in slowly and casting again. Presently, she had a good rushing strike that nearly jerked the rod from her hands. Despite the drag, the reel was humming. It was a big one. The fish jerked the crank from her fingers, stripped the reel, and cut such monkeyshines away off up the river that she could barely hang onto the rod.

"Can't you keep that crank in your fingers?" asked Charles.

"No, I cannot, or I would," she replied, half provoked. For fifteen minutes she worked, the fish stripping the reel with no restraint. Then in the distance came a familiar sound. The afternoon boat was coming! Loaded with one hundred to three hundred passengers, it would pass within fifteen feet. Day after day, fishermen on the river responded to an unwritten law: those who failed to show their catch to the tourist boat were subject to hoots and catcalls.

The opportunity was too good to pass up. She was determined to land the fish just as the boat passed. If Charles wanted to add to the effect by holding up their day's catch, that was quite all right, but she would give these tourists a performance they would remember. The same thought occurred to Charles: "Now here is your chance," he said, "keep him deep and get ready to reel. The boat will drive him down to you and you can land him for the entertainment of the passengers."

It happened that way to a point. It was a fine day, and the boat was crowded. People took in the situation at a glance and began to shout and wave.

> "She'll never land it!" "No woman has the wrist to land a fish like that!" "Why don't the man take it?" yelled the men.
> And the women answered: "Yes, she can land it!" "You think it takes a man to do any big thing!" "Why there it is!" "You can see it!"

With all her might, Gene tried to swing the fish in reach of Charles's outstretched net. Crack! The bass sprang clear of the water, doubled, and with a back-action jerk smashed her thirty-five-dollar rod. Away up the river he went. One wildly dancing man on the boat mopped his beady brow and shouted: "Reel's busted—rod's smashed—fish gone—I told you so. Why didn't she let the MAN take it?"

The rod was in pieces at her feet, but the line was still in her fingers and the fish was still on the end of it. Grimly, Gene set out to haul him in. She worked quickly. Then, about twenty feet from the boat, the fish dashed sideways and was lost in the logs of the dock.

"Unchain the boat and back it up until I say stop, then hold it firm," she ordered Charles. Again she hauled in the line. When the boat was steady, she dove into the water, head first. The fingers of her left hand entered the bass's gills, and her thumb curled into its jaw. She came up triumphant, with a yell that would have done justice to a Comanche.

The entire steamer broke out in white, waving handkerchiefs and hats; the whistle blew, and the onlookers cheered. Just as they went from sight came the faint soprano strains of "Glory, Glory Hallelujah."

She sat down grinning. In her hands was the catch of her life, the gamest bass she had ever seen. Charles was prostrate with laughter. "Only to think," he groaned, "what a man could save if he knew. I spent fifty dollars laying around Petoskey a couple of days last week, waiting to go to a show, and here I've had a show, the biggest circus of my life and not a cent to pay."

"Oh! Do you think so?" Gene retorted. "What was it you paid for that rod and reel?"

"Gee!" said Charles, "I didn't think of that!"[29]

Her Very Good Friend

BACK home again and well rested, Gene Stratton-Porter settled down to work in earnest. Now equipped with the latest in camera and darkroom equipment, she needed nothing but a few extraordinary photographs on which to base her forthcoming articles. Then one day she received a curious message from a man who owned a portion of the Limberlost. From him she learned that, deep in the recesses of the swamp, far inside the hollow of a giant felled elm, lumbermen had reported seeing a white baby bird as big as a gosling. Beside it was a brown speckled egg, pale blue, shaped like a hen egg but as large as that of a turkey. This was wonderful news. She had never seen the type of egg described. Anxious to photograph such a find, but reluctant to go that deep into the Limberlost without assistance, she asked Charles if he would help her. Knowing that she would go alone if he refused, he agreed to accompany her.

A few days later they set out shortly after dawn. Prepared for the worst, each carried a revolver. A rod inside the swamp their carriage mired to the hubs. Forced to proceed on foot, they secured the horse and began to hack their way through

Robin, photographed by Gene Stratton-Porter

Young black vulture, photographed by Gene Stratton-Porter

dense underbrush with ax and hatchet, Charles in high heavy leather boots, lighting one cigar after another to drive away the bugs, Gene in waist-high rubber waders. As she later described it:

> We forced our way between steaming, fetid pools, through swarms of gnats, flies, mosquitoes, poisonous insects, keeping a sharp watch for rattlesnakes. We sank ankle deep at every step, and logs we thought solid broke under us. Our progress was a steady succession of prying and pulling each other to the surface. Our clothing was wringing wet, and the exposed parts of our bodies lumpy with bites and stings.[1]

Two hours into the swamp, Charles spied the dead elm. Once in its general vicinity, this felled tree was easy to spot because of its great size, even though it was lying on the ground. It measured forty feet in length. Its hollow trunk, lying on the ground, was nearly three feet high. Scrambling up onto the smallest end of this mammoth log, Charles began walking along it, tapping gently to drive out the mother bird. As Gene sat poised with a camera, the mother bird came out on wing, in a rush. The lens caught only a swipe. The bird was frightened off, and Charles went after her baby and the egg by entering the trunk and creeping its cavernous length.

He brought the baby and the egg out in his leaf-lined hat. Gene was ecstatic. It was the nest of a black vulture, an unusual find. At maturity the black vulture is enormous; its wingspan approaches five feet. But there would be a problem working around this nest. The eating habits of the black vulture are nauseous. It feeds on carrion. To counteract the awful stench, the Porters bound their mouths and nostrils with handkerchiefs dipped in disinfectant. This done, they set to work clearing underbrush and small trees. It was hot and humid, and they worked hard. Little light penetrated this section of the swamp. Good photographs would be difficult without substantial clearing. In mid-afternoon, as the shadows length-

ened, they quit for the day. Wordlessly, at the point of pros-
tration, they packed up and headed home, survival gear again
at the ready. On reaching the carriage, they were overheated.
Once aboard, both began to chill. Wrapped in side curtains
and the carriage robe, they started home, exhausted. Out of
the blue, Charles asked: "Do you think that paid?" Never had
she been as uncomfortable, as bone tired, and as much in need
of a long hot bath. Yet her weariness paled beside the privilege
of studying such an uncommon nesting place. Struck dumb
by Charles's question about the possible profitability of their
undertaking, she pretended she had not heard him. The next
morning she produced her photographs: "Do *you* think it
paid?" Charles must have thought it had because he returned
with her to the bird nest once or twice a week for the next
three months, until they knew that Little Chicken, as she had
named the baby vulture, had taken wing and could fend for
itself. When he was almost fully grown, he would follow her
across the swamp and take food from her hand as readily as
from his mother. With his queer rocking gait, humping his
shoulders and ducking his head, he looked so uncanny and
threatening in that dark, inhospitable place that she had to set
her muscles hard, "to keep from giving a scream and running
for my life."[2]

The whole vulture business tried her sorely. It was an aggravating experience, made worse by a man who farmed not
far from this section of the Limberlost. When Gene tried to
set up a feeding station on his land for the parent vultures,
about two miles from their nest, the farmer would not co-
operate. One day she moved a dead calf from Charles's farm
onto the farmer's land, hoping to coax the adult vultures to
feed within range of her camera. The farmer spoiled her
scheme by burying the calf and ordering her not to make his
land a dumping ground for her dead stock. Gene was stumped
for a reply. She could not tell a farmer she was feeding vultures. So she swallowed hard and explained nothing, although

she was much aggrieved and aggravated, especially when the farmer began to charge her for using the road now being forged through the swamp, while lumbermen, now beginning to invade the Limberlost, were allowed to use the road every day at no charge.

Yet the aggravations of fieldwork were often offset by better days, when good fortune seemed to follow her. While working on a magazine article one morning, she was desperate for a certain photograph. Later that day she obtained it in an unexpected manner. All day she had wondered where she could find a picture of an owl. That night, passing through the back rooms of the cabin, she heard the tremulous wail of a screech owl, close by in the orchard. Turning out the lights, she opened a kitchen window, lit a candle to make a dim inviting glow, and then crouched low, imitating the owl's doleful cries. The owl began to answer, drawing ever nearer. When its shadow passed over her head, her heart stood still. She slammed shut the window and there he sat, perched on the back of a kitchen chair. All the next day she photographed him from every angle, releasing her lucky catch at dusk.

With a regular income now coming her way from the sale of articles about wild birdlife, Gene Stratton-Porter was still not completely satisfied, and she would not be satisfied until she had accomplished something else. Overshadowing her success to date as a writer was the specter of that unnamed critic who had belittled her first literary efforts as a high school girl. She still wanted to write poetry—if not poetry, at least fiction. Yet she was afraid to try because any rejected manuscript would be delivered to Charles at the bank along with the balance of the Porter household mail. She avoided this prospect by quietly renting a post office box in her own name. Then she sat down to write a short story.

For the setting of this story she relied heavily on the current editorial and public preference for a romance set in a mythical kingdom, a craze for stories about royalty that had reached epidemic proportions five years earlier. Readers could not get enough of such books as *The Princess Aline* by Richard Harding Davis. Gene capitalized on the prevailing public appetite for castles and kings by inventing a commoner in love with a highborn heroine, changing the setting for her tale from a feudal castle to a small midwestern agricultural community. When finished, she mailed her manuscript to Perriton Maxwell, editor of *McFadden's* fiction magazine, otherwise known as *Metropolitan*.

Weeks and weeks she waited for word of what had happened to it. In the meantime, unbeknown to her, her story was published. Due to a mixup in *Metropolitan*'s office, her address had been lost: "I decided in my own mind that Mr. Maxwell was a 'mean old thing' to throw away my story and keep the return postage." Then one day on a routine visit downtown, she was in for a shock when one of Charles's clerks addressed her: "I read your story in the *Metropolitan* last night. It was great! Did you ever write any fiction before?" "No. Just a simple little thing! Have you any spare copies? My sister might want one."[3]

Back home, in the seclusion of the cabin, she sat down to look it over. She quite agreed with the clerk: "It was great!" The title of Gene Stratton-Porter's first short story should come as no revelation, *Laddie, the Princess, and the Pie.* Twenty-nine years had elapsed since the death of her brother Laddie, yet she still remembered him with great affection. The plot in this short story revolves around an upstanding young man named Laddie, his girl friend the Princess—a lass with royal blood—and a piece of juicy rhubarb pie.

What makes this lighthearted story so thought provoking is its sober addenda. An anguished postscript is set off from the main body of this otherwise happy tale by asterisks. In this unrelated postscript to her first published short story, Gene Stratton-Porter places the blame for Laddie's drowning

not on his own inability to swim the Wabash River, but on
the boy who had tried to rescue him:

> O Laddie! Laddie! I know you had to do it. You never
> could have seen a companion drown and not make even
> an effort to save him. But when the cruel water shut
> the light from your dear eyes forever, it killed your
> mother, struck joy from the life of the Princess, and
> left forever an ache in the heart of your little sister.[4]

After Gene wrote to Perriton Maxwell and identified herself as the author of "Laddie, the Princess, and the Pie," she
received a quick reply: "It was a letter that warmed the deep
of my heart."[5] Maxwell enclosed a check and asked her to
write another story in a similar vein to be used as a Christmas
leader. So she wrote "How Laddie and the Princess Spelled
Down at the Christmas Bee." Maxwell liked this second story
idea well enough, but this time he also wanted photographic
illustration: a frontispiece, head and tail pieces, and six or
seven other photographs as well.

This request for illustrations had come with the mail on an
early morning train. With less than twenty-four hours to meet
Maxwell's deadline, Gene set briskly to work. First she telephoned Fort Wayne and made arrangements for delivery of
print paper and chemicals on the afternoon train. Then, because she needed pictures of persons dressed in the manner
of the 1870s, she ransacked the cabin for costumes. Next she
hitched up her little black horse and drove to the homes of
potential subjects and arranged for sittings. By ten in the
morning she was photographing an old gentleman seated
beside her fireplace. At eleven she was dressing a young girl
to be depicted as the princess in her story. At noon she was
in one of her bedrooms photographing another child who
served well as another character in her story. An hour later
she trotted this child three miles out in the November air to

a cemetery where she posed her among mounted butterflies from her cases in the cabin and potted plants from the conservatory. At four in the afternoon she was at the schoolhouse, working with models on spelling bee scenes, and by six she was in her bathroom, developing and drying the plates, every one of which was good enough to use. She selected twelve, and Maxwell would use all of them. At three in the morning she began to type captions, and by four o'clock a parcel stood in the front hall ready for the six o'clock morning train: "I realized that I wanted a drink, food, and sleep, for I had not stopped a second for anything from the time of reading Mr. Maxwell's letter until his order was ready to mail."[6] And that is the way she would continue to work, to the exclusion of both her own personal needs and also the needs of her family.

Buoyed by the acceptance of her fiction by *Metropolitan*, early in 1902 Gene Stratton-Porter mailed another short story illustrated with her photographs to Richard Watson Gilder, editor of *Century* magazine. Because she did not offer *Century* the exclusive use of these photographs, and because some of them had appeared previously in other magazines, Gilder rejected her work. In an unusual display of vulnerability, she wrote to him again, describing herself as a country girl who was ignorant of publishing practice. Would Gilder publish her wild bird studies if she submitted unused photographs? She had on hand material and illustrations for four small books similar to those being published by the naturalist Ernest Thompson Seton, and she was in a fever to have them published. If she had ruined them for book form, she would be devastated. Richard Watson Gilder would never publish her work, although he would help her. It would be Gilder who would call her work to the attention of a major book publisher two years hence.

Meanwhile, *Metropolitan* published two more of her short stories, and six detailed bird studies, illustrated with her photographs, were published by *Outing* magazine. These articles reflect hours and hours of homework. Legends surrounding various birds abound in her work. Her field observations were buttressed with scientific terms and historical comparisons. She was apparently continuing to read both scientific literature and that of general American interest.

For one of her short stories in *Metropolitan* she chose a contemporary title, "The Real Babes in the Woods," a direct adaptation from a lecture by Artemus Ward, king of American drol'ery. Yet "The Real Babes in the Woods" is not a humorous story. It can only be described as poignant. The characters include a man named Reginald, husband of a nature lover, who finds himself subordinate to his wife's complete absorption in her work. The story culminates when this neglected husband, married to a lady called the Bird Woman, tells his wife he has never forgiven her life choice of the woods, but he accepts it:

> I would have ruined you. I wanted to make you happy with society and the fashionable amusements. . . . The secrets of the birds and flowers and all the finest miracles of God in nature are for you. Your choice was right and wise. Let me hereafter be your very good friend.[7]

The Bird Woman, then left alone, sits staring vaguely. Great dry sobs begin to rise in her throat. In that hour she realizes both her mistake and her heart's hunger. This short story ends abruptly, in midair: "In that hour he who had been her lover approved of her wisdom in denouncing him. It was what she would have had him do, and yet——."[8]

In addition to her husband's understanding and his occasional help, Gene Stratton-Porter had other assistance with her fieldwork. Many of her neighbors, like the Hawbakers, willingly opened their gates to her, although there were a few farmers in the area who merely tolerated her in their fields, and still others who charged her to drive down lanes they

used every day themselves. A farmer's refusal to grant access
was not unusual. Charles Porter would not tolerate trespassing on *his* farmland either. As a constant reminder that he
would brook no violators, he ran an ad in the local weekly
stating that anyone caught trespassing on his farm would be
prosecuted.

Gene Statton-Porter's fullest cooperation afield came from
the oil workers in Adams County. Of these oilmen, she had
the highest regard for one Bob Burdette Black. After he had
his belts running smoothly, his rod lines pulsing steadily, his
powerhouse in order, and all of his men at their stations, Bob
Black liked to go out among the feathered friends he had
known and befriended for years.

Like Gene's father, Bob acted as if he could do anything.
He could improvise a raft and pole across the Wabash. He
could climb a tree so tall and rotten that it swayed with his
weight. He even seemed to be able to scent the nest of a bird
when his pointer dog failed. When Bob Black came upon a
bird nest, he could scarcely wait to show it to Gene, to reserve
it for her camera.

One day while trying to corner several baby quail, all at
once Gene realized that both she and Bob had a higher priority: "A million tiny red lice were swarming up his neck and
over his face and arms. Only a quarter million fell to my share
and drove me frantic."[9] Leaping into the carriage, she raced
madly for the cabin. Glancing back, she saw Bob flying from
his powerhouse with a bundle, in a dead heat to reach the
river.

Bob Black seems to have understood what Gene Stratton-
Porter was trying to accomplish. The residents of Geneva,
however, were less understanding. Because she continued to
be cryptic about gathering material for her articles and stories,
inevitably some of her neighbors began to buzz with stories.
There had to be something the matter with a lady who lived

in such a grand house and liked to run all over the countryside clad in khaki, taking pictures of birds. No normal woman would leave the comfort of such a fine home to drive a drafty buggy through swamp and field in all kinds of weather on such strange business. Beyond this, when such a woman went trotting all over the countryside without her husband, some of the locals liked to speculate about any possible relationship she might have with the teenager who helped grapple with her long ladders and forty pounds of photographic equipment.

The town gossips need not have worried. Young Raymond was an employee, not a lover. Had these villagers known Gene Stratton-Porter better, they might have speculated that the rhythms which permeated her being were those of nature and poetry, not the bedstead. In her own words: "I like paragraphs that swing through a story with rhythmic sweep. I have juggled with sentences for days, and taken them to bed with me at night, in an effort to combine music with truth and realism."[10]

On the other hand, perhaps it was *not* the music of the spheres that dominated Gene's bedtime fantasies. In a story about Bob Burdette Black, she wrote: "As he came swinging down the path in corduroys, flannel shirt and flopping old hat, the Bird Woman saw a vision of him on a ball room floor in dress suit and patent leathers showing the most clinging wall flower of the occasion the time of her life."[11]

Without a certain skill in photography, Gene Stratton-Porter would have been severely handicapped. Lacking the benefit of prearranged studio lighting, she was daily required to make the best of ever-shifting sunlight and shadow. Nevertheless, her bird photographs startle because of their lifelike quality. She attributed these animated photographs to more than skill, however, or even luck: "There comes a time in amateur photographic work when your plate is fresh and faultless, your light all you could wish, and your subject poses with a spirit as well as a body. In such cases you record, not details, but the light of the soul shining through the eyes and illuminating the countenance."[12] She was referring to the soul of a bird. Birds, from earliest times a symbol of the human soul, would always be the focal point of her work, and in all of her writing they would take on human characteristics.

Gene Stratton-Porter believed the various birds suited their melodies to their life stories:

> If they have an emotional complex, then they sing passionately, richly, thrillingly—and their songs are love songs. If they rejoice in the warm spring air, in the sunshine, their notes are clear and flute-like—as for instance, the meadow lark, whose clear whistle always seems to be floating or soaring on a tenuous beam of light.[13]

One spring morning while working along the banks of the Wabash, she had the good fortune to encounter closeup one of bird land's loudest singers. She scarcely had time to attach a hose to her camera and dive for cover before he came full tilt toward her, landing forcefully on a limb directly in front of her. He was breast front to the camera, his wings drooping half-folded, his crest flared to a greater degree than she had ever seen it, his snowy collar and bright coloring flashing in the light, his liquid eyes gleaming: "Almost as he struck the limb he turned his head riverward and let out a prolonged whoop—the shrill, discordant, laughing cry of a kingfisher lover calling his mate to follow him."[14]

Gene was shaking so hard she was unsure whether she had even squeezed the bulb to make an exposure, but straightaway she headed for home to develop whatever her plate might hold. She had previously made four studies of a kingfisher in fairly favorable attitudes; however, upon developing her most recent print she made a fresh discovery. Here was a new ele-

Wood robin, photographed by Gene Stratton-Porter

Kingfisher, photographed by Gene Stratton-Porter

ment of kingfisher's character and a new cry, yet she knew
what he said when he struck that limb:

> Come on, old sweetheart, let us play! Our beaks are
> scarred with tunneling! Our breasts are bruised with
> brooding! We are worn with baby raising! Our chil-
> dren are grown and gone! Now we are free! This is our
> playtime! I'll race you to the dam! I'll beat you to
> horseshoe bend! I'll show you plunges of flight you
> never saw before! Let us riot in the sunshine! Let us
> rock on the wind! Let us taste the intoxication of per-
> fect freedom, with no thought of care! Hurrah! Hur-
> rah! Come on, old girl! It is kingfisher holiday![15]

A Full Mailbox

RIVALING Gene Stratton-Porter's determination to become established as a writer was her intense devotion to what she regarded as her family duty. Invariably when a family crisis occurred, the youngest Stratton was the first to respond. Perhaps her most magnanimous gesture would be the rearing of Lemon's adolescent daughter as her own after his death. Generous with her money as well as her time, she also contributed substantially to the support of Jeannette after her marriage and to the support of Ada and Florence in their old age. Expecting nothing in return and never complaining about additional responsibility or expense, she helped her family without being asked. An intense loyalist who placed a high value on family and personal privacy, Gene Stratton-Porter was customarily silent about her generosity. By the same token, she was equally quiet in regard to family disagreements.

One such divisive matter, a family free-for-all, came to a head in 1902. Understandably, no reference to this prickly matter is found anywhere in Gene Stratton-Porter's published remarks. It is fairly easy, however, from various court records and newspaper accounts to reconstruct the facts of the matter.[1]

Gene Stratton-Porter

This family uproar centered around a touchy subject, the one subject Gene Stratton-Porter could not contemplate even briefly without becoming highly agitated: her father and his money.

By the spring of 1902, although twelve years had passed since Mark Stratton's death, his financial affairs were at loose ends. His estate was still open, supposedly under the watchful eye of Ada's husband Frank, estate administrator. One day, however, Frank Wilson took a sudden notion to leave Indiana for California. With him went the little black book he had carried for several years that recorded how much he had spent, and how much he had taken in, on behalf of the Stratton heirs. When Frank first left, no one missed him. Few of the Strattons even knew he was gone. They were geographically scattered. Most lived far from Wabash and did not know that Frank Wilson had been neglecting their interests in the estate. Catherine resided in Los Angeles, and Florence was still in Michigan. Although Lemon was nearby, dealing in timber, Jerome and Irvin were in Kansas. Jerome had a sizable law practice there in Erie, the seat of Neosho County. Irvin, also active as a lawyer, but in Wichita, had become well known in that area as a breeder of fine cattle and horses.

A few months after Frank Wilson took off for California, the question arose as to when Mark Stratton's affairs could be wound up. Unbeknown to others in the family, Irvin stepped in to find out. He decided to go to California, specifically to San Bernardino where Frank Wilson then resided. Irvin had in mind selling two of his thoroughbreds there, as well as some Jersey cattle, and he intended to look the place over with a view to moving to southern California if conditions suited. Unfortunately, Irvin's tentative plans for his future, as well as an opportunity to talk estate settlement matters with Frank Wilson, went sadly awry. On 2 April 1902, two days after Irvin's arrival in San Bernardino, he died several hours after his rig collided with a Southern Pacific electric.

As if this shock to the family were not enough, immediately thereafter Frank Wilson tried to take steps to wash his hands of Mark Stratton's affairs without accounting for any of the heirs' money that had passed through his hands over the past several years. From what he no doubt hoped would be the safe distance of the West Coast, Frank told the Wabash Circuit Court, which had jurisdiction of this matter, that he owed the Stratton heirs nothing. It made no difference, even if it could be determined that he owed them something, because he was broke. He also had the gall to state that, because the statute of limitations had expired on his old house loan from Mark Stratton, now many years delinquent, he had no obligation to pay that off either. To top it off, he wanted to be reimbursed for various expenditures on behalf of the Stratton estate that he claimed had come out of his own pocket. At this, Alvah Taylor, who had been acting as Frank Wilson's attorney, immediately filed a petition with the court in Wabash demanding that Frank be ordered to turn over his little black book for examination. It would remain to Alvah, who by this time must have wished he had never heard of, let alone met, a Stratton, to finally clear up this financial quagmire, and it would take him six more years to do so.

It is understandable that Gene had nothing to say about the myriad problems attendant to settling her father's financial affairs, although it is curious that, in later years, she failed to mention the fatal accident of her brother Irvin. After Laddie, he was her most beloved brother. Perhaps, as in the case of her father, but for different reasons, she was unable to write easily of Irvin's death. Immediately after her brother's death, she began to write furiously, as if chased by another apparition. As always, it was birdlife that triggered her inspiration.

While walking a road late one afternoon, Gene came upon the body of a cardinal. Like those long-ago birds in her father's orchard, it had been shot. The sight of this lifeless redbird inspired both her sympathy and her imagination. The result was a short story that she sent to Richard Watson Gilder. Gilder liked her story and thought it had possibilities as a novel. He advised her to expand it. It took Gene a month to expand the story, and no one, least of all Charles and Jeannette, knew she was attempting a full-length book until she was unable to execute a legal contract for its publication without Charles's signature: "With them [Charles and Jeannette] I was much more timid than with the neighbours. Least of all did I want to fail before my man person and my daughter and our respective families; so I worked in secret, sent in my material, and kept as quiet about it as possible."[2]

Gene Stratton-Porter's first novel, *The Song of the Cardinal*, replete with her photographic illustrations, was published the following spring by Bobbs-Merrill. It is the tale of a redbird who lives along the banks of the Wabash, an affectionate bird who loves its mate. She dedicated the book to her father and hyphenated her own last name so that everyone would know she had been born a Stratton. This book dedication was her father's only epitaph, as no marker had yet been erected over his grave, another estate matter Frank Wilson continued to neglect.

The most striking aspect of Gene Stratton-Porter's first book is not so much the voice of her father, but the hand of her mother, mother earth.

> Up in the land of the Limberlost, old Mother Nature, with strident muttering, had set about her annual house-cleaning. With her efficient broom, the March wind, she was sweeping every nook and cranny clean. With her scrub-bucket overflowing with April showers, she was washing the face of all creation, and, if these measures failed to produce cleanliness to her satisfaction, she gave a final polish with storms of hail. . . . The ice and snow had not altogether gone; but the long-pregnant earth was mothering her children. . . . The sap was flowing, and leafless trees were covered with swelling buds.[3]

Nationwide, Gene Stratton-Porter's first book was well received by the literary establishment. One reviewer felt it would do for the birds of the forest what *Black Beauty* had done for the horse. Its author was distressed, however, because *The Song of the Cardinal* seemed to find the pulse of only a small audience: "The book started so slowly that soon I came to the realization that, if I could not reach people faster, so far as my work was concerned, the cardinals might all go as had the pigeons."[4]

So she wrote another book, this time with a different focus. Her second novel is about people, not birds. In the background hovers a bird woman who rejoices in photographing birds and wildflowers, in the foreground a light romance. The main character, an orphan known as Freckles, guards a large tract of timber for a lumber firm. Freckles boards near a swamp known as the Limberlost with a charitable family named Duncan. It is curious that the Mrs. Duncan of this novel has the same name as the widow, Mrs. Sarah Duncan, who had boarded with the Strattons those many years ago.

It is not difficult to construe one of the sentences in Gene Stratton-Porter's second novel as personally applicable to its writer: "The utter loneliness of a great desert or forest is not so difficult to endure as the loneliness of being constantly surrounded by crowds of people that do not care in the least whether one is living or dead."[5] The dedication page reads: "To All Good Irishmen in general and one Charles Darwin Porter in particular."[6]

As first written, *Freckles* was titled *The Falling Feather*. It ended tragically when the central character was crushed by a falling tree. With great reluctance Gene Stratton-Porter ceded to the demands of her publisher to change the title and add a conventional happy ending: "I walked the floor two days and a night before I gave in. I had no audience and no funds to publish and exploit my own work. . . . The true flavor of the book was spoiled for me. . . . I still mourn for my little classic that might have been."[7]

Her publisher was Doubleday, Page and Company, a firm that had been established four years earlier by Frank Doubleday, Walter Hines Page, and Sidney Lanier. Almost at once Doubleday had begun to publish a stream of well-advertised nature books, both fiction and nonfiction. By October 1904, when *Freckles* was released, the reading public was avidly receptive to Doubleday's nature lore push. A widespread interest in the great outdoors had developed, instigated by Theodore Roosevelt. The times were especially right for Gene Stratton-Porter's particular frame of reference; her readers had a high curiosity about all things natural, and she appeared to supply certain insights.

About two months after the publication of *Freckles*, Gene Stratton-Porter found herself hopelessly bogged down in a subject to which she had previously given no serious thought. She was asked by a genealogist for a delineation of the Stratton family tree. There is no evidence to show that she had been interested prior to this time in substantiating any of her father's tales about his illustrious forebears. To the contrary, five years earlier she had erroneously declared her father to have been born in Pennsylvania, not New Jersey. This certainly suggests that either she did not know at that time where he had been born, or at least felt that his birthplace was inconsequential. Early in 1905, however, she was asked to clarify her paternal ancestry by an experienced genealogist, Harriet Stratton. Stratton was then examining eleven colonial lines of Strattons and attempting to trace more than five thousand of their descendants, an arduous undertaking that involved painstaking research and strict documentation.

In her correspondence with Harriet Stratton, Gene Stratton-Porter ran into difficulty with several aspects of her family history. One of her misunderstandings concerned her great-grandfather. She cited her ownership of a prized family possession, a carved black walnut chest that had supposedly been made by this paternal great-grandfather. On it was penciled "made by Daniel Stratton in 1760." Inasmuch as Gene Stratton-Porter's great-grandfather Daniel had not been born until the late 1750s, she was unprepared to explain to the genealogist how that carved walnut chest had been made by a child under the age of three. It is perhaps significant that no such family chest appears on the inventory of the estate of Gene's grandfather, Ohio pioneer Joseph Stratton, where it presumably should have been, either in the chattels apportioned to his widow or in the list of his personal property disposed of at public vendue. This inventory appears to be complete, down to a teakettle valued at twenty-five cents. Where such a chest may have originated remains a mystery.

After careful research, the Stratton researcher finally determined that Gene's great-grandfather had indeed been one Daniel Stratton of Sussex County, New Jersey, although the genealogist was unable to find Daniel's point of origin nor was she able to find proof of this Daniel Stratton's parentage. Moreover, even the first Mark Stratton, the colonial immigrant for whom Gene's father claimed he had been named, had no retrievable ancient warrior in his background. No clue could be unearthed verifying the parentage or former residence of the first Mark Stratton to American shores, thus the Stratton historian assigned him number one on her charts, denoting the commencement of a colonial line and showing no connection whatever to any earlier Englishman. A Mark Stratton of a later generation than the first one did turn up on her charts. This Mark Stratton had brothers who registered in Frederick County, Virginia, in 1770 at a Hopewell meeting of Friends. The Quaker name Hopewell does suggest a connection between this later Mark Stratton and Gene's father. He had so cherished the name of Hopewell, one he associated

with his forebears, that he had bestowed it on his church, the
Hopewell Methodist Church of Lagro.

The Stratton family historian made small progress in her
attempt to modify Gene's misunderstanding of the family
tree, although she did manage to have the last word. Her
compilation of colonial Strattons, as eventually published,
enabled any interested descendant to verify his or her family
connections immediately by means of a system using either
a plus or a minus. Mark Stratton's progeny were not accorded
either a plus or a minus.

One of Gene Stratton-Porter's letters to Harriet Stratton
carries an almost desperate quality, as if she felt her credentials
would be somehow incomplete without proof of an august
lineage. She may have had a glimmer at that time that she
would be asked by her publisher for biographical information.
On 22 February 1905, in response to Harriet's letter asking if
she would like to see a Stratton crest, one of many, Gene
leaped to reply, with bold underscoring: "Sure I want the
tracing and photograph of crest, *and* I want the right to *repro-
duce* and *use* crest—mighty bad. I know I am entitled to 'S' if
I can only prove it."[8]

Meanwhile, *Freckles*, her second book of fiction and wood
lore, had begun to find an appreciative audience. In this book,
set in the Limberlost, Gene Stratton-Porter hits her stride as
a writer with certain unique powers of presentation. Bugs
wing. Insects hum. A spunky goldfinch skips, flirts, and
swings. Drumming and piping frogs compete with chatter-
ing wild ducks and grebes. Freckles, the main character, is
awed as a snowy moth, lined with a lavender band, emerges
from a large cocoon and unfolds its velvet down in the morning sun. In the privacy of the Limberlost, Freckles constructs
for himself a cathedral. Part of his walls were mallow, part
alder, thorn, willow, and dogwood. At one side the swamp
came close, and cattails grew in profusion. In front of them

he plants a row of water hyacinths. Nearby he tenderly transplants lacy vines and ferns, dainty blue-eyed Mary and wild
geranium, cardinal flower, columbine, trillium, pitcher plant,
hepatica, jack-in-the-pulpit, wild clematis, and climbing
bittersweet.

Soon after the publication of *Freckles*, Gene Stratton-
Porter's post-office box began to overflow. Many of the letters
she received were from unfortunates, critically ill in body and
spirit. Buoyed by the wholesome tale of Freckles, they wrote
to thank her for writing such an uplifting work. A nurse
wrote, on behalf of a spinal patient unable to walk, that her
charge had lost himself in Freckles's pictures of swamp and
forest for an hour. From a reform school, its warden wrote
that fifteen hundred little sin-besmirched souls in his care
were reading *Freckles* to rags. Recalling Gene Stratton-Porter's
early contempt for academia, it is a strange twist that the
highest praise upon the publication of *Freckles* came from one
of America's most distinguished scholars. Oren Root, professor of mathematics, college president, clergyman, lawyer,
and author, penned a tribute to Gene Stratton-Porter's second
book that moved her more than any other. Root read *Freckles*
in one absorbed sitting. The next morning, seated beside the
fireplace in his beloved "Hemlocks," he wrote her a grateful
letter. In it he told her how much he liked what he had read.
It was this tribute by Oren Root that Gene Stratton-Porter
recalled most often and cherished above all others. It is this
tribute by Oren Root that best personifies how readers worldwide have felt about the rustic novels of Gene Stratton-Porter:
"I have a severe cold this morning, because I got my feet very
wet last night, walking the trail with 'Freckles,' but I am
willing to risk pneumonia any time for another book like
that."[9]

Camera Fever

A
S soon as her mailbox began to run over,
Gene Stratton-Porter was off and running
too, afield by day and at home by night, writing feverishly. She had long ago abandoned
writing in longhand in favor of the type-
writer and had taught herself to operate it
using three fingers on each hand. In the past she had enjoyed
secretarial help from her daughter, by this time a teenager,
who had borrowed a second machine. About the time *Freckles*
was published, however, she lost Jeannette's assistance. Possibly because of its bigger and better school system, the Porters had dispatched Jeannette to Wabash, as a boarder with
Frank and Ada, who had returned from California.

With her daughter elsewhere, the house was quiet, con-
ducive to reflection. Free to work unimpeded, Gene Stratton-
Porter began to gather and organize material for several books
simultaneously. One work in progress was a book about all
the birds mentioned in the Bible. Night after night she pored
over her Bible, making notes about the birdlife mentioned in
its pages. For this forthcoming book, and for other nature
works to follow, she was determined to procure photographic
illustrations.

Gene Stratton-Porter felt the sketched illustrations in standard ornithologies, such as those by John James Audubon, were inferior to photographic illustrations. To her, Audubon's drawings looked unlifelike and stiff, "as if they had been cut out with a scroll saw."[1] She was anxious that her future nature books, such as that projected about the birds of the Bible, bear animated illustrations, and she worked tirelessly to that end. From the first dove of March to the last migrant of October she carried her heavy camera equipment and long ladders through swamps and up and down country lanes, searching for birdlife.

Nostalgia for her childhood also drew her camera to field and barnyard. When a flock of baby ducks came tearing to possess a puddle at her feet, nothing stopped her from a quick snap. In the pasture, in her fever to catch the beautiful Jersey on her way home, she would forget she had seen six massasaugas in that same spot at haying time the year before. She drove herself relentlessly, because she must: "To whom it is given to go afield because driven by an inward fever every step is its own compensation. Who goes with the camera fever added goes with something of the fascination of a gambler."[2] Why she loved fieldwork, she could not explain: "It is beyond me; but it is probably for the same reason that Kepler numbered stars and Agassiz hammered rock—because they couldn't help themselves."[3]

One day when the temperature ranged between 104 and 108 degrees, she was out working with set cameras for a shot at a hawk. The weather was so hot that the rubber slide of her plateholder would curl if not laid flat and held by a heavy weight. On her way home, it was so stifling in the buggy that she passed out. An old farmer roused her, disentangling her horse from a thicket of wild briers. The farmer said that if she did not have enough sense to stay indoors in such weather, somebody should appoint her a "guardeen." She reached home worn in body and spirit. As she dragged herself up the front steps and swung her equipment onto the veranda, she stopped, nearly paralyzed. There on the top step, newly emerged, slowly exercising a pair of big wings, was the finest cecropia moth she had ever seen. Recalling her loss of that cecropia many years ago, she recovered with a start, quickly netted it, and took it in the house: "On the most delicate . . . curtain there, I placed my cecropia, and then stepped back and gazed at it with a sort of 'Touch it over my dead body' sentiment in my heart."[4] What luck. What extra golden luck!

Gene Stratton-Porter had many fortunate and unusual experiences afield. One morning on the way to the river she observed a cedar waxwing intoxicated on fermented pokeberries. Another day, as her camera was focused on a nest of chewinks, she watched a bird roll with laughter. The male came within a yard of her blind, scratching for food like a busy hen. When a small rootlet appeared in his way, he pulled on it with all his might. As it broke, he fell over backward and then picked himself up, a most astonished expression on his face, and then he laughed and so did she.

Once, as she rested momentarily in the bottom of a rowboat, a tiny red-eyed vireo came peeking at her, softly chirring, "Du, du, du!" When nothing happened he hopped a little closer, until he was only three feet away. "Peai? Peai?" he asked. When Gene did not respond he raised his voice and screamed, "Tishvoo! Tishvoo!" It awakened the woods. All kinds of birds came flocking in to have a look. It was a rare treat, interrupted only when a drove of pigs appeared, and she feared for her best camera hose lying onshore.

Her rarest sighting came one morning as she was hidden in a fence corner, her camera focused on a nest. A wild pigeon, then nearly extinct, flew over and perched on a telegraph wire above her. It was a big and beautiful male bird, gleaming in the light with a metallic luster. It seemed frightened and ner-

King Birds, photographed by Gene Stratton-Porter

Bird Nest, photographed by Gene Stratton-Porter

vous, its head erect. Looking in all directions, it uttered a few call notes and then took a high and uninterrupted flight, so far as she could see, straight west. Because she was working with a set camera, there was no opportunity to photograph him.

When it was necessary to photograph baby birds in the nest, Gene Stratton-Porter handled her subjects with reverence: "I most emphatically do not go about tearing out nests, changing their locations, handling and killing young birds."[5] Casualties occurred, however, and she kept a precise record of them. One of her notebooks read: "One ground sparrow nest abandoned through my work on it; one nest and eggs taken for scientific purposes; one young flycatcher and one shrike killed by dropping from tree tops."[6] This small number contrasted with the over one hundred twenty negatives obtained during the same time frame, representing one to six subjects on each.

Gene Stratton-Porter's careful observational methods differed sharply from those of Audubon, whom she denounced for his collection practices. Audubon noted that the bittern would freeze in terror when encountered until he knocked it down with an oar or a stick. "May heaven preserve me," Gene wrote. "No, may heaven preserve the birds" from ornithology of Audubon's sort. She felt it unnecessary to kill a bird as common as the bittern for examination purposes. The timid bittern had been anatomically studied for years. Audubon could have consulted established authorities about its innards yet he chose to see for himself, a practice Gene Stratton-Porter pronounced "a bloody work."[7]

Late in 1904 her camera fever paid large rewards. Edward Bok, a nature lover and the flamboyant editor of *The Ladies' Home Journal*, wrote asking to see her portfolio. They met in Chicago, and impressed by her fine prints, Bok ordered an illustrated series of articles for his magazine. The six-month series, titled "What I Have Done with Birds," exposed Gene

Stratton-Porter's work to its widest audience to date. At that time *The Ladies' Home Journal* had passed the million mark in circulation.

A few months later an Indiana publisher reprinted "What I Have Done with Birds" in book form. Its sales were a disappointment, although by this time Stratton-Porter's *Freckles* was selling steadily. The reviews of *Freckles* had been mixed, but none constituted high praise. One reviewer wrote: "The story is not so ingenious nor so well written as *The Song of the Cardinal*, by the same author. She has carried sentiment a trifle too far this time and made it ridiculous."[8] The public disagreed wholeheartedly with the literary critics. Over the next ten years American readers would express their delight with *Freckles* by purchasing more than six hundred thousand copies. Eventually sales would amount to more than two million in the United States and Great Britain. Up until this time, however, there had been no recognition for Gene Stratton-Porter's work from the academic community, although she did receive early praise from a prominent paleontologist. R. R. Rowley of Missouri was so impressed with *What I Have Done with Birds* that he named a trilobite for her: *Phillipsia Stratton-Porteri*.

In the fall of 1906 Gene Stratton-Porter accepted an assignment from Doubleday, Page and Company to write an article about a famous ranch for its magazine, *Country Life in America*. In October she boarded a train for Buffalo County, Nebraska, where she photographed Watson's Ranch, a large expanse covered with sheep, dairy cows, and orchards. Her photographs of this ten thousand-acre spread, along with an interview with the tycoon who owned it, were published three months later.

Although this magazine assignment had been a challenge, it was outside the mainstream of her interests. She had no inclination to become a camera for hire. On her return to Indiana, Gene Stratton-Porter began work on her third novel, *At the Foot of the Rainbow.* Like *Freckles*, this hunting and fishing story sings with blackbirds who swing on rushes and talk over the seasons. Sapsuckers scold and blue jays form investigating committees.

At the Foot of the Rainbow was written with ease, as were all of Stratton-Porter's novels. The facility with which she wrote is remarkable. Revising, cutting, and rewriting were virtually unknown to her. Her manuscripts as first written were in need of few revisions. She could not comprehend the rarity of this gift for facile expression. In her naïveté about her talent, she could not believe that the majority of writers struggle, at least occasionally. She was unaware that several rewrites would not be unusual. She once said with much surprise: "I know one author who sometimes writes the manuscript for a book as many as three times."[9]

Despite the ease with which she wrote, she was yet handicapped by the lack of a secretary. Every day brought more and more letters from an admiring public, which she felt compelled to answer. There was no prospect of any further help from Jeannette. When Jeannette graduated from high school, the Porters promptly enrolled her in an eastern seaboard college.

In 1908, to help with her burgeoning correspondence, Gene Stratton-Porter hired Lorene Miller, an ex-schoolteacher who was a good typist. With Lorene's assistance, as well as that of a domestic to cook and clean, matters went along smoothly for several months. Then Jeannette came home and shattered the peace and quiet. She had been at loose ends for a year or two. After she returned to Indiana from Chestertown, Maryland, where she had been enrolled in Washington College, the Porters arranged for her to attend a private school in Indianapolis, Indiana, known as Knickerbacker Hall. The emphasis at Knickerbacker, an Episcopalian school, was on general culture and European travel.

Jeannette, then twenty-one, did not take to Knickerbacker Hall. If she was headstrong, that was understandable. She came by it honestly. Jeannette had other things on her mind.

Studio profile portrait of Jeannette Porter Meehan taken in 1907

She was infatuated with a man who did not have her parents' approval. On the sly, she was seeing G. Blaine Monroe of Warren, Pennsylvania, one of the oil men who frequented Adams County. On 4 February 1909 she and Blaine obtained a marriage license at the county seat. License in hand, Blaine telephoned the Porter home and asked if they should be married away from Geneva, or at home. The wedding took place at the cabin two days later, on a Saturday afternoon. Shortly thereafter, the newlyweds left for Pennsylvania.

Never one to dwell on what could not be helped, Gene Stratton-Porter suppressed her reservations about her daughter's marriage and continued to concentrate on her work. That year saw the publication of two more books, *A Girl of the Limberlost*, a novel that gave impetus to butterfly and moth collecting and, finally, *Birds of the Bible*, the illustrated reference work on which she had long labored. For publication of the latter, she turned to a religious publishing house. Jennings and Graham's rendition of *Birds of the Bible* was impressive. Printed on heavy paper with a simulated wood binding, it contained eighty-one photographs and was issued in a handsome slipcase.

Stratton-Porter first attracted worldwide attention, however, with the publication of a new novel. Wholesome fiction, with the stamp of high ideals on every page, *A Girl of the Limberlost* rings with the universal song of hope. She said she had written this story of earth and sky for those confined: "I wrote 'A Girl of the Limberlost,' to carry to workers inside city walls, to hospital cots, to those behind prison bars, and to scholars in their libraries."[10] This novel is the story of a strong individualist, a swamp girl in calico and cowhide who struggles to pay for her education by selling moth specimens. It was a fifty-cent reprint of *A Girl of the Limberlost*, along with a like reprint of *Freckles*, that catapulted Gene Stratton-Porter into the public eye permanently. Through inexpensive reprints of these two books, distributed both at home and abroad, she reached a stratum of society that did not read reviews, shop in new bookstores, or come from an economic level generally equated with a higher education. Gene Stratton-Porter's readers were home-loving, homekeeping people. Many were troubled and poor. Through her rustic inspirational novels these readers were uplifted. From Alaska and South Africa, from China and Burma, from Australia, and from every corner of the United States letters began to come by the hundreds, each testifying that her Limberlost novels of swamp and field helped readers meet life with a braver front, to find a new joy in the out-of-doors previously unknown. A typical reader wrote to her: "You have set my discouraged heart singing. Your Limberlost has been made a haven of peace for me to live in. Thankfully yours."[11]

Gene Stratton-Porter reveled in the growing popularity of her books. The best thing about it was her new financial independence. What a pleasure, finally, to be generating her own income. As soon as she realized her freedom to spend was not a temporary aberration, she went on a spree in an Indianapolis department store, sailing out of its French Room in a double-weave, full-length motor coat of lavender, trimmed in white, with matching bonnet and silk veil. Then she motored to Wabash, her old hometown, in a seven-passenger automobile driven by a chauffeur. Her motives were mixed. First she turned to housebound old folks and shut-ins and gave them a ride. Then she looked up her former schoolmates. She remembered keenly her miserable experiences in the Wabash school system, and she could not resist flaunting her success, later describing her triumphant return to Wabash as "pure, unadulterated joy."[12] After spending an entire month there with Ada, she returned to Geneva ready to work with renewed effort.

Because of various commercial inroads, however, field-work in Adams County became increasingly difficult. Lumbermen had been gradually clearing the Limberlost, leaving it crisscrossed with roads and drainage ditches. As its salable timber was removed, shrubs and vines were eradicated and brush burned, destroying wildlife. Canadian lumbermen had come first, seeking tall timber for ship masts and heavy trees for beams. Lumbermen from Grand Rapids, Michigan, followed and stripped the hardwood for the city's furniture factories. Now hoop and stave men and local mills were taking the best of the softwood, and a ditch had been dredged across the north end of the Limberlost to drain its water into the Wabash River. Agriculture was on the increase in Adams County, thanks to the draining of the swamp. Also by 1909 there were 650 wells pumping in the Geneva area, producing over a million barrels of oil annually.

All of this commercial expansion meant that few bird habitats remained undisturbed. So in order to obtain sufficient photographs from the wild for a forthcoming book, Gene Stratton-Porter had to move far afield. She chose familiar ground, the untouched shoreline of Sylvan Lake, about two hours by train north of Geneva, where she and Charles had continued to vacation since chautauqua days. A large portion of the photographs in *Music of the Wild*, a Stratton-Porter nature book published in 1910, were taken at Sylvan Lake. It was easy to work at the lake. The lake was man-made, with trees that overhung the water, making it ideal for observational work.

For the publication of *Music of the Wild*, once more Gene Stratton-Porter found herself turning to Jennings and Graham, the religious house that had published *Birds of the Bible*. Shortly thereafter, however, she worked out a long-term publishing arrangement with Doubleday, Page and Company. Frank Doubleday believed in the great sales potential of Gene Stratton-Porter's novels, not her nature works, but he was anxious to represent her exclusively. However, Gene Stratton-Porter believed in the long-lasting worth of her nature books, as opposed to her fiction. In a compromise,

Doubleday agreed to publish her novels and her nonfiction books on an alternate annual basis.

Gene Stratton-Porter's rise to public prominence paralleled that of Doubleday, Page and Company. Doubleday had, since its inception, published works primarily in praise of country life, including several well-received books by Neltje Blanchan, Frank Doubleday's wife. In 1910, to further its back-to-nature image, the company moved its publishing operation from New York City to Garden City, on Long Island, making it the first major publishing house to leave Manhattan. The new thirty-acre tract in the suburbs was a showpiece of ornamental landscaping. Teddy Roosevelt laid the cornerstone. From this symbol of Arcadia, Doubleday continued successfully "to foster a love of the wide outdoors." Between 1910 and 1913 the company doubled its business, thanks in part to the record-breaking sales of the fiction of Gene Stratton-Porter, including a new novel titled *The Harvester.* From number five on the best-seller list in 1911, this latest Stratton-Porter title rose to number one in 1912.[13]

The Harvester depicts a woodsman of simple nobility who gathers seeds, plants, and bark for medicinal purposes. The background of this best-seller was based on firsthand experience and observation. For years Charles had bought wild herbs such as ginseng for resale at his pharmacy, and both he and Gene knew several persons locally who gathered various herbs for market.

The year *The Harvester* appeared was exceptionally busy. Breaks in daily routine were frequent. The Doubledays arrived unexpectedly in May for a short visit, followed by Edward Bok. Knocking at the door of the cabin had begun to reach a fever pitch. Callers came often. Some merely wanted to meet the author whose work they liked so much. Others brought sick or wounded birds, dangling cocoons, unusually constructed bird nests, or various kinds of nature

freaks in need of identification. Lorene was instructed to turn
away well-wishers, although there was one request that was
never refused, and that was to aid an injured bird or animal.
Lorene recalled one day when she and Gene doctored a bird
fished from an oil pool: "That meant more to Mrs. Porter
than a week of uninterrupted work."[14]

When these interruptions consumed the morning, that
meant no work on any novel in progress. Gene Stratton-
Porter had an unalterable routine, writing fiction only in the
morning. After lunch she usually napped for an hour. Then,
later in the day, she liked to take a constitutional. On days too
busy for a long walk, she and Lorene went to a bridge span-
ning a small stream not far from the cabin, where Gene would
enjoy a few minutes of calisthenics. One day an old lady who
lived nearby asked Lorene: "Jest what does that woman mean
by them crazy moves on the bridge?" When Lorene tried to
explain her employer's need to exercise after sitting at a desk
all morning, the neighbor replied: "Well, I jest 'lowed, she'd
worked her brain so hard she'd gone plum daffy."[15]

Evenings at home were apt to be filled with literary fireworks. After dinner, what had been written that morning
dominated the conversation. Charles had a good ear for plot
and was not afraid to use it. According to Lorene: "Frequently
a war of words followed these criticisms."[16] It was a friendly
war, however. By this time the Porters had achieved a marital
understanding. Charles was his wife's helpmate in all things,
and she tolerated his criticisms of her work. He was her financial adviser as well, steering her toward sound real estate
investments. In turn, she invested heavily in his bank, becoming a majority stockholder. Their relationship had come to
rest solely on this financial quid pro quo and a respect for
each other's drive and intellect. As such, Charles was free to
come and go from home whenever he pleased, and this he
did often, sometimes vacationing by himself, with old friends,

or with his brother, occasionally venturing as far afield as Mexico, where he liked to pursue various collecting interests.

In the spring of 1911 the Porters learned they would become grandparents in the fall. Ordinarily, that is wonderful news. However, in recent months Jeannette's hasty marriage had begun to confirm her parents' worst fears. Her husband could not seem to hold a job. Most recently, he had lost his position as a sales representative when the gas fixture company for which he worked in Buffalo, New York, went out of business.

Late in 1911 the Monroes relocated to Emporium, Pennsylvania, where their first child, Jeannette Helen, was born 27 November. In her book Jeannette puts the best face on her early marital instability, stating how much her parents enjoyed a Christmas visit to her Pennsylvania home in 1911. Her recollection is faulty, however, as the Porters spent Christmas at home in Geneva, where Jeannette and her new baby joined them for a prolonged visit.

Meanwhile, Stratton-Porter books continued to sell well. A new edition of *Freckles* was just going to press. The first edition of *The Harvester* had been exhausted, and 25,000 additional copies were being printed. A third edition of *Music of the Wild* was in the works, as well as a second edition of *At the Foot of the Rainbow*. Over 90,000 copies of *A Girl of the Limberlost* were in print, and another nature book, about the moths of the Limberlost, was in progress.

For years, while tramping the woods and fields, Gene Stratton-Porter had been collecting cocoons. She hung them in her conservatory and, when it rained, in imitation of Mother Nature, she sprinkled them. She had learned the art of raising moths by trial and error. Her first moth experiment had been a failure. One morning while working in the swamp, she had noticed an unusual caterpillar eating its way around a grape leaf. It was over four inches long, with no horn, and of a deep, red wine color. After clipping the vine

Gene Stratton-Porter with moth collection

on which it fed, she carried it home where she placed it in a large box with sand on the bottom, lined with grape leaves. Every few hours she replaced wilted leaves with fresh.

The caterpillar ate for three days, then began to race frantically around the box. She thought perhaps it disliked confinement and turned it loose in the house. When its travels stopped two days later at a window screen, she was puzzled to discover it had shrunk to half its former length. Not knowing it was in the process of changing into a pupa from which she could have secured an exquisite moth, she discarded it.

Further experimentation and investigation led to a general knowledge of the habits and characteristics of the big nonfeeding night moths of the Limberlost and some of the day moths. By 1912 she had collected enough specimens for a book. And there was a need for such a book geared toward the layman. In Gene Stratton-Porter's opinion, the lepidopteral books then on the market were too technical for the average person. She wanted to write a moth and butterfly book that anyone could use and understand, with illustrations prepared by herself. When the book was finished, she was proud of it. She felt her photographic illustrations, done from live moths, contrasted most favorably with those made from mounted specimens in which the colors were faded and the bodies shriveled: "I would quite as soon accept the mummy . . . as a fair representation of the living man, as a mounted moth for a live one."[17]

In April 1912 there was another family wedding, this time a happier occasion. Ada's daughter married a recent college graduate who was employed by the United States Department of the Interior. The groom's hobby, outdoor photography, immediately endeared him to the family photographer. Years later Gene Stratton-Porter would dedicate a book to James Sweetser Lawshe, who shared her interest in bird and plant life.

That summer, as usual, she vacationed at Sylvan Lake, near Rome City, taking Lorene along. This time she would stay over four months. When he could get away from the bank, Charles came up on weekends. Developments at the Geneva Bank, however, were very unsettling that summer. An unexpected visit from examiners uncovered a shortage of thousands of dollars in certificates of deposit. The day the bank examiners descended, a pale assistant cashier was seen leaving the bank for home. Later that day he was found hanging in his barn. Despite the local scandal, there was no loss of confidence on the part of the bank's depositors. It was common knowledge that Gene Stratton-Porter's substantial royalties were on deposit there.

When Charles was finally able to join his wife and her secretary at Rome City, he found them in a small cottage. Instead of staying at Triplett's Hotel, as they had in the past, Gene Stratton-Porter had decided to buy a summer home on the lake. Early in June she had purchased a bungalow known locally as the Hofmann cottage on the north side of Sylvan Lake. She knew when she bought it, however, that this small cottage would only be temporary summer quarters. Once settled, she had begun a private scouting operation up and down Sylvan Lake, looking for vacant property. She had an idea. She wanted to build a year-round home here, in the nature of a workshop.

Her rationale was sound. At home in Geneva, interruptions to her work by well-meaning callers were costing her both time and money. She needed more privacy, and she could have it at Rome City. Here also, along the wild stretches of the lake, she could observe birdlife to her heart's content for many years to come. In Adams County the best birding haunts had been lost to lumber cutting, oil wells, and agriculture. She also wanted a more convenient workplace, one with every photographic convenience. The cabin in Geneva had no darkroom. She was also ready for a modern kitchen.

One day while poking around the south shore of Sylvan Lake, she found a five-acre tract with possibilities. About one acre of it was covered with blue-eyed grass, a wildflower of

the iris family. The balance of the property was virgin timber.
She liked the looks of it. A house built on this curving water-
front could face the lake on two sides. It could be lovely. It
was her vision of what she could do with the grounds, however, that was the most elaborate. She envisioned at least one
species of every wildflower native to Indiana growing here,
as well as extensive plantings to attract and protect every bird
native to the region. She thought it over. She was forty-nine
years old, and her finances were sound. She had the vitality
to build again, and this time she could pay for it herself, with
no help from Charles. She could live here year-round. Charles
could stay in the cabin in Geneva and ride the train to Rome
City on weekends, if he chose. Their marital separation
would not be official, and there would not be much buzzing
about it. The temptation was overwhelming.

Gene Stratton-Porter's decision to abandon her fine home
in Adams County, Indiana, and build a workshop and birdlife
refuge eighty-five miles to the north was one that she made
one day while talking it over with Ada. In July 1912 she
obtained an easement over the lakefront site she had in mind,
and by mid-October she had purchased it and plunged headlong into plans for a new log cabin and grounds. Ada always
said that Gene had paid the full purchase price for an acre of
blue-eyed grass. Ada was half right. The other half of the
equation was a wood duck. Two different times Gene saw
him floating among the lily pads only a few rods from shore,
his bright plumes glistening in the afternoon sun: "I bought
the wood duck and the blue-eyed grass, with a wealth of tall
hardwood trees for good measure."[18]

Wildflower Woods

WILDFLOWER Woods, the estate created by Gene Stratton-Porter on the shores of Sylvan Lake at Rome City, Indiana, stands today, maintained as a historic site by the state of Indiana. The well-kept Stratton-Porter homestead is a monument to Indiana's respect for her accomplishments, its lush grounds a reminder of her long endeavors. Out of more than fourteen thousand trees, vines, shrubs, and wild-flowers that she found or bought and planted, 90 percent were set by her own fingers. These botanic specimens came not only from the swamps and woods of the upper Midwest, but also from her readers. Over the years letters and packages filled with seeds arrived from readers all over the world.

Gene Stratton-Porter's development of this birdlife sanctuary in Noble County, Indiana, began with an acre by acre inspection by Frank Wallace, tree surgeon and later Indiana State Entomologist. In the spring of 1913 Stratton-Porter hired Frank Wallace to work with her small tangled tract. To establish birdlife here, she knew that she must have a healthy stand of timber. Wallace's first job was to clear brush and administer first aid and surgery to all diseased and damaged trees. Many varieties needed attention—chestnuts, hackberries, elms, oaks, maples, lindens, beeches, and several other native Hoosier specimens, including a rare blue ash.

From April until November 1913, at great expense, a corps of workmen supervised by Frank Wallace swarmed over the grounds, clearing away dead trees and logs and filling tree cavities. Raccoons, owls, squirrels, and rabbits were encouraged to remain; hollow trees were left standing so that these animals might find homes. Poison vines and nonfruit and nonflowering trees and bushes were replaced with growths having fruits and berries. Flowering plants were introduced according to a color pattern. Beginning at the shoreline, large, separate sections were marked off for planting red, white, pink, blue, lavender, and yellow wildflowers.

The site for the cabin fell within the yellow area. A number of splendid beeches, seven fine tulip trees, and a pair of oaks ringed the cabin site. The construction of this cabin, like that of its predecessor, was a personally superintended affair: "I was on the job from the drawing of the line for the back steps between the twin oaks to the last stroke of polish that finished the floors."[1] She also took on a heavy aspect of the construction. She designed and helped build the stone fireplaces in the living room and the library.

This was not her first experience with masonry. For years she had slowly gathered rocks from the bed of the Wabash River to form a low wall around the grounds of her home in Geneva. At her hearth in Rome City, however, Gene Stratton-Porter wanted pudding stone. Dozens of front yards in and around Sylvan Lake were decorated with pudding stone. Some of the stones were only a few inches in diameter; others were huge formations weighing tons. When split, pudding stone is most attractive, revealing roundish red, white, and blue stones against a light background. To find enough of this special stone, she scoured the countryside with a stonemason for several weeks.

Along with constant work on the house and grounds in 1913, there was also time to write another novel. Like *The Harvester*, which had appeared the previous year, *Laddie: A True Blue Story* was another best-seller. This book, a reflection of the current trend toward sentimental romanticism, resurrects the memory of Gene Stratton-Porter's devoted brother Laddie. In this autobiographical work, she looks back at her early childhood on the farm through rose-colored glasses, with one exception. She felt that, in the beginning, she had been unwanted, that her unexpected arrival had been a shock to her middle-aged parents and an embarrassment to her twenty-three-year-old sister Mary Ann, whom she had never been able to forgive. But she also felt that Laddie had wanted her from the first. As with her short story about him, she writes again with much affection about this wonderful big brother who whistled behind his plow, and of kindly neighbors, spelling bees, and young romance. She intended this novel as a true representation of her preadolescent years: "I could write no truer biography. To the contour of hill and field, to the last stripe on the wall paper and knot on the door, that is the home in which I was born."[2]

While working on her novel about Laddie, she was overcome with nostalgia for her childhood home. She even had a fleeting impulse to end her days there, on her father's former acreage: "I went back with my mind fully made up to buy that land at any reasonable price, restore it to the exact condition in which I knew it as a child, and finish my life there."[3] Her desire was short-lived. The house had been burned; the trees set by her mother's hands were gone; and the hills had been plowed down, filling and obliterating creeks and springs. Most of the woods had been cut and planted with corn.

Her old catalpa, a Bartlett pear, and a few gnarled apple trees were all that was left. The garden and lanes had been moved. The only creek remaining, out of three, flowed sickly over a dredged bed. She was sick at heart: "The whole place seemed worse than a dilapidated graveyard. . . . All my love and ten times the money . . . never could have put back the face of nature as I knew it on that land."[4]

Satisfied that she could never restore her former home, Gene Stratton-Porter dropped her quest and began to concentrate on the construction of her new home on Sylvan Lake. At this time she and Lorene were living in the small cottage she had purchased the previous summer, on the other side of the lake. Charles came up on weekends, mostly to putter. Then sixty-three, he was slowing down and not entirely well. As his wife's fame had grown, he had developed ulcers. Fame had complicated both of their lives.

By 1913 reporters and historians, as well as her publishers, were clamoring for facts about Gene Stratton-Porter's background to satisfy an inquisitive public. She was ill-prepared for this personal scrutiny, and the biographical material she eventually supplied was largely faulty, especially that detailing her family history, which she based primarily on hearsay and wishful thinking. Convinced of the importance of high ancestral connections, she concocted an impressive lineage for publication. Drawing on her imagination and the arms of the Strattons of Nottingham, she designed her own coat of arms, adding three shells, or escallops, to indicate that her forebears had made a pilgrimage to the Holy Land during the Crusades. She topped this home creation with a bird of prey, to signify that the heads of her family had been warriors. Gene Stratton-Porter's family history, as she presented it, first appears in Clarkson Weesner's *History of Wabash County*, published in 1914, and again a year later in an anonymously written booklet about her published by Doubleday, Page and Company.

In the spring of 1914 the Stratton family tree expanded. Jeannette gave birth to another girl, whom she named Gene Stratton. It was a busy year. Work at the construction site of the cabin and on its grounds consumed the summer; business

Gene Stratton Monroe, granddaughter of Gene Stratton-Porter

interests were piling up. As various enterprises presented
themselves, Gene Stratton-Porter took advantage of them.
One example is the turning of raw materials from her new
lake property into a finished product. With Charles's help she
established a broom factory in a nearby community, where
she served actively as its president. At the same time she was
also appointed a member of the board of directors of Charles's
bank.

In the fall of 1914, rather than returning to Geneva after
Labor Day, Gene and Lorene stayed on at the cottage in company with a cook and a driver. During cool September days
they motored many miles searching for plants and wildflowers that could be transplanted to the site of the new cabin.
One morning Gene met a farmhand who was removing a rail
fence full of bittersweet, a colorful woody-stemmed vine.
When she asked him if he thought the owner of the land
would mind if she took the roots he was casting aside, he
cackled with glee, "Well now, since Henry's paying three dollars a day to have that 'tarnal stuff grubbed out, I don't reckon
he would object much if you took it out for nothin'."[5] So she
took the vines and set them near the cabin. When this bittersweet matured, it formed a green hedge in spring and a golden
wonder later in the year. All winter its orange-red berries
lifted above the snow. Each October she cut and dried great
boxes of it to send to her sisters, where for months it hung
in wreaths and festoons of brightness.

On her plant-hunting expeditions, Gene Stratton-Porter
was always on the lookout for rarities. She was especially
interested in finding a fringed gentian, a dainty violet-blue
wildflower that blooms in late summer. Doubleday, Page and
Company was offering a prize to the first person who could
induce this wildflower to bloom from seed in a cultivated
location. She found her fringed gentian one brisk October
morning, clinging to an embankment, head down in a ditch
and wide open in bloom. A short distance down the road,

May Apples, photographed by Gene Stratton-Porter

Flowering Shrub, photographed by Gene Stratton-Porter

beyond a bog surrounded with waving marsh grass, she came upon a larger expanse of lovely gentian blue. In the days to come she kept careful watch over these wildflowers, waiting for their seeds to ripen. In the meantime she cultivated a seedbed along the shoreline near the construction site of the cabin. When the gentian seeds were ripe, she planted them prayerfully in her newly prepared seedbed and mulched the spot with leaves, trusting they would push up in the spring.

When winter winds began to howl, she made arrangements to board in the home of a neighboring farmer where she, along with her driver, spent the winter overseeing the completion of the cabin. Workmen added the finishing touches early in February. Gene telephoned Lorene that it was ready for occupancy and arranged to pick her up at the village railroad station. She met her in a bobsled. Snow had fallen a few days earlier, but the road to the cabin had been worn smooth by workmen and trucks. A deep white blanket covered the remainder of the grounds. Giant trees lifted their naked limbs toward the clear blue skies, intensifying the whiteness. From a snow-covered brush heap there suddenly appeared a snow bunting, a small finch, the first they had ever seen, a harbinger of hope that things would go well for them in this new home.

As they trotted up to the cabin, Lorene was impressed. This two-story house had been modeled after Limberlost Cabin in Geneva. Built on sturdy lines of the same Wisconsin cedar logs, it rested on a stone foundation. A large, long porch faced the lake, with sleeping rooms overhead. And, as with the Porters' first cabin, no expense had been spared on the interior. The entrance hall and dining room were paneled in wild cherry, rubbed and waxed to a sheen. The chandeliers were handmade. Several Toltec stone heads, collected by Charles on his sojourns to Mexico, fronted the living room fireplace. Upstairs there were seven bedrooms and a bath, trimmed in maple and pine. And there was a darkroom, a place to compound chemicals and print photographs. The finishing touch was an old English knocker on the front door.

They settled quickly and comfortably into these new quarters. A few days later, in a letter to her tree surgeon, Frank Wallace, Gene wrote:

Dear Frank:

We have been in the new Cabin about two weeks and nearly all we possess has found its permanent location except pictures and curtains. On these I am going slowly. But you may think of us as toasty warm and happy on these days of furious wind and storm. On snowy days Lorene and I go from window to window to see the picture of the snow gracefully whirling through the big trees in Wildflower Woods and nights of white moonlight are so lovely the sight actually hurts.

I shall wait to tell you about my plans for spring planting when you come, which I hope is very soon. You will enjoy seeing my feathered friends feasting on the suet, nuts and parings that they always find on the sills of the conservatory windows. I have titmice, chickadees, nuthatches, sap suckers, flickers and cardinals there daily.

Have had no time as yet, for picture taking, but I've seen signs and wonders and miracles in Wildflower Woods this winter just waiting to be recorded with my camera in the spring.

I am expecting to begin my new novel this week and when a new book is a-borning, as you know, all things at the Cabin must be pushed into the background. Wish me luck.[6]

Later that week they awoke to a still, white world. All around the cabin and across the lake as far as one could see, new snow covered the ground to a depth of several inches. As they opened the door to scatter a fresh supply of birdseed, it was as if they had received a special dispensation: "We are really and truly snowbound, Lorene! Not even the mailman can reach us for days."[7] Work on her next novel, *Michael O'Halloran*, began in this peaceful setting. She allotted more daily time to this book than she customarily gave to fiction as, come April, she knew the pull of the woods would be irresistible. In addition, she knew that Lorene and Frank Wallace were planning to wed and that Lorene would be leaving her employ in June.

Early springtime on a lake was a new experience for both women. There were no sounds quite like those heard as the ice gave way. With loud booms and cracks, ice sixteen inches thick and a mile long set up reverberations that hit the side of the cabin like the blow of a felled tree. Another loud sign of spring was the cry of the great horned owl. It was the mating season for these birds, who cry almost incessantly as they breed. A magnificent pair with a yard of wingspread homed near the cabin in a huge hollow beech. Ordinarily the penetrating cry of the great horned owl while breeding is worse than that of a cat. In late spring, when hunting food for its young, its scream is bloodcurdling.

Toward the first of May, when the racket of the owls had diminished and the weather had improved, Gene moved her bed to the porch, where she could awaken to bird song. One morning she was roused before dawn by men's voices, talk of bait, and the rattle of oars. Unalarmed, she dozed off without investigating. Later that morning, however, when she walked down to the water's edge to keep a tryst with her newly sprouted fringed gentians, she nearly fainted. Her flower bed had been spaded from end to end. Somewhere out on Sylvan Lake fishermen were angling with the worms they had taken from her gentian bed. This ruined flower bed was the first of several wildflower losses to follow.

She again planted another fringed gentian bed in the fall, as Doubleday's medal had not yet been awarded. One triumphant morning the following spring she cut several fine blooms and sent them to her publishers, but to no avail. According to Lorene: "Doubleday & Page's reply brought her the bitterest of disappointments. A flower grower in New York had claimed the medal by a margin of only ten hours."[8]

Later, when Frank Doubleday was a guest at the cabin, he reproached her for failing to telegraph: "All you had to do was to state the hour at which your flowers opened, to say that you had cut them and that they were on the way, specifying the train and hour and the medal would have been yours."[9]

She tensed before she answered: "Having had a Methodist minister for a father and a Benjamin Franklin training in economy, I have not yet learned—even after ten years of successful authorship—that I dare telegraph, when a letter might possibly answer as well."[10]

A New Way of Life

B Y 1915 life in the new cabin at the lake had settled into a steady routine. It was a humdrum existence that would not last for long. As usual, winter and early spring were consumed by a book, usually finished and in the hands of Doubleday sometime in June. Summertime was playtime after the book was on its way. On a typical day Gene Stratton-Porter would leave the cabin after breakfast with a camera, armed with a revolver for stray snakes. Her cook recalls: "We never disturbed her unless something important turned up. . . . Then we would ring a large bell near the lake."[1] Fall was always absorbed by the annual planting of the grounds, with the continued assistance of Frank Wallace and his new bride Lorene.

In the summer of 1915 Jeannette came home for an extended visit with the children, then four and one. They were beautiful girls, and their grandmother took so many pictures of them that summer that she soon had enough for a book. When Charles came up on weekends, he enjoyed working in his strawberry bed or cruising the lake in his motor launch. White with mahogany trim, with seating for eight to ten, it was one of the finer boats to ply Sylvan Lake. He also had a rowboat, used mostly for fishing, although on Sundays he liked to row to the drugstore in Rome City to pick up a newspaper, about a four-hour trip down along the north shore and back along the south.

One morning he came in saying the black bass were bait fighting. That meant the females were preparing their nests and getting ready to spawn, while the males were in shallow water, rushing toward anything that struck the surface. He wanted Gene to row so he could cast, at least one trip around the head of the lake. So she grabbed a rod and stepped quickly into the boat. Afterward, when Charles had resumed rowing, in a sort of pocket formed by a big log extending from the shore, they saw a large wader, the brown bittern. As they approached, the bird froze. Compressing his feathers tightly to his body, he drew down his neck and pointed his daggerlike beak almost straight up, in a position of camouflage.

"I have no camera, but let me make a test of what I could do if I had one,"[2] said Gene. Slowly dropping to her knees in the boat, she went through the motions of picture taking, over and over, using a small tackle box and an old coat. The bird stood motionless for several minutes, a part of his sur-roundings, as they pulled quietly away. For the remainder of the season she hunted him along this same stretch of lakeshore and often saw him flying over or alighting in bays nearby, but she could never get within working distance of him when equipped with a camera.

That year which passed so quickly and was so perfect in many ways ended on a solemn note. During the Christmas holidays word came from southern Indiana that Lemon was seriously ill. Fifty-five and totally disabled by heart disease, he was not expected to live more than a few days. Lemon's life had been difficult, complicated both by the hand of fate and his own reckless behavior. As a young man he had been inclined to long bouts of drunkenness. His first marriage ended in divorce; his first child died in infancy. Death claimed his second wife in 1911, leaving him with a seven-year-old daughter, Leah Mary. Recently remarried and in the throes of his last illness, Lemon trusted that his third wife, Luella, would care for his twelve-year-old daughter. It was not to be. Luella did not want her. At her father's death Leah Mary Stratton was taken into the Porter home, under Gene's guardianship, where she remained for several years.

As his heart ran like a waterfall, Lemon made light of his last few hours. When Gene offered to summon a heart specialist, he replied: "My dear, there is no specialist special enough for such a blow-out as this—just put your ear to my chest and hear me soozle!" She hoped God would grant her the grace to go unafraid and with as much dignity: "To the very last he kept his doctor and nurses and friends laughing, and then said: 'It's all right,' and went to sleep."[3] The Strattons would have been proud of their most ornery member. At the time of his death Lemon was president of the Bible class of his Sunday school and one of the most active members of the Waldron, Indiana, Methodist Episcopal Church.

The next year passed routinely, with Leah Mary making a swift adjustment to life at the cabin. Lorene and Frank were guests there in the spring, and Gene was happy to see them. On one memorable day, while plant hunting in a nearby swamp, she and Frank stumbled upon several acres of orchids in full bloom. Overcome, they sank to a log and gazed at this fragile field in total silence. For half an hour they drank in this unforgettable scene. She had heard people say that such sights were to be seen when the country was first settled, but had never expected to have the good fortune to see one herself.

By this time, with the help of the Wallaces, Wildflower Woods was nearly overrun with wildflowers. Several acres of them were growing here, including fragrant evergreen partridgeberry, dainty goat's rue, lavender toadflax, yellow Saint-John's-wort, rose mallow, orange hawkweed, aromatic bergamot, scarlet painted cup, pennywort, moth mullein, dewberry, feathery Dutchman's-breeches, bouncing bet, wild columbine, blue-eyed Mary, and countless others, including her old favorite, sweetbrier rose.

No novel appeared in 1916 because Gene was working on a book of children's nature verse begun the previous summer while entertaining her grandchildren. *Morning Face*, dedicated to her first grandchild, was published in October 1916. About the same time she made a gift to Jeannette of the cottage on the other side of the lake.

Matters went smoothly for Gene Stratton-Porter until the spring of 1917. Then, when war was declared in April against Imperial Germany, she lost her chief of fieldwork, Bill Thompson. He was also her driver and most reliable employee. When he enlisted, she was devastated. They had worked hand in hand for over a year. Together they had waded swamps and gone hungry without complaining. Afield, Bill knew exactly what was needed next and had it there. In the basement, above the purr of the household machinery, a low whistle was always on his lips. As long as Gene heard that whistle, she knew that the gasoline engine that pumped the water supply would run, that the chimneys would draw, and that the roof would not leak. With Bill gone she would be without transportation, as she did not drive, and she would have no man at the cabin except Charles, who came only on weekends, and who was no maintenance man. Due to the war, it would be hard to hire a new driver.

The day Bill Thompson went to war he and Gene set a big basket of painted trillium and made and sowed a bed of its seed. Dusk was on them when they finished. She was slow to gather their paraphernalia: "Every nerve in me ached. I could give money, any degree of talent I possessed, cheerfully, but not the boy."[4] As the last seed was smoothed over, Bill lifted a deep spade of earth, slipped off his field gloves, and dropped them in the hole. When he was gone, she laid her head on that tiny grave and almost cried herself to death.

Lobby Cards

Nothing went well that year, and little was accomplished. For the first time in her life, she contracted poison ivy, a stubborn case that flared up four separate times. Her business matters were also an aggravation. Paramount produced *Freckles* as a movie in 1917, although she was unhappy with it because the screenplay did not follow the novel. A book was released that year, but *Friends in Feathers* was merely a rehash of *What I Have Done with Birds*, an earlier nature work. Meanwhile, the critics continued to pan her novels as unrealistic. That was nearly the last straw: "Such a big majority of book critics and authors have begun to teach, whether they really believe it or not, that no book is *true to life* unless it is true to the *worst in life*, that the idea has infected even the women."[5]

Gene Stratton-Porter was cranky and bored. Fall brought the onset of a bitter winter that claimed the master singer of her woods, a song sparrow. He had homed here for the past four years, giving a short morning concert, until claimed one morning by the January cold. Christmas had been festive on the outside, but bleak on the inside. For the sake of the grandchildren, she and Jeannette made an effort to celebrate. The larder was full, and the table groaned, laden with fat turkey, fruitcake, homemade wine, and fancy cookies. A red-ribboned holly wreath hung in each window; Spanish moss draped lights and mantels. Even the birds and squirrels had their own Christmas tree, decorated with tin baskets brimming with seeds and nuts and yards of strung popcorn and suet.

After the holidays Gene Stratton-Porter began her next novel with a heavy heart, but soon rallied to produce another best-seller. *A Daughter of the Land* is the story of a young woman of grit named Kate. Kate fights a father who feels a daughter's duty is to scrub and drudge, in order that her brothers might have land and opportunity. This novel received high praise from one of the nation's most respected pundits.

William Lyon Phelps of Yale, writing in *The Bookman*, was generous with his praise:

> An admirable story, with a real plot and real characters.
> . . . Here was a girl who really loved the country; loved
> living on a farm; loved all kinds of agricultural work;
> loved to make and see things grow. And, as presented
> in the novel, this love is understandable and intelligi-
> ble. There are not many such girls. But it would be
> well if there were more.[6]

Like the strong characters in her novels, Gene Stratton-Porter was blessed with an iron constitution and boundless energy. She had always worked long hours with little thought about the state of her health. Other than a crack on the head as a teenager, she had seldom been unwell for more than a few days. And it was a wonder. For years she had neglected herself, eating on the run and driving herself compulsively. In 1918 this self-neglect caught up with her. With the coming of spring she was tired and out of sorts. Traipsing about in the damp and cold aggravated her joints. Then fifty-four, she decided to seek expert medical help. Also, she had begun to think about her health for other reasons. She had recently had to confront her own mortality. In February word came of the unexpected death of Frank Doubleday's wife, Neltje, a fond acquaintance two years her junior. Then three months later Charles's nephew and namesake, son of his brother Miles, died at a relatively young age of pneumonia. Overshadowing all of this were her anxieties about Jeannette, whose marriage was fast deteriorating.

Concerned about her total well-being, Gene Stratton-Porter opted for a complete checkup at a New York clinic. Clifton Springs Sanitarium and Clinic, a spa dotted with sul-phur springs, mild athletic facilities, and restful gardens, had been founded in 1850 on the principle of the water cure. Al-

Gene Stratton-Porter, 1918

though its specialty was thermoelectric baths, during the early part of the twentieth century this health spa was known primarily as a retreat for the famous. Ill or simply worn out, most preferred to remain anonymous during their stay. In the fall of 1918, accompanied by her new secretary, Phoebe, Gene Stratton-Porter registered at this clinic under the name of Mrs. John Comstock and placed herself under the care of two general internists. Reassured and rested, she emerged a month later with a better idea of what the human body could tolerate and a resolve to take better care of herself. That resolve did not last five minutes. Back once more at the lake, health considerations were the first to go as she undertook one strenuous project after another.

First, with the help of Frank Wallace, she went into a frenzy of planting. In ten days they moved onto the grounds of Wildflower Woods 1,204 flowers, vines, shrubs, and trees. Then she tackled an even harder job. For some time she had been undecided about how to use the pile of pudding stone that remained after the cabin had been constructed. That fall she decided to use it to build a pair of gateposts, three feet square and nine feet high, at the road entrance to the cabin. As always, she gave it her best, and this time it wiped her out: "Frequently I was so tired I could scarcely reach the cabin at night. Many days I dressed the seams after Bates had laid the stone until the lime in the mortar cut my fingers to bleeding."[7]

These new gateposts were so handsome that she was encouraged to use pudding stone to wall in a natural spring down near the shoreline and also to build a runway for it. In the meantime, oblivious to her doctors' orders to slow down, she breezed through the semiannual housecleaning and then turned her attention to an adjacent farm she had recently acquired, where she made sauerkraut and supervised the butchering. At this time there was absolutely no hint that Gene Stratton-Porter was feeling restless and ready to bolt in a new direction. She was expecting Jeannette to motor up from Fort

Wayne with the babies for Thanksgiving, and she seemed content. As she wrote to an invalid she had met at Clifton Springs Sanitarium, things were going well:

> I have a fairly good cook, an excellent man, and Phoebe is still on the job. She will be wanting to write to you one of these days, I know, and she will tell you the latest word from our dear soldier! We are overjoyed with the prospect of the end of the war coming nearer, so we can begin to plan to live once more, in some respects, as we did in the good old days. There are some ways in which I think a number of us will not want to come back, and I sincerely hope, for the sake of posterity that we never do. We are very much pleased over the election, because we are Republican in politics and not sympathizers in a one man admin-istration. If you are not well enough to write . . . please have your husband or daughter send us just a few lines to let us know how you are feeling.
>   With much love, I am
>   Your friend,[8]

In the weeks that followed winter worked its usual despair. The worst of it was the notorious influenza that swept the nation, killing thousands. Gene Stratton-Porter was thankful to survive it. When spring appeared she was ready for sunshine, and she knew where she could find it: southern California, where the sun shines over three hundred days per year.

Gene Stratton-Porter was not a person who made hasty decisions. Obviously, thoughts of investigating southern California, possibly even residing there, had been brewing for some time, and logically so. Southern California was not the great unknown. She had several relatives there. Her oldest sister, Catherine, now a widow, had resided in Los Angeles nearly twenty years. Ada's daughter Gladys, who had married the photographic hobbyist, had been in Los Angeles more than five years, as had Gene's niece Cosette, Jerome's daugh-

Gene Stratton-Porter and her brother Jerome

ter. And Jerome, then seventy-five and still practicing law in Kansas, was thinking about a California retirement.

In the spring of 1919, ready for a new challenge and fresh from the strain of the most miserable winter in her experience, Gene Stratton-Porter set her sights on southern California and did not waver until she got there. But first she had a book to finish. She was working on a book about the habits and characteristics of birdlife as displayed in nest building, brooding, and feeding. To illustrate this book, she wanted to capture with her lens those behavioral traits described by Auguste Forel, Swiss entomologist and psychiatrist. In his *Senses of Insects*, published in 1910, Forel had attributed several humanlike characteristics to ant life: hatred, devotion, activity, perseverance, and gluttony. To these, with respect to birdlife, Gene Stratton-Porter added fear, surprise, ecstasy of song, and the mating emotions: timidity, boldness, and pride. She felt the birds capable of expressing many humanlike emotions: "Today, if I go into the fields and fail in photographing a living, free wild bird, not only in a characteristic location, attitude and occupation, but also with a distinct facial expression, I discard my work as a failure."[9]

The spring of 1919 was consumed by a book supported by Forel's observations and her own. Titled *Homing with the Birds*, it was set for publication the following November. By mid-June the galleys for this book were at Doubleday, and Gene Stratton-Porter's plans for her future were fast taking shape. By the summer of 1919 she had made a momentous decision. Bored with her present surroundings and eager to explore new horizons, she had decided to break completely with Indiana. It would be a tidy leave-taking, with no loose ends. She called her lawyers and instructed them to set up lifetime trusts for Ada and Florence, both now widowed and living in Fort Wayne. At the same time retaining Wildflower Woods, she disposed of most of her other real estate holdings. In the meantime, the war was grinding to a halt, and Bill Thompson would soon be home. But it no longer mattered. Her mind was made up. Unfettered and optimistic, Gene Stratton-Porter was on her way to sunny California and a new way of life.

Open to
Change and Possibility

BY 1919, because of its bracing climate and productive soil, the population of Los Angeles was vaulting. Twenty-five years earlier, before the advent of the automobile, the City of the Angels had not a single paved street. Now, however, over twelve hundred miles of boulevards radiated to all parts of the southland through orange groves and rose hedges. This city on the go had much to recommend it: several theaters, a fine library, a public transportation system, and over twenty public parks, not to mention the scenic and recreational wonders of its gentle foothills and winding canyons and the accessibility of its nearby seaside resorts. Next to its wonderful weather, the chief attraction, according to the Los Angeles Chamber of Commerce, was its beautiful homes and their spacious grounds. The residences here were built with wood, pine, and redwood. Architecture varied. The bungalow style was popular, and for more pretentious residences, the mission style was often used.

A fine home had always been important to Gene Stratton-Porter, although when she arrived in California in the fall of 1919 she was in no hurry to acquire a permanent residence. For the first six weeks she rented. Then, late in November, she bought a small bungalow near her Stratton relatives in the Hollywood District, between Second and Third streets. Catherine, her oldest sister, resided one mile north, and Jerome's daughter Cosette lived about two miles south. Ada's daughter Gladys and her husband James were only two blocks away.

After her move to the Sunshine State, the first thing from the pen of Gene Stratton-Porter was an optimistic magazine article, "Why I Always Wear My Rose-Colored Glasses." For a woman who had once craved the rural isolation of a swamp, she was making a quick adjustment to metropolitan bustle: "I sorter like this glorious sunshine, the pergola of Cherokee roses, the orange trees and blood-red poinsettias, and the mocking birds tame as robins at home."[1] When Charles wrote and enclosed the papers for the sale of the cabin in Geneva, she signed and returned them without a blink.

Now approaching seventy, but still active in the bank, Charles was residing in a Geneva boardinghouse. It was rumored in Rome City that Gene had told a neighbor she did not want Charles with her in California. And Charles did tell a friend that there was no room for him in her small California bungalow. Totally abandoned by his wife and ignored by his daughter, who had problems of her own, Charles was left to his own devices. After his wife's westward move, he was known to winter quietly in Daytona Beach with an old friend, Emery Routsong from Rome City.

No Stratton-Porter book appeared in 1920. She was unsettled, and not only because of her recent move. She had not been in California six months before she sped back to Indiana to lend support to Jeannette, whose marriage was near collapse. Her only acknowledgment of this family crisis was a vague expression of regret that, because of it, she could not buy her younger granddaughter a pony: "I promised one of my little granddaughters a pony, and I meant it. But when the little Gene grew old enough for a pony, things happened, as things will, and I could not buy the pony."[2]

Things surely did happen. Jeannette was in an apartment in Fort Wayne, cooped up with the children, while Blaine spent his time carousing. In June, buoyed by her mother's return, she summoned the courage to leave him. Three weeks later she filed for divorce, alleging habitual drunkenness, as well as cocaine abuse and infidelity. In mid-October the court granted the divorce to Jeannette, along with an order restraining Blaine from molesting her or their children. The court also granted her the sole care and custody of the children, which was all she needed to board a train with them for Los Angeles.

One week after Jeannette and the girls arrived on her doorstep, Gene Stratton-Porter purchased a large colonial house with a colonnaded porch on the corner of Serrano and Fourth streets. Its chief attraction was a beautiful garden, a hummingbird haven blooming with seventy varieties of roses. Settled at last, with her daughter and grandchildren around her once more, Gene Stratton-Porter exhibited her increasing well-being by beginning to socialize.

Among her new friends were Charles Brown, oil promoter and financier, also a newcomer to Los Angeles, and his wife Helen. Gene had much in common with Helen Brown, a woman nearly her own age, who was also a native of northern Indiana and who liked to write light verse. Other new friends and acquaintances included the photographer Edward S. Curtis, Charles Lummis, noted scientific authority and librarian, and Jack Wilkinson Smith, California artist. It was an enriching experience to rub shoulders with the likes of these. In Indiana she had been an outsider, uncomfortable with the locals. The residents of Rome City, as in Geneva, had been respectful of her books but not her aloof personality, nor what they perceived as her sorry marriage. Those who knew the

Porters in Rome City admired Charles greatly and felt she had treated him poorly. None of that was an issue in California. Los Angeles was looking better to her every day: "It is a blaze of colour, a voice of rapture, a deep note of earnestness, a gay note of entertainment. Fine folk these artistic and creative people be!"[3]

Experiencing a burst of creativity of her own, poetry written by Gene Stratton-Porter suddenly began to appear in national magazines, a simple expression of the freedom welling within her since her move to the West Coast. "Symbols," expressing her love for birdlife, appeared in *Good Housekeeping* magazine in January 1921, followed by "Blue-Eyed Mary" four months later, an obvious double tribute to her mother and to a wildflower of the same name.[4] Her major efforts, however, were centered on a novel with a southern California setting. Unacquainted with southwestern plant life, she relied heavily for the background of this book on the expertise of her niece's husband. *Her Father's Daughter* is dedicated to James Sweetser Lawshe, "To whom I owe all that I know about the flowers of California."[5]

The characterizations in this Stratton-Porter novel differ considerably from those in her earlier works, reflecting the intemperate racial climate of the southwest. *Her Father's Daughter* is especially biased against the Japanese, yet its portrayal of the Asian as inferior caused no ripples in Gene Stratton-Porter's readership. Even the experts were preaching distrust of aliens during the early 1920s. At that time it was fashionable, even honorable, to be anti-Oriental in southern California. The Los Angeles Anti-Asiatic Society was at its peak, its membership drawn mainly from the Native Sons of the American West, organized labor, and the American Legion. The state of California had a long history of anti-Asiatic bias, beginning with the Chinese Exclusion Act of 1882, denying immigration and citizenship and culminating in a state law passed in 1913 forbidding aliens to own agricultural land.

California was not alone. Nationwide, racial prejudice held full sway. Segregation in the South was firmly entrenched. In the aftermath of World War I, Americans saw Bolshevists in the bushes, embraced the Ku Klux Klan, and deported aliens wholesale. Governor William Dennison Stephens of California was especially anxious to see its Asiatic population leave: "Unless the race ideals and standards are preserved here at the gateway the conditions that will follow must soon affect the rest of the continent."[6]

Despite its bias, *Her Father's Daughter* met with few complaints. *The Literary Review* remarked about its "wholesome charm." The strongest comment about its racism came from William Lyon Phelps, writing in *The Bookman*: "Somebody in California has been stuffing our novelist, who is more gullible in international politics than in the study of nature."[7] So great was the demand for this new novel that half the printers at Doubleday's Country Life Press were working day and night to fill advance orders numbering 250,000 copies.

The year *Her Father's Daughter* appeared was one of the busiest of Gene Stratton-Porter's career. She spent the summer vacationing in Indiana, granddaughter Gene, age seven, in tow, but soon returned to California to launch a major undertaking in conjunction with a West Coast filmmaker, Thomas Ince, whose slogan was "Clean Pictures for Clean People." She had recently granted the photoplay rights to one of her novels to Ince's film company, along with exclusive options on five other novels, pending the satisfactory completion of the filming of the first, *Michael O'Halloran*. Under her arrangement with Ince, she would oversee the filming and assist personally in the direction of these motion pictures. The principal director would be James Leo Meehan, an actor and journalist whom Gene Stratton-Porter liked and trusted instantly, as did Jeannette, who would write the screenplays.

At the same time there was another challenge on her horizon. Late in 1921 she was approached by Harry Burton,

Gene Stratton-Porter, Jeannette Porter Meehan, and James Leo Meehan

editor of *McCall's* magazine. When asked by Burton if she had a message for the women of America, she replied: "Not one, but one hundred," and signed a contract for a series of monthly editorials in his magazine. Gene liked *McCall's*, and she liked Harry Burton: "He is a brilliant chap, clean as a ribbon, and . . . a live wire."[8] His magazine was growing in circulation, and she took much pride in being asked for a major contribution to it. Her first editorial appeared in the January 1922 issue. It was the beginning of a working relationship that would prove satisfactory not only to herself but also to the ownership of *McCall's*, which had previously operated at a loss.

Gene Stratton-Porter's editorials in *McCall's* were directed toward those cheerless women yoked to the endless circle of housework. Hers was a formidable task: to make the American woman feel good about her role as a housewife. Culturally, Stratton-Porter was pulling against a tide that devalued the art of homemaking. So she wrote about how to get the joy out of life every day and how to make Christmas last a year. She also wrote about how to cultivate talent in children, how to have the courage of one's convictions, how to make a garden, how to have fun with or without money, how to grow old gracefully, how to help one's brother, and, a subject long on her mind, how to help one's mother. Stratton-Porter remembered her own mother's domestic toil and felt a kitchen revolution was long overdue. She was a witness to women who continued to live as her mother had lived, who trailed up and down stairs with crocks of milk from the cellar, pails of water from the outdoor pump, and baskets of wood.

Gene Stratton-Porter's editorials in *McCall's* reflected a strong personal concern about the younger generation. She read a great deal into city pallor and a tendency to overapply face paint: "The round-shouldered, flat-chested, hollow-eyed, little painted girls so frequently in evidence on the streets, in the parks, and at social occasions of today are the most shocking sign of deterioration that our age presents."[9]

Gene Stratton-Porter's strongest charge to her 1920s readers of *McCall's* can be faulted more for its lack of finesse than its message. In it she placed the blame for what she regarded as the questionable conduct and standards of the younger generation squarely at the door of lax breeding practices:

> Degeneracy is a thing that would be remedied did the people of our country pay as much attention to the breeding of their children as they pay to the selection of the right sires and to bringing about the right conditions for the production of stock. No land in the world has finer blooded horses and cattle and better hogs than ours, but the same cannot be said of the human element.[10]

She suggested that every American couple bear and rear to patriotic citizenship four or five children, and she advocated censorship in the home: "It is difficult for me to understand why . . . characters that would not be admitted into a home or a family circle in person . . . should be allowed to come there between the covers of a book."[11] She was known to deem a book a waste of paper and ink and use it for kindling.

Reader response to Gene Stratton-Porter's bold editorials was heavy, and it was positive. The collective American conscience shared her strict views and was thankful for her articulation of their values. Letters poured into *McCall's*: "From women in lovely ranch houses, from wardens of prisons, from pastors and educators, from young girls and boys, from brides and mothers, have come thousands and thousands of letters telling what Gene Stratton-Porter meant to them."[12]

At this point in her career, the only print medium Gene Stratton-Porter had not fully explored was poetry, and it was not for want of trying. For years she had wanted to write a book of poetry. Doubleday, however, was reluctant to publish such a work: "My publishers always assured me that poetry would never pay."[13] She agreed with this assessment, noting ruefully that the average individual had no more use for poetry than a rooster would have for skates. Yet one morning she changed her mind: "I stood it as long as I could. . . ." She said to her secretary: "We'll put away what we are doing and try something different."[14] Three days later her first long narrative poem, *The Fire Bird*, was finished.

Inspired by a private screening of Edward Curtis's Indian pictures, she had combined what she had seen with a flood legend in which a redbird figures prominently. An Indian tragedy, *The Fire Bird* is a poetic confession, the story of a squaw tortured by conscience. While writing this poem Gene Stratton-Porter discovered something new about herself. Whenever she wrote fiction, she wrote the "featheriest kind of romance." Poetry differed: "It is the queerest thing, but the only time I see life in the raw, see it as it is really lived by aching, sinning, suffering, struggling, rejoicing humanity, is when I try to express myself poetically."[15]

The Fire Bird was published in April 1922. To celebrate its release, she invited over one hundred people to an evening gala at her home. The guest list leaned heavily to singers, poets, and artists, including Edward Curtis, to whom *The Fire Bird* is dedicated. Her most famous guest was Charles Russell, renowned painter of deserts, Indians, and cowboys. It was an original party, different from the usual Hollywood bash. Russell took center stage to relate an Indian story in sign language, his wife interpreting as he made the signs. As the evening drew to a close, each guest received an autographed copy of *The Fire Bird* containing three Indian wishes especially fashioned to suit the recipient.

The ink on *The Fire Bird* was scarcely dry when Gene Stratton-Porter commenced another long work in blank verse, its protagonist a downtrodden woman who survives a mean husband and years of domestic hardship. *Euphorbia* was eventually serialized in *Good Housekeeping* magazine. A polished work, conveying both anguish and hope, *Euphorbia* was hard to write, according to the blurb accompanying its first installment: "A story that the author rewrote seven times 'in an effort to plumb the depth of a woman's soul, to picture poignant pain, to paint the healing power of God through nature.'"[16] Her sister Catherine, a product of the old school who did not appreciate blank verse, was critical of *Euphorbia*: "It's a heartbreaking story. It flows the smoothest of anything I ever read in print, but for God's sake don't publish that and call it poetry!"[17]

A third poem, of a religious nature, followed *Euphorbia*. The poem was inspired by a letter received from one of her Australian readers. This letter and its contents rekindled Gene Stratton-Porter's interest in a subject long dormant. Years earlier, while researching *Birds of the Bible*, she had encountered a thought-provoking book about the Lentulus legend published by the Methodist Book Concern. The legend purports to set forth the whereabouts of Jesus Christ during those years unaccounted for in the Holy Bible and further purports to describe his personal appearance. In the spring of 1922 Gene Stratton-Porter received a letter from Charles Anderson, of Melbourne, Australia, that again brought the Lentulus legend and the possible personal appearance of Christ to mind.

Anderson, a former employee of the British Museum, enclosed with his letter a photograph allegedly made by him thirty years earlier from a negative held by the British Museum. This photograph depicted an ancient emerald, on it a head carved in the likeness of Jesus Christ. The emerald, of course, from earliest times has been a symbol of eternal life. According to Anderson, this emerald carved with the countenance of Christ had reposed among the treasures of the Vatican for many years, although this cannot be confirmed. An inscription photographed with the emerald stated: "The only true likeness of 'Our Saviour' taken from one cut on an emerald by command of Tiberius Caesar, and given from the Treasury of Constantinople by the Emperor of the Turks to Pope Innocent VIII for the redemption of his brother, then a captive of the Christians."[18]

Gene Stratton-Porter was skeptical, but intrigued. She had long been curious about the personal appearance of Jesus Christ, and the photograph of his likeness on the emerald agreed with her own visualization: "I was delighted with the picture because it fulfilled my personal conception of Jesus Christ."[19] Based primarily on what she had previously read in the Lentulus legend, a picture had emerged in her mind's eye of a comely man with a short thick beard, gray far-seeing eyes, and hair the color of a ripe chestnut, curling and waving over broad shoulders.

When she showed Anderson's photograph of the carved emerald to Bishop John Joseph Cantwell of the Diocese of Los Angeles, he claimed that he knew of such a sacred object among the treasures of the Vatican. Cantwell's substantiation set her mind churning. Perhaps Anderson's photograph *had* been made by the British Museum. Perhaps the emerald it depicted *did* date to ancient times. Perhaps the physical description of Christ as set forth in the Lentulus legend and confirmed by the photograph *was* more truth than fiction. She buried herself in ancient history, poring over the works of established authorities. She emerged convinced that Anderson's photograph and the legendary description of Jesus could be genuine: "To my mind there is the strongest possibility that both the description and the picture are genuine, that the description [set forth in the Lentulus legend] might have been attributed to a Lentulus one generation later, [than] the first Publius. . . located 63 B.C."[20]

She felt the personal magnetism of Anderson's photograph keenly and carried it and his letter with her on a motor trip through southern California: "I had a wonderful journey . . . my mind was full of the picture and the description."[21] In the old mission garden at San Juan Capistrano, while looking over the hills green with the annual resurrection, it occurred to her that she was in the same geographical latitude as the Holy Land. She returned home filled with beauty and wonder and rolled into bed exhausted. As she lay there quietly, a poem began coming to her, a poem fulfilling her personal conception of the appearance of Jesus Christ. Far into the night she punched her pillow, but sleep would not come. Perhaps the Lord did not want her to go to sleep and take the risk of forgetting what He had revealed. So she got up and went to her study, where she wrote out the poem *Jesus of the Emerald* as it was eventually published in book form. Set in the seven hills of Rome, the poem describes the quest of Tiberius Caesar for information about the works and personal appearance of Jesus.

Although it was truly inspired, *Jesus of the Emerald* is not a work of high merit. Gene Stratton-Porter was not an accomplished poet. She lacked the discipline to revise again and again. Yet the poem that came to her that sleepless night is important not only because of its inspired genesis but also because of the personal information that accompanied its publication. In an afterword to *Jesus of the Emerald*, Gene Stratton-Porter explains in depth her personal theology. Hers was a Christian mind open to possibility, lacking the arrogance of those who would explain the inexplicable. She was especially taken with a controversial work published by Nicolas Notovitch in 1893. She wondered if there might be some truth in Notovitch's book, *The Unknown Life of Jesus Christ*. To summarize, Notovitch contends that the biblical gap in the young adulthood of Christ could be explained by his presence in the Far East, where he studied the religion, laws, and customs of other countries.

Gene Stratton-Porter's afterword in *Jesus of the Emerald* also sets forth in detail her overall perspective concerning man's place in the universe. She believed that God had created an orderly system, uniform and predictable, and that personal salvation was not only plausible but compatible with His overall design:

> To my mind it is absurd to look to the Heavens above us and believe that other innumerable bodies circling their orbits, other suns, other moons, other solar systems, can differ widely from ours. . . . They must evolve life in the same way. I do not understand how there can be any doubt in the mind of any one touching natural science even lightly that these other worlds, many of them larger and more favourably situate in the universe than we, have evolved life and living conditions and have been peopled possibly aeons before our time. . . . Neither in my mind is there any doubt but that God, at the right time and in His own way, has worked out for these other worlds the same plan of salvation that has been vouchsafed to us. In the economy of Nature nothing is ever lost. I cannot believe that the soul of man shall prove the one exception.[22]

On the Move Again

LATE in 1922 Gene Stratton-Porter returned to Indiana for a short visit. It was time for the annual fall planting. This time her return was marked by apprehension. She could no longer move about without heavy publicity, especially in her home state. Once at the lake, as she had anticipated, her homecoming was marred with frequent interruptions. Curiosity seekers were a constant nuisance, wandering her grounds at will, trampling flower beds, and appearing at the door uninvited. Wildflower Woods was no longer private.

The highlight of her short stay at the lake was the opportunity to go plant hunting with Frank and Lorene. One day while picnicking, they had the good fortune to come upon a patch of wildflowers they had sought for years: the harebell, a nodding, bell-shaped blue flower sentimentally known overseas as bluebells of Scotland. With happy hearts they dug up several of these tall grass-like flowers and transplanted them to a bed near the cabin, among a clump of maidenhair ferns.

After a brief stay at the lake Gene returned to Los Angeles where several book and magazine commitments awaited. For the first time she had granted the serialization rights of a novel to an American magazine publisher to run prior to actual book publication. The first installment of this novel was scheduled to run the following April. It was now August, and she had not yet begun the book. Also she had been asked for help by the Izaak Walton League whose fledgling monthly magazine, *Outdoor America*, was just getting off the ground. The request from the Izaak Walton League came first. She wrote two articles for this new monthly, the second of which voiced a powerful plea for land conservation:

> If we do not want our land to dry up and blow away, we must replace at least part of our lost trees. We must save every brook and stream and lake . . . and those of us who see the vision and most keenly feel the need must furnish the motor power for those less responsive. Work must be done. It is the time for all of us to get together and in unison make a test of our strength. All together, Heave![1]

Among Gene Stratton-Porter's many commitments, there remained the film production of *Michael O'Halloran* in nearby Culver City. In the winter of 1922 she was maintaining a torrid pace, a pace she could not continue without help. Her family suggested that, instead of typing or writing her manuscript in longhand, she hire a stenographer and learn to dictate. Gene was reluctant: "I found it almost impossible at first . . . the sound of my own voice bothered me."[2] The idleness of her hands also bothered her. To contain her restless hands, she began to finger a little string of beads, a gift from one of the grandchildren. That string of beads proved her salvation and was always at hand. The stenographer she hired, a capable young woman named Frances Foster, would prove to be a loyal and devoted employee.

To no one's surprise, in the spring of 1923 Jeannette announced her engagement to the movie director, James Leo Meehan, with whom she had been working on the screenplay of *Michael O'Halloran*. After the announcement, in a burst of generosity, Gene Stratton-Porter bought them a house, nine blocks east of her own. However, she did not tell her daughter and future son-in-law of this purchase. It was to be a Christmas gift. The marriage took place 2 June 1923. Two weeks later, satisfied that Jeannette was now married to a stable individual, Gene Stratton-Porter set about putting her own affairs in order.

First, she revised her Last Will and Testament. Then, after consulting with her lawyers, she again left for Indiana where she had unfinished business. She needed to decide what to do with Wildflower Woods. Frank and Lorene met her there early in July. All of them were appalled by the latest evidence of trespass on the grounds. The bluebells they had planted near the cabin were gone. The explanation came one morning in the mail.

> Dear Lady:
> You do not know me, but I have been on my knees working for you. I passed through Wildflower Woods Thursday and seeing the grass among your maidenhair fernbed, I got down on my prayer bones and pulled it up for you. I do not even want you to thank me, so will just remain,
> A Friend, and lover of your work.[3]

As an interim solution, "No Admittance" signs were posted at the front gate. Yet there was no effective way to discourage those who intruded by boat. One evening as Gene and Lorene fished from the dock, enjoying the sunset, a boatload of summer people passed, not realizing, or not caring, how voices carry over water. Their comments were amusing—and embarrassing.

"Oh, which one is Mrs. Porter, the slim one or the fat one?"

The answer was a revelation, "The one with the red scarf around her head. Red is Mrs. Porter's favorite color. She has spent thousands of dollars to have all her mahogany furniture in the cabin upholstered in red morocco."

"Mrs. Porter has an Indian tent set up in the hall of the cabin that has all sorts of Indian relics and old Indian blankets in it," another voice added with authority.

"I'll bet it smells in that hall," a loud voice continued.

"That is a choice version of my fondness of scarlet, isn't it," sighed Gene, as they took in their fishing lines and headed up the path to the cabin. Recovering quickly, she added with a laugh, "Let's go in and sniff the old Indian blankets."[4]

The next morning she received a telephone call from a guest at Triplett's Hotel who had been a member of the boating party the night before. He asked if his party might come up to the cabin that evening, just to shake her hand. She denied his request, but agreed to see them briefly that morning. The crowd arrived by boat shortly before noon, interested and enthusiastic. They looked in vain for the smelly Indian tent in the hall. Their tour ended at the pudding stone spring down along the shoreline. As they were getting ready to leave, one of the women left the group and hurried toward Gene: "Would you, O dear lady, would you allow me the honor of sitting in that chair at your desk where you wrote those wonderful books?"[5]

They returned to the study for less than five minutes. Later in the day Gene discovered that her worshipful admirer had made off with one of her best pens.

The following week, as she was working in a flower bed near shore, another excursion party landed who did not recognize her. One of them strolled over and began to ask questions. Did she work for Mrs. Porter? Was the cabin beautifully furnished? Was Mrs. Porter good to her help? Did she pay them well? Directing this nosy trespasser and his companions to flower beds on the other side of the cabin, she scurried inside.

These and other continuous violations of her privacy contributed to Gene Stratton-Porter's decision in 1923 to abandon

Wildflower Woods. In the fall she wrote to Gov. Warren T. McCray of Indiana, offering her property on Sylvan Lake to the state as a bird and wildflower preserve, with certain stipulations. She expected to be reimbursed for her improvements, including the cost of bringing in and setting the wild things she had gathered there. Over the years her secretaries had kept a record of every tree, shrub, bush, vine, and wildflower that had been planted, as well as a record of every bird that had nested in the grounds and all animals habitually on the property.

The birdlife list was lengthy. Over fifty varieties had nested at Wildflower Woods. Several acres of wildflowers had also been established there. Her botanical records listed thousands of separate plantings and, as she advised the governor: "This collection is peculiar in Indiana, a unique thing, the like of which is not in existence in any State in the Union."[6] Whether from lack of interest or lack of funds, the state of Indiana was unresponsive. Her offer would be pigeonholed for many years.

Meanwhile, as she awaited a reply from Indiana's governor, there was an unexpected development. Her latest novel was selling slowly. *The White Flag* would not make the best-seller charts, her first lackluster performer. And, as usual, the reviewers were panning it. One critic deemed this novel a long lachrymose tale with an excessive casualty list.[7] Another described it as melodrama.[8] It no longer mattered. Gene Stratton-Porter's career focus had shifted. She was more interested in producing movies than in pleasing book reviewers or producing best-sellers. The motion picture adaptation of *Michael O'Halloran* had recently premiered successfully at Graumann's Third Street theater, and she was now working on the filming of *The Girl of the Limberlost*, again at Ince Studios in Culver City.

When Charles showed up in the winter of 1923, Gene had little time for him. She had agreed to do a fourteen-part nature series for *Good Housekeeping* magazine, commencing in

Charles Dorwin Porter, 1923

January, and at the same time she was on location every day with *The Girl of the Limberlost*. On the set from eight in the morning until six in the evening, and often even longer, she was enjoying film work immensely. When they finally wrapped it up, she counted it a fine experience: "I had a grand time every minute, and gained ten pounds."[9] Contrary to the prevailing stereotype, she found members of the acting community to be educated and extremely interesting and passed many beneficial hours in conversation with them, learning much: "Do not criticize actors—they are an industrious lot, and they have much to their credit—look at the doughnut, and not at the hole."[10]

Now familiar with the ins and outs of movie production, in January 1924 Gene Stratton-Porter broke with International Higher Culture Films and incorporated a film production company of her own. She was looking forward to producing movies that paralleled her uplifting novels, movies that would dramatize the values she continued to expound through the editorial columns of *McCall's*: "As a motion picture producer I shall continue to present idealized pictures of life, pictures of men and women who inspire charity, honor, devotion to God and to family."[11]

Her own family relationships yet played an important part in her everyday life. Despite a busy schedule, to the end of her days Gene Stratton-Porter maintained close relations with her Stratton relatives. All of them were well except her sister Catherine, then eighty-six and confined to a wheelchair. Catherine was being cared for in her own home in the Hollywood District by Jerome and his wife, who at long last had retired to Los Angeles. Gene Stratton-Porter visited there frequently, always bearing magazines and fresh flowers, or occasionally a reminder of their old days on the farm, such as a ham and greens. On one such visit she found her elderly sister despondent. During her afternoon nap Catherine had dreamed that her room was full of big black birds, picking and tearing at her. Twice before she had had the same dream, and each time there had been a death in the family. As she was the oldest Stratton, and the most frail, she believed that this time the call was for her. Not a superstitious person, Gene joked with her and tried to divert her. The next morning came word by telegram of the death of a distant relative. Shortly thereafter, Catherine died in her sleep.

Gene Stratton-Porter could not have known that her time too was nearly at hand. She was only sixty, and she was feeling well and greeting each day with her usual incredible energy. Part of this zest was generated by thoughts of building again. Ready to abandon her summer home in Indiana, plans for a new vacation retreat in California were on the drawing board, along with plans for a large combination workshop-residence.

In love with the mountain peaks and low-hung stars of California's Catalina Island, early in 1924 Gene Stratton-Porter bought two lots and prepared to build a fourteen-room redwood vacation home. About twenty-five miles by steamer from the harbor of Los Angeles, Catalina Island had recently been purchased by William Wrigley for development as a playground. A wild place, dotted with thousands of wild goats and seals, it was an ideal place for a nature lover. As Gene expressed: "I like the quiet and the big immensities of the mountains and the sea . . . maybe . . . I can do some bigger and better work here than I ever have done before."[12]

Plans for a permanent home-workshop in the city of Los Angeles proceeded more slowly, although by March 1924 she had selected the site, a secluded undeveloped tract directly west of present-day Beverly Hills, between two canyons. Shaped like a baby mountain, its wooded terrain was wild and steep. Gene Stratton-Porter loved her small mountain so much she began bringing her work to the site after her driver made her a table and benches out of rough boards. As construction at this site was not scheduled to begin until July, she and her secretary frequently worked here in the spring and early summer of 1924, surrounded by birds and wildflowers and the clean smell of sage. Gene Stratton-Porter felt both energized by this wild setting and at peace here: "I am more deeply convinced than ever that this is the only place I have seen in California where I really wanted to build a home . . . I have long since decided that I so love California that this is the land in which I wish to finish my living and to do my dying."[13] She hoped to replicate here the birdlife sanctuary she had left behind in Indiana, stating: "Give me a few years and I will guarantee to make my little mountain say to all and sundry, 'My name is Floraves,' because Flora means flowers and Aves means birds."[14]

Her plans for this permanent residence were grand: twenty-two rooms and, although she still did not drive, a four-car garage, with servants' quarters overhead. When completed, this palatial home would contain approximately eleven thousand square feet, exclusive of basements and attics. Outside there were fish ponds, a greenhouse, and a tennis court. Separate quarters would be built for Charles. With his retreat at Wildflower Woods now offered to the state of Indiana, she felt obligated to provide a place for him: "I do not abuse the man of the house. . . . The plans encompass a suite consisting of a large room having a beautiful fireplace, shelves for the relics and curios, a fine light for a writing desk, a beautiful view, and a bedroom and bath adjoining; a little world where no one may intrude except at the discretion of the owner."[15]

For the general contour and specific blueprints of this house, she hired an architect with a reputation for vision and cooperation. She explained to him that she wanted the outline of her residence and its color so conformed to the color of the mountains and their summits that not one bird in its migration would change its course because she lived here. The house was to be set on a special spot, directly under the flight path of two great white Arctic owls she had observed while working here one day. She was also explicit about the style of this new home. It must be predominantly English, English Tudor to be exact.

Hers was to be the first residence in a subdivision to be known as Bel Air, and she wanted to build quickly, to develop her grounds and get them to a state of settled seclusion before others bought surrounding land and began cutting down trees and tearing out shrubbery. When construction started, the workmen were instructed to be careful. She felt if she restricted them to one entrance, she might not frighten away roadrunners and quail, chewinks and thrushes, hummingbirds and warblers, not to mention the blue jay that played rocking horse every day on the top twig of the biggest oak on the front part of the grounds. She was delighted to find her little mountain already covered with native wildflowers, including the rare yellow mariposa lily. Great was the day when she found the same flame of Indian paintbrush growing on her mountain that had grown back in Indiana.

One day she had a letter from a landscaping establishment stating that representatives of the company had gone to her homesite, looked it over, and designed a landscape. They asked if they might come and show her their design. She recalled a poem children once recited about the bootblack's apple, the climax of which was: "There ain't goin' to be no core." With these lines in mind she said softly to her secretary: "There ain't goin' to be no landscaping."[16]

Gene had other letters, one from an individual who offered to "interpret" her house for her. She replied: "Some way I hadn't expected that. It hadn't occurred to me that anybody would think he could come into my home and tell me how I wanted it decorated and furnished." She was not prepared for someone who thought he knew better about what she wanted in her home and how she wanted it, than she knew herself. So again she said to Frances: "There ain't goin' to be no interpretation . . . here and there is going to be tucked away all over this home of mine every single treasure that any nature lover ever sent me from topmost Alaska to bottommost Africa. . . . [but] the fellow that 'interprets' my home for me will do it over my dead body, because so long as I live I will put my own interpretation on my own home."[17]

Gene Stratton-Porter's last summer was one of relaxation and self-indulgence. In the latter part of June she moved into her new vacation redwood home on Catalina Island, taking with her Jeannette, straight from the hospital with a baby boy, and the girls. Leo stayed behind in the city, supervising the construction of the house in Bel Air. Lorene came out that summer for several days, most spent relaxing on the smooth beaches of Catalina Island's Avalon Bay.

When Lorene left, Gene Stratton-Porter went back to work and, once again, it was masonry that drew her full daily attention. She had designed a complex fountain, incorporating stones and seashells, for the grounds of her Catalina summer property. Gathering the raw materials for this fountain took time. With the help of her driver and a little Yaqui Indian, she ranged the mountains of Catalina Island looking for appropriate stones. Although Wrigley permitted no private vehicles on his primitive island, in Gene Stratton-Porter's case he had made an exception. She was allowed a field car, which permitted her to cover Catalina Island from end to end. Clad in boots and breeches, sleeves rolled up, her hair tucked in a floppy old Panama, she combed the nooks and crannies of Catalina Island during the month of July 1924. In August she hired a small barge and spent several days in a small cove on the west side of the island while the tide was out, gathering large seashells. The morning her intricate fountain was finished, she sat on the porch and studied her achievement. As the water trickled from one large shell to another, thirty-two in all, it made such a constant rippling song that she named her new island home "Singing Water."

When Labor Day rolled around, there was good news from Graumann's Third Street theater. *The Girl of the Limberlost*

Gene Stratton-Porter in California, about 1924

was doing well. Gene reported: "The managers of the theatre
tell me that . . . on Labour Day they had the biggest house
. . . in the history of the theatre."[18] The next week, after
Jeannette went back to the city to put the girls in school, Gene
Stratton-Porter headed for the hills behind Catalina Island's
little village with Frances. There, from a hammock strung
between two trees, she began to dictate her next book, *The
Keeper of the Bees*. As with her last novel, it was not important
to Gene Stratton-Porter whether or not *The Keeper of the Bees*
reached the best-seller list. The plan was for Leo to write a
screenplay for this new novel as soon as possible. Then a
motion picture version of the novel would be released simultaneously with its serialization in *McCall's*, due to begin the
following spring.

The Keeper of the Bees was finished in record time. Jeannette
said her mother worked faster out in the open air of Catalina
than she had ever worked previously: "Her inspirations were
the lazy hum of the bees, the chirp of the birds, the blue haze
hanging over the hills, and the flecks of sunlight dancing
through the trees."[19] In November 1924 Gene Stratton-Porter
left these hazy hills for the mainland to supervise the finishing
details of her house in Bel-Air. When pudding stone for its
fireplaces arrived from Indiana, she put in long days with a
stonemason, directing the placement of each stone. When its
fireplaces were completed, the house in Bel-Air was nearly
finished. The contractor promised occupancy by the end of
December. As she waited for moving day, Gene Stratton-
Porter took two brief motor trips. She first traveled to nearby
Lake Arrowhead, then went north by way of the Santa Cruz
mountains with Leo, Jeannette, and Leo's mother.

The coastline between Mission San Buenaventura and
Mission Santa Barbara was scenic beyond her expectations.
Shanties connected with strings of hot peppers dotted the
beaches. As they rumbled over the famous wooden piles of
Rincon Boulevard, crashing ocean breakers deadened the

sound of the motor. Traveling as far up as San Francisco, they explored John Muir's giant redwoods before turning for home. On the way back, two miles in from the sea in the foothills, they paused at Mission Santa Barbara. Here they tarried, drawn by the ancient fountain in front under an old stone washing table. It was a secluded setting from the past. Tonsured monks in brown moved slowly under arched, rose-covered cloisters. From the inner garden, forever barred to womankind by papal authority, Gene Stratton-Porter left laden with rare cuttings to plant atop her baby mountain.

Two days later the busy hands of the Bird Woman were forever stilled. She died 6 December 1924 from injuries received in an automobile accident. An inquest attributed the cause of death to a fractured pelvis and crushed chest. She had left her home about eight o'clock that Saturday evening with her chauffeur, on her way to spend a few hours with Jerome. Less than a block from home, her large Lincoln collided with a speeding streetcar. She was thrown to the pavement and rendered unconscious. She died at a nearby hospital less than two hours later.

Jeannette, in charge of the final arrangements, deferred the question of where her mother should be buried to her father, on his way to California by train. In the meantime, she arranged for temporary interment nearby. When Charles arrived, he chose not to change these arrangements, a decision contrary to one of Gene Stratton-Porter's last wishes: "When I am gone, I hope my family will bury me out in the open, and plant a tree on my grave; I do not want a monument. . . . A refuge for a bird nest is all the marker I want."[20]

Private funeral services were conducted at Gene Stratton-Porter's South Serrano residence by a Reverend Haywood of the Wilshire Methodist Episcopal Church, assisted by the church choir. Reverend Haywood had presided at services for her sister Catherine the previous April. In a letter to Florence, who had been looking forward to a California visit, Gene Stratton-Porter's secretary described this sad morning:

> The doors were wide open to the morning, and outside on the pergola the roses bloomed in riotous profusion and little ruby-throated hummingbirds darted from flower to flower. The strains of "Lead, Kindly Light" and "Rock of Ages" came softly. Dr. Haywood spoke of her wonderful life. There was a simple prayer and then sweet voices were lifted in Tennyson's "Crossing the Bar." Her friends and dear ones came together for a moment to look again on that peaceful face and then she was carried out into the morning sunshine.[21]

Afterword

IN a cruel twist of fate, there is no tree on Gene
Stratton-Porter's grave, as she had requested, nor any
refuge for a bird nest above her final resting place. She
lies behind marble. When she died, in 1924, her body
was shunted to a temporary receiving vault. There it
remained for ten years, until 1934, when she was in-
terred in Crypt 217 Foyer "F" of the Hollywood Cemetery.

The executor of Gene Stratton-Porter's sizable estate was
James Sweetser Lawshe, husband of Ada's daughter and a
virtual stranger to Charles Porter. The sole legatee of this
estate, which approximated half a million dollars, was her
daughter Jeannette. Charles Porter was not mentioned in
his wife's Last Will and Testament. How ironic. Charles
Porter was the only person who ever cared enough about
Gene Stratton to give her what she needed most. Charles, in
his quiet support and even in his neglect, gave his ambitious
and talented wife her personal freedom.

As a married man, Charles Porter never had a real home.
Neither did his wife. The wilderness was the only home Gene
Stratton-Porter ever knew. As a child she ran barefoot down
lonely country lanes. As a young woman she lived in the
shadows of an uncharted swamp. As her life drew to a close

she was seeking fulfillment as she alone understood it, on a steep secluded mountainside, teeming with birdlife and rare woodland flowers.

Charles Dorwin Porter died in 1926; Jeannette Porter Meehan died in 1977.

Notes

CHAPTER I

1. Grant Overton, *American Nights Entertainment* (New York: D. Appleton & Co. [etc.], 1923), 287.

2. Jeannette Porter Meehan, *The Lady of the Limberlost: The Life and Letters of Gene Stratton-Porter* (Garden City, N.Y.: Doubleday, Doran & Co., 1928).

3. David G. MacLean, *Gene Stratton-Porter: A Bibliography and Collector's Guide* (Decatur, Ind.: Americana Books, 1976), vii.

4. Gene Stratton-Porter, "My Life and My Books," *The Ladies' Home Journal*, Sept. 1916, 13.

5. Ibid.

6. Ibid.

7. Ibid.

8. Gene Stratton-Porter, *The Song of the Cardinal* (Indianapolis: Bobbs-Merrill Co., 1903).

9. Gene Stratton-Porter, *Freckles* (New York: Doubleday, Page & Co., 1904).

10. Frederic Taber Cooper, "The Popularity of Gene Stratton-Porter," *The Bookman* 41 (Aug. 1915): 671.

11. Book Review, *Independent*, 30 Aug. 1915, 302.

12. Review of *The Keeper of the Bees, The Saturday Review of Literature* 2 (12 Sept. 1925): 128.

13. Meehan, *Lady of the Limberlost*, 211.

14. Review of *Music of the Wild, The Spectator*, 9 Sept. 1911, 385.

15. Stratton-Porter, "My Life and My Books," 80.

16. Gene Stratton-Porter, "Why I Wrote 'A Girl of the Limberlost,'" *World's Work* 19 (Feb. 1910): 12547.

17. William Lyon Phelps, "The Why of the Best Seller," *The Bookman* 54 (Dec. 1921): 301.

18. Gene Stratton-Porter, *A Daughter of the Land* (Garden City, N.Y.: Doubleday, Page & Co., 1918).

19. In her complaint for divorce filed in the Allen Superior Court on 28 July 1920, Jeannette Helen Monroe alleged that George Blaine Monroe "for the past nine (9) years has been a habitual drunkard, that during said time he at periods would consume a great quantity of alcohol and become intoxicated for days at a time; that when he could not secure alcohol, he took cocaine and other drugs which caused a drunken condition; that he has contracted the alcohol and cocaine habit and is now and has been for the past several years a habitual drunkard." A restraining order was issued against Monroe by the superior court judge. (*Jeannette Helen Monroe* vs. *George Blaine Monroe*, Allen Superior Court Case No. 21273, Office of the Clerk of the Allen Superior Court, Fort Wayne, Indiana.)

20. New York State Conservation Commission, *Annual Report* (New Albany, 1926).

21. "Memorial Trees Will Be Planted," *Los Angeles Times*, 13 Nov. 1925.

22. "Gene Stratton-Porter Dies after Auto Wreck. . . ," *New York Times*, 7 Dec. 1924.

23. S. F. E. [attributed to both Eugene Francis Saxton and Samuel F. Ewart], *Gene Stratton-Porter: A Little Story of the Life and Work and Ideals of the Bird Woman* (Garden City, N.Y.: Doubleday, Page & Co., [1915]), 3.

24. Gene Stratton-Porter, interview by J. J. Lowman, "The Revolt," published posthumously, *Los Angeles Times*, 6 Feb. 1925.

25. Gene Stratton-Porter, "Helping Father," *McCall's*, Aug. 1924, 48.

26. Gene Stratton-Porter, *Homing with the Birds* (Garden City, N.Y.: Doubleday, Page & Co., 1919), 347.

27. Stratton-Porter, "Helping Father," 48.

28. Letter from Frances Foster to Florence Compton, 12 Dec. 1924, in possession of author.

29. Ibid.

30. Gene Stratton-Porter, "What My Father Meant to Me," *American Magazine* 99 (Feb. 1925): 23.

31. Clarkson W. Weesner, ed., *History of Wabash County, Indiana*, 2 vols. (Chicago: Lewis Publishing Co., 1914), 2:609.

32. S. F. E., *Gene Stratton-Porter*, 7.

33. Gene Stratton-Porter, interview by Emma Lindsay Squier, "The Lady from the Limberlost," *Los Angeles Times*, 11 June 1922.

34. Ibid.

35. Margaret Day Briggs, "Gene Stratton-Porter," in *1872–1972 Geneva and Area Centennial*, ed. Alan S. Baumgartner (n.p., n.d. [Geneva, Ind., ca. 1972]), 45.

36. Gene Stratton-Porter, "Let Us Go Back to Poetry," *Good Housekeeping*, Apr. 1925, 200.

37. Overton, *American Nights Entertainment*, 270.

38. Gene Stratton-Porter, "How to Open Doors of Literary Fame," reported posthumously without byline in the *Los Angeles Times*, 25 Apr. 1926.

CHAPTER 2

1. Clarkson W. Weesner, ed., *History of Wabash County, Indiana*, 2 vols. (Chicago: Lewis Publishing Co., 1914), 2:606.

2. Harriet Russell Stratton, comp., *A Book of Strattons*, 2 vols. (New York: The Grafton Press, 1908; New York: Frederick H. Hitchcock, 1918), 1:239, 2:477.

3. Gene Stratton-Porter, "Why I Always Wear My Rose-Colored Glasses," *American Magazine* 88 (Aug. 1919): 36.

4. Deed, marriage, guardianship, and probate records, 1820–1850. Office of the County Recorder, the Clerk of the Court of Common Pleas, and the Probate and Juvenile Court offices of Wayne and Wood counties, Ohio.

5. Gene Stratton-Porter, "Fixing Our Fences," *McCall's*, Feb. 1925, 58.

6. Application for membership of Florence Stratton Compton to the DAR, Fort Wayne, Indiana, 11 Feb. 1921, referencing the "Public Records of Sussex & Orange Counties, New Jersey."

7. Military history of Thomas Stratton, April 1777–July 1780, Military Service Records, S.40,507, National Archives.

8. David M. Ludlum, *Early American Winters 1604–1820* (Boston: American Meteorological Society, 1966), 232; C. F. Volney, *View of the Climate and Soil of the United States of America* (London: J. Johnson, 1804).

9. Ludlum, *Early American Winters 1604–1820*, 190–94; C. Edward Skeen, "'The Year without a Summer': A Historical View," *Journal of the Early Republic* 1 (Spring 1981): 51-67.

10. Ben Douglass, *History of Wayne County, Ohio, from the Days of the Pioneers and First Settlers to the Present Time* (Indianapolis: Robert Douglass, 1878), 775.

11. Ibid.

12. Stratton, *A Book of Strattons*, 1:294.

13. Douglass, *History of Wayne County*, 775.

14. Stratton, *A Book of Strattons*, 1:294.

15. John Muir, *The Story of My Boyhood and Youth* (Boston: Houghton Mifflin Co., 1913), 31.

16. S. F. E. [attributed to both Eugene Francis Saxton and Samuel F. Ewart], *Gene Stratton-Porter: A Little Story of the Life and Work and Ideals of the Bird Woman* (Garden City, N.Y.: Doubleday, Page & Co., [1915]), 4.

17. Court of Common Pleas of Wayne County, Ohio, Case No. 0115, May 1818.

18. Record of Marriage Certificates, Probate and Juvenile Court, Wooster, Ohio, 4A:48.

19. Office of County Recorder of Wayne County, Ohio.

20. Probate Court Records, Wayne County, Ohio.

21. Ibid.

22. County Recorder, Wayne County, Ohio.

23. Court of Common Pleas of Wayne County, Ohio, 7:161.

CHAPTER 3

1. Ronald L. Baker and Marvin Carmony, *Indiana Place Names* (Bloomington: Indiana University Press, 1975), 172.

2. Paul Fatout, *Indiana Canals* (West Lafayette, Ind.: Purdue University Studies, 1972), 28–29.

3. Stratton quoted in T. B. Helm, ed., *History of Wabash County, Indiana* (Chicago: John Morris, 1884), 339.

4. Ibid.

5. *Illustrated Historical Atlas of the State of Indiana* (Chicago: Baskin, Forster & Co., 1876), 283.

6. Helm, *History of Wabash County*, 340.

7. Ibid.

8. Ibid.

9. Office of the Recorder of Kosciusko County, Indiana, 5:460.

10. Leola Hockett, "The Wabash and Erie Canal in Wabash County," *Indiana Magazine of History* 24 (Dec. 1928): 302.

11. Clarkson W. Weesner, ed., *History of Wabash County, Indiana*, 2 vols. (Chicago: Lewis Publishing Co., 1914), 2:609–10.

12. Kosciusko County Recorder, 7:568.

13. Wabash County Recorder, 1:416; Kosciusko County Recorder, 7:460.

14. Population Schedules of the Seventh Census of the U. S., 1850, Wabash and Warren counties, Indiana, The National Archives, Washington, 1963.

15. Ibid.

16. Wabash & Erie Canal Lands—Indiana, Commission on Public Records, Archives Division, Indiana State Library, Indianapolis, "J," 2:331.

17. 1852 Discipline of the Methodist Episcopal Church, The Archives of Indiana United Methodism, Roy O. West Library, DePauw University, Greencastle, Indiana, 74–75.

18. Helm, *History of Wabash County*, 156.

19. S. F. E. [attributed to both Eugene Francis Saxton and Samuel F. Ewart], *Gene Stratton-Porter: A Little Story of the Life and Work and Ideals of the Bird Woman* (Garden City, N.Y.: Doubleday, Page & Co., [1915]), 4.

CHAPTER 4

1. S. F. E. [attributed to both Eugene Francis Saxton and Samuel F. Ewart], *Gene Stratton-Porter: A Little Story of the Life and Work and Ideals of the Bird Woman* (Garden City, N.Y.: Doubleday, Page & Co., [1915]), 9.

2. Gene Stratton-Porter, *Homing with the Birds* (Garden City, N.Y.: Doubleday, Page & Co., 1919), 4.

3. S. F. E., *Gene Stratton-Porter*, 11.

4. Jeannette Porter Meehan, *The Lady of the Limberlost: The Life and Letters of Gene Stratton-Porter* (Garden City, N.Y.: Doubleday, Doran & Co., 1928), 10.

5. Stratton-Porter, *Homing with the Birds*, 15–16.

6. Ibid., 14–15.

7. Ibid., 16–18.

8. Gene Stratton-Porter, "Let Us Go Back to Poetry," *Good Housekeeping*, Apr. 1925, 199.

9. Stratton-Porter, *Homing with the Birds*, 22–23.

10. Gene Stratton-Porter, "What My Father Meant to Me," *American Magazine* 99 (Feb. 1925): 70.

11. Meehan, *Lady of the Limberlost*, 7.

12. Gene Stratton-Porter, "Why I Always Wear My Rose-Colored Glasses," *American Magazine* 88 (Aug. 1919): 112.

13. Gene Stratton-Porter, "Books for Busy People," *McCall's*, Jan. 1924, 28.

CHAPTER 5

1. Gene Stratton-Porter, "The Bible in the Schools," *McCall's*, May 1925, 2, 78.
2. Gene Stratton-Porter, "Under My Vine and Fig Tree," in *The American Annual of Photography and Photographic Times-Bulletin Almanac for 1903*, ed. W. I. Lincoln Adams (New York: Scoville Manufacturing Co., 1902), 28.
3. Gene Stratton-Porter, "How to Make a Home," *McCall's*, May 1922, 65.
4. Gene Stratton-Porter, *Laddie* (New York: Charles Scribner's Sons, 1916), 60–66.
5. Ibid.
6. Jeannette Porter Meehan, *The Lady of the Limberlost: The Life and Letters of Gene Stratton-Porter* (Garden City, N.Y.: Doubleday, Doran & Co., 1928), 22.
7. Gene Stratton-Porter, "What My Father Meant to Me," *American Magazine* 99 (Feb. 1925): 23.
8. Gene Stratton-Porter, "Religion as a Stimulus to Success," *McCall's*, Dec. 1925, 2. See also Stratton-Porter, "What My Father Meant to Me," 70, and Gene Stratton-Porter, "Let Us Go Back to Poetry," *Good Housekeeping*, Apr. 1925, 194.
9. Letter to the author from the Secretary to the Archivist of the Archives of Indiana United Methodism, 11 Nov. 1976.
10. Stratton-Porter, "Let Us Go Back to Poetry," 195.
11. Meehan, *Lady of the Limberlost*, 14.
12. Ibid., 22–23.
13. Stratton-Porter, "What My Father Meant to Me," 70.
14. Gene Stratton-Porter, "Division of Labor in the Home," *McCall's*, Sept. 1927, 2.
15. Gene Stratton-Porter, "Why I Always Wear My Rose-Colored Glasses," *American Magazine* 88 (Aug. 1919): 114.
16. Gene Stratton-Porter, "Getting the Joy out of Life," *McCall's*, May 1923, 46.
17. Gene Stratton-Porter, *Homing with the Birds* (Garden City, N.Y.: Doubleday, Page & Co., 1919), 201–2.
18. Stratton-Porter, "Why I Always Wear My Rose-Colored Glasses," 36.
19. S. F. E. [attributed to both Eugene Francis Saxton and Samuel F. Ewart], *Gene Stratton-Porter: A Little Story of the Life and Work and Ideals of the Bird Woman* (Garden City, N.Y.: Doubleday, Page & Co., [1915]), 6.
20. Stratton-Porter, "What My Father Meant to Me," 70.
21. S. F. E., *Gene Stratton-Porter*, 8.
22. Gene Stratton-Porter, *After the Flood* (Indianapolis: Bobbs-Merrill Co., 1911).
23. Stratton-Porter, "What My Father Meant to Me," 23.
24. Stratton-Porter, "Let Us Go Back to Poetry," 194.
25. S. F. E., *Gene Stratton-Porter*, 11.

CHAPTER 6

1. *Wabash Plain Dealer*, 19 Feb. 1872.
2. Ibid., 11 July 1872.

3. Ibid., 9 Jan. 1873.

4. Ibid., 30 Jan. 1873.

5. Ibid., 2 Jan. 1873.

6. Ibid., 12 Feb. 1874.

7. Ibid., 12 June 1873.

8. Ibid., 5 June 1873.

9. Ibid., 19 Mar. 1874.

10. Ibid., 9 July 1874.

11. Ibid., 15 July 1881.

12. Ibid., 9 Jan. 1874, and various business ads throughout the month.

13. Ibid., 30 June 1877.

14. Ibid., 22 Mar. 1878.

15. Ibid., 21 Mar. 1879.

16. Ibid., 30 Nov. 1877, 1 Mar., 14 June 1878.

17. Gene Stratton-Porter, *Moths of the Limberlost* (New York: Doubleday, Page & Co., 1912), 92.

18. Ibid., 100.

19. Gene Stratton-Porter, "Why I Always Wear My Rose-Colored Glasses," *American Magazine* 88 (Aug. 1919): 117.

20. Jeannette Porter Meehan, *The Lady of the Limberlost: The Life and Letters of Gene Stratton-Porter* (Garden City, N.Y.: Doubleday, Doran & Co., 1928), 41.

21. Gene Stratton-Porter, "What My Father Meant to Me," *American Magazine* 99 (Feb. 1925): 72.

22. Gene Stratton-Porter, "Having Fun with Your Money," *McCall's*, Nov. 1923, 2.

23. Stratton-Porter, "What My Father Meant to Me," 72.

24. Gene Stratton-Porter, "Educating Mother," *McCall's*, July 1924, 41.

25. Meehan, *Lady of the Limberlost*, 41.

26. *Wabash Plain Dealer*, 31 Dec. 1880.

27. Ibid., 7 Jan. 1881.

28. Ibid., 8 Mar., 1 Nov. 1878, 11 Feb. 1881, 20 Jan. 1882.

29. Stratton-Porter, "What My Father Meant to Me," 72

30. Ibid., 76.

31. Ibid., 72.

32. Ibid.

33. Meehan, *Lady of the Limberlost*, 42–43.

34. Stratton-Porter, "What My Father Meant to Me," 76.

35. Ibid.

36. Ibid.

37. Ibid.

38. Gene Stratton-Porter, "The Lost Talent in the World," *McCall's*, Mar. 1923, 30.

39. Gene Stratton-Porter, "Personal Adventures of an Author," *McCall's*, June 1927, 2.

40. Stratton-Porter, "The Lost Talent in the World," 30.

41. Stratton-Porter, "What My Father Meant to Me," 76.

42. Stratton-Porter, "The Lost Talent in the World," 30.

CHAPTER 7

1. Merle Curti, *The Growth of American Thought*, 2d. ed. (New York: Harper & Bros., 1925), 595–603.
2. M. F. Owen, *History of Orange Township* (n.p., n.d. [ca. 1930]), 54–82.
3. *Recollections of Thomas R. Marshall, Vice-President and Hoosier Philosopher: A Hoosier Salad* (Indianapolis: Bobbs-Merrill Co., 1925), 297–98.
4. Obituary, *Wabash Plain Dealer*, 4 May 1883.
5. Clarkson W. Weesner, ed., *History of Wabash County, Indiana*, 2 vols. (Chicago: Lewis Publishing Co., 1914), 2:607.
6. Ibid.
7. *Wabash Plain Dealer*, 4 Nov., 2, 23 Dec. 1881; 13 Jan. 1882; 27 Apr., 4 May 1883; Jeannette Porter Meehan, *The Lady of the Limberlost: The Life and Letters of Gene Stratton-Porter* (Garden City, N.Y.: Doubleday, Doran & Co., 1928), 35–36.
8. Ada M. Wilson, Deposition before a Special Examiner of the Pension Office filed 2 Oct. 1905 at Wabash, Indiana, in the case of Lemon M. Stratton, No. 1251.011.
9. Meehan, *Lady of the Limberlost*, 36.
10. Gene Stratton-Porter, "My Life and My Books," *The Ladies' Home Journal*, Sept. 1916, 13.
11. Meehan, *Lady of the Limberlost*, 44.
12. "Gene Stratton-Porter, the Fourth in Our Series of Pictorial American Romances," *The Delineator*, May 1920, 24.
13. A question exists concerning the correct spelling of Charles D. Porter's middle name. Some sources refer to him as Charles Darwin, while others use Dorwin. Based on information obtained from his daughter's book, *Lady of the Limberlost*, from the *Dictionary of American Biography*, and from Margie Sweeney, curator at the Gene Stratton-Porter State Historic Site at Rome City, in this biography Dorwin will be used.
14. Meehan, *Lady of the Limberlost*, 50–51.

CHAPTER 8

1. Gene Stratton-Porter, "Making Your Vote Count for Something," *McCall's*, Nov. 1925, 67.
2. *Wabash Plain Dealer*, 12 Sept. 1884.
3. Stratton-Porter, "Making Your Vote Count for Something," 67.
4. Ibid.
5. *Biographical and Historical Record of Adams and Wells Counties, Indiana* (Chicago: Lewis Publishing Co., 1887), 235, 238, 379, 399–400.
6. Ibid., 325.
7. Scrapbook in possession of Walter Burgin, Geneva, Indiana, Dec. 1985.
8. Jeannette Porter Meehan, *The Lady of the Limberlost: The Life and Letters of Gene Stratton-Porter* (Garden City, N.Y.: Doubleday, Doran & Co., 1928), 58.
9. Ibid., 56.
10. M. F. Owen, *History of Orange Township* (n.p., n.d. [ca. 1930]), 66.

11. Meehan, *Lady of the Limberlost*, 61–62; Exceptions to Final Report of Frank P. Wilson: The Estate of Mark Stratton, in the Wabash Circuit Court, April Term, 1901.

12. Meehan, *Lady of the Limberlost*, 62.

13. Ibid., 63–64.

14. Claim against the estate of Mark Stratton, Promissory Note and Affidavit to Claims, Estate No. 2423, Office of Clerk of the Wabash Circuit Court, Wabash, Indiana.

15. Meehan, *Lady of the Limberlost*, 83–85.

CHAPTER 9

1. S. F. E. [attributed to both Eugene Francis Saxton and Samuel F. Ewart], *Gene Stratton-Porter: A Little Story of the Life and Work and Ideals of the Bird Woman* (Garden City, N.Y.: Doubleday, Page & Co., [1915]), 19.

2. Jeannette Porter Meehan, *The Lady of the Limberlost: The Life and Letters of Gene Stratton-Porter* (Garden City, N.Y.: Doubleday, Doran & Co., 1928), 95–98.

3. Ibid., 87–88.

4. Ibid., 117.

5. M. F. Owen, *History of Orange Township* (n.p., n.d. [ca. 1930]), 67.

6. Meehan, *Lady of the Limberlost*, 90–94.

7. Gene Stratton-Porter, "The Gift of the Birds," *The Youth's Companion*, Part Two, 26 Mar. 1914, 159.

8. Gene Stratton-Porter, *Homing with the Birds* (Garden City, N.Y.: Doubleday, Page & Co., 1919), 38.

9. Gene Stratton-Porter, "A Message to the Working Women," *McCall's*, July 1926, 2.

10. Gene Stratton-Porter, "Having Fun with Your Money," *McCall's*, Nov. 1923, 2.

11. Gene Stratton-Porter, interview by Grace Wilcox, "Great Composers Stole Music from Bird Songs," *Los Angeles Times*, 19 Nov. 1922.

12. Stratton-Porter, *Homing with the Birds*, 45–46.

13. Wabash County Deed Records, Book 49, p. 263, Wabash County Recorder's Office, Courthouse, Wabash, Indiana.

14. S. F. E., *Gene Stratton-Porter*, 8.

15. Meehan, *Lady of the Limberlost*, 95.

16. Stratton-Porter, *Homing with the Birds*, 44.

17. *The Strike at Shane's: A Prize Story of Indiana* (Boston: American Humane Society, 1893), 6.

18. Ibid., 7.

19. *Geneva Herald*, 24 Jan. 1894.

20. Meehan, *Lady of the Limberlost*, 99–110.

21. Ibid., 100, 103.

22. Max J. Herzberg, *The Reader's Encyclopedia of American Literature* (New York: Thomas Y. Crowell Co., 1962), 1223.

23. Meehan, *Lady of the Limberlost*, 108.

24. Ibid., 110.

25. Gene Stratton-Porter, "Individual Homes," *McCall's*, Nov. 1926, 2.

CHAPTER 10

1. Jeannette Porter Meehan, *The Lady of the Limberlost: The Life and Letters of Gene Stratton-Porter* (Garden City, N.Y.: Doubleday, Doran & Co., 1928), 113–14.

2. *Geneva Herald*, 14 June 1895.

3. Ibid.

4. Gene Stratton-Porter, "Why I Always Wear My Rose-Colored Glasses," *American Magazine* 88 (Aug. 1919): 117.

5. Gene Stratton-Porter, *Homing with the Birds* (Garden City, N.Y.: Doubleday, Page & Co., 1919), 48.

6. Gene Stratton-Porter, "The Gift of the Birds," *The Youth's Companion*, 26 Mar. 1914, 159.

7. Gene Stratton-Porter, interview by Grace Wilcox, "Great Composers Stole Music from Bird Songs," *Los Angeles Times*, 19 Nov. 1922.

8. Gene Stratton-Porter, "Why the Biggest One Got Away," *Recreation*, Apr. 1900, 265.

9. Ibid.

10. Gene Stratton-Porter, *Music of the Wild* (Garden City, N.Y.: Doubleday, Page & Co., 1911), 273–74.

11. Gene Stratton-Porter, "Sight and Scent in Birds and Animals," *Outing* 40 (June 1902): 298.

12. Ibid., 296–97.

13. Gene Stratton-Porter, "The Birds' Kindergarten," *Outing* 40 (Apr. 1902): 70.

14. Ibid., 73.

15. Ibid., 74.

16. Gene Stratton-Porter, "From the Viewpoint of a Field Worker," in *The American Annual of Photography and Photographic Times Almanac for 1902*, ed. Walter E. Woodbury (New York: Scoville Manufacturing Co., 1901), 219.

17. Gene Stratton-Porter, "Under My Vine and Fig Tree," in *The American Annual of Photography and Photographic Times-Bulletin Almanac for 1903*, ed. W. I. Lincoln Adams (New York: Scoville Manufacturing Co., 1902), 28.

18. S. F. E. [attributed to both Eugene Francis Saxton and Samuel F. Ewart], *Gene Stratton-Porter: A Little Story of the Life and Work and Ideals of the Bird Woman* (Garden City, N.Y.: Doubleday, Page & Co., [1915]), 21.

19. Margaret Day Briggs, "Gene Stratton-Porter," in *1872–1972 Geneva and Area Centennial*, ed. Alan S. Baumgartner (n. p., n. d. [Geneva, Ind. ca. 1972]), 44–49.

20. Meehan, *Lady of the Limberlost*, 117.

21. Letter to the author from a private source in Decatur, Indiana.

22. S. F. E., *Gene Stratton-Porter*, 24.

23. Gene Stratton-Porter, "A New Experience in Millinery," *Recreation*, Feb. 1900, 115.

24. Gene Stratton-Porter, "In the Camps of Croesus," *Recreation*, July 1900, 21–22.

25. Ibid.

26. Ibid.

27. Ibid.

28. Ibid.

29. Gene Stratton-Porter, "My Great Day," *Outdoor America*, June 1924, 12–14.

CHAPTER 11

1. S. F. E. [attributed to both Eugene Francis Saxton and Samuel F. Ewart] *Gene Stratton-Porter: A Little Story of the Life and Work and Ideals of the Bird Woman* (Garden City, N.Y.: Doubleday, Page & Co., [1915]), 33.

2. Gene Stratton-Porter, "Character Sketches of Twelve Birds," in *Biennial Report of the Commissioner of Fisheries & Game for Indiana* (Indianapolis, 1908), 1093.

3. S. F. E., *Gene Stratton-Porter*, 25.

4. Gene Stratton-Porter, "Laddie, the Princess, and the Pie," *Metropolitan Magazine*, Sept. 1901, 421.

5. S. F. E., *Gene Stratton-Porter*, 26.

6. Ibid., 27.

7. Gene Stratton-Porter, "The Real Babes in the Woods," *Metropolitan Magazine*, Aug. 1902, 213.

8. Ibid.

9. Stratton-Porter, "Character Sketches," 1088.

10. Gene Stratton-Porter, "Choosing Words," *McCall's*, Oct. 1926, 2.

11. Gene Stratton-Porter, "Bob's Feathered Interloper," *Metropolitan Magazine*, Nov. 1903, 194.

12. Gene Stratton-Porter, "When Luck is Golden," *Metropolitan Magazine*, Apr. 1902, 440.

13. Gene Stratton-Porter, interview with Grace Wilcox, "Great Composers Stole Music from Bird Songs," *Los Angeles Times*, 19 Nov. 1922.

14. Stratton-Porter, "When Luck is Golden," 442.

15. Ibid., 443ff.

CHAPTER 12

1. Records pertaining to the Estate of Mark Stratton, No. 2423, filed with the Wabash Circuit Court, Wabash, Indiana: Petition for an Order to an Action on a Contract, 11 Mar. 1890; Division of Property and Petition to Sell Personal Property, 19 Mar. 1890; Inventory and Appraisement of Goods, 21 Mar. 1890; Petition to Sell Personal Property, 24 Mar. 1890; An Account of the Sale of Personal Property, 4 Jan. 1892; Report of Sale of Personal Property, 11 Jan. 1892; Current Report, 18 Feb. 1892; Current Report, 14 Oct. 1893; Petition for a Movement, 9 Sept. 1895; Exceptions to Final Report of Frank P. Wilson, ? Apr. 1901; Affidavit for Inspection . . . , 27 May 1901; and Final Report of Frank P. Wilson, Administrator, 15 May 1901; Final

Report of Alvah Taylor, Administrator *de bonis nom*, 17 July 1908. See also the *San Bernardino* (Calif.) *Daily Sun*, 3, 4 Apr. 1902.

2. S. F. E. [attributed to both Eugene Francis Saxton and Samuel F. Ewart], *Gene Stratton-Porter: A Little Story of the Life and Work and Ideals of the Bird Woman* (Garden City, N.Y.: Doubleday, Page & Co., [1915]), 23.

3. Gene Stratton-Porter, *The Song of the Cardinal* (Indianapolis: Bobbs-Merrill, 1903), 33–34.

4. Gene Stratton-Porter, "My Life and My Books," *The Ladies' Home Journal*, Sept. 1916, 13.

5. Gene Stratton-Porter, *Freckles* (New York: Doubleday, Page & Co., 1904), 27.

6. Ibid., dedication page.

7. Stratton-Porter, "My Life and My Books," 13.

8. Gene Stratton-Porter, letter to an unidentified person dated 22 Feb. 1905, in the possession of Miss Freda Cobourn.

9. Gene Stratton-Porter, "Why I Wrote 'A Girl of the Limberlost,'" *World's Work* 19 (Feb. 1910): 12546.

CHAPTER 13

1. Gene Stratton-Porter, "The Camera in Ornithology," in *The American Annual of Photography and Photographic Times-Bulletin Almanac for 1904*, ed. W. I. Lincoln Adams (New York: Scoville Manufacturing Co., 1903), 55.

2. Gene Stratton-Porter, "From the Viewpoint of a Field Worker," in *The American Annual of Photography and Photographic Times Almanac for 1902*, ed. Walter E. Woodbury (New York: Scoville Manufacturing Co., 1901), 226.

3. Ibid., 219.

4. Gene Stratton-Porter, *Moths of the Limberlost* (Garden City, N.Y.: Doubleday, Page & Co., 1912), 111.

5. Ibid., 221.

6. Ibid.

7. Stratton-Porter, "The Camera in Ornithology," 61.

8. Book Review, *The Independent*, 20 July 1905, 153.

9. Gene Stratton-Porter, "The Disadvantages of Authorship," *McCall's*, May 1927, 136.

10. Gene Stratton-Porter, "Why I Wrote 'A Girl of the Limberlost,'" *World's Work* 19 (Feb. 1910): 12546.

11. Mrs. Frank [Lorene] Wallace, "Gene Stratton-Porter's Secretary Tells of Last Visit with Author at Catalina Island Home," *Indianapolis Star*, 1 Dec. 1935.

12. Gene Stratton-Porter, "Having Fun with Your Money," *McCall's*, Aug. 1924, 38.

13. Peter J. Schmitt, *Back to Nature: The Arcadian Myth in Urban America* (New York: Oxford University Press, 1969), 30–31.

14. Mrs. Frank Wallace, "Secretary," *Indianapolis Star*, 16 Feb. 1936.

15. Mrs. Frank Wallace, "Gene Stratton-Porter Started Famous Story *The Harvester* on Valentines Day 28 Years Ago," *Indianapolis Star*, 12 Feb. 1939.

16. Ibid.

17. S. F. E. [attributed to both Eugene Francis Saxton and Samuel F. Ewart], *Gene Stratton-Porter: A Little Story of the Life and Work and Ideals of the Bird Woman* (Garden City, N.Y.: Doubleday, Page & Co., [1915]), 44.

18. Gene Stratton-Porter, *Homing with the Birds* (Garden City, N.Y.: Doubleday, Page & Co., 1919), 120.

CHAPTER 14

1. Gene Stratton-Porter, "Ready," *McCall's*, Apr. 1924, 2.

2. Jeannette Porter Meehan, *The Lady of the Limberlost: The Life and Letters of Gene Stratton-Porter* (Garden City, N.Y.: Doubleday, Doran & Co., 1928), 170.

3. S. F. E. [attributed to both Eugene Francis Saxton and Samuel F. Ewart], *Gene Stratton-Porter: A Little Story of the Life and Work and Ideals of the Bird Woman* (Garden City, N.Y.: Doubleday, Page & Co., [1915]), 13.

4. Ibid., 14.

5. Gene Stratton-Porter, "No Lazy Man Can Make a Garden," *McCall's*, June 1922, 2.

6. Mrs. Frank [Lorene] Wallace, "Snowbound at Limberlost," *Indianapolis Star*, 25 Feb. 1940.

7. Ibid.

8. Mrs. Frank Wallace, "Extended Search for Renowned Fringed Gentian with the Late Gene Stratton-Porter Is Described," *Indianapolis Star*, 18 Oct. 1936.

9. Ibid.

10. Ibid.

CHAPTER 15

1. Glen Elsasser, "Memories of Limberlost," *Indianapolis Star Magazine*, 2 Sept. 1962.

2. Gene Stratton-Porter, *Homing with the Birds* (Garden City, N.Y.: Doubleday, Page & Co., 1919), 139.

3. Jeannette Porter Meehan, *The Lady of the Limberlost: The Life and Letters of Gene Stratton-Porter* (Garden City, N.Y.: Doubleday, Doran & Co., 1928), 146.

4. Gene Stratton-Porter, "Ready," *McCall's*, Apr. 1924, 78.

5. S. F. E. [attributed to both Eugene Francis Saxton and Samuel F. Ewart], *Gene Stratton-Porter: A Little Story of the Life and Work and Ideals of the Bird Woman* (Garden City, N.Y.: Doubleday, Page & Co., [1915]), 39.

6. William Lyon Phelps, "The Why of the Best Seller," *The Bookman*, Dec. 1921, 301.

7. Stratton-Porter, "Ready," 2.

8. Gene Stratton-Porter, letter to Mrs. Levin, Limberlost Cabin, Rome City, Indiana, 15 Nov. 1918, in the possession of the author.

9. Gene Stratton-Porter, "From the Viewpoint of a Field Worker," *The American Annual of Photography and Photographic Times Almanac for 1902*, ed. Walter E. Woodbury (New York: Scoville Manufacturing Co., 1901), 214.

CHAPTER 16

1. Jeannette Porter Meehan, *The Lady of the Limberlost: The Life and Letters of Gene Stratton-Porter* (Garden City, N.Y.: Doubleday, Doran & Co., 1928), 212.

2. Gene Stratton-Porter, "Broken Promises," *McCall's*, July 1927, 2.

3. Meehan, *Lady of the Limberlost*, 219.

4. Gene Stratton-Porter, "Blue-Eyed Mary," *Good Housekeeping*, May 1921, 52.

5. Gene Stratton-Porter, *Her Father's Daughter* (New York: Grosset & Dunlap, 1921), dedication.

6. Robert F. Heizer and Alan F. Almquist, *The Other Californians* (Berkeley and Los Angeles: University of California Press, 1971), 193.

7. William Lyon Phelps, "The Why of the Best Seller," *The Bookman*, Dec. 1921, 302.

8. Meehan, *Lady of the Limberlost*, 188.

9. Gene Stratton-Porter, "Once It Was 'Home Sweet Home,'" *McCall's*, Aug. 1922, 30.

10. Gene Stratton-Porter, "Our Thanks," *McCall's*, Nov. 1924, 2.

11. Gene Stratton-Porter, "Gene Stratton-Porter Calls on Our Government to Curb Indecent Literature," *McCall's*, July 1922, 18.

12. "In Memoriam Gene Stratton-Porter," *McCall's*, Feb. 1925, 27.

13. Gene Stratton-Porter, interview by Emma Lindsay Squire, "The Lady from the Limberlost," *Los Angeles Times*, 11 June 1922.

14. Ibid.

15. Meehan, *Lady of the Limberlost*, 248.

16. *Good Housekeeping*, Jan. 1923 [accompanying *Euphorbia*, Part I] 11.

17. Meehan, *Lady of the Limberlost*, 250.

18. Gene Stratton-Porter, *Jesus of the Emerald* (Garden City, N.Y.: Doubleday, Page & Co., 1923), xii.

19. Ibid., xi.

20. Ibid., xiii.

21. Gene Stratton-Porter, "How I Write," *McCall's*, May 1926, 2.

22. Stratton-Porter, *Jesus of the Emerald*, xvii-xviii.

CHAPTER 17

1. Gene Stratton-Porter, "All Together, Heave," *Outdoor America*, Dec. 1922, outside cover.

2. Gene Stratton-Porter, "Personal Adventures as an Author," *McCall's*, June 1927, 2.

3. Mrs. Frank [Lorene] Wallace, "Intimate Glimpses Into Gene Stratton-Porter's Life Written by Former Secretary as Anniversary Nears," *Indianapolis Star*, 11 Aug. 1935.

4. Ibid.

5. Ibid.

6. Lester C. Nagley, "Limberlost on Sylvan Lake," *Indianapolis Star Magazine*, 18 Nov. 1923.

7. *Literary Review*, 22 Sept. 1923, 75.

8. *New York Tribune*, 2 Sept. 1923, 20.

9. Gene Stratton-Porter, "Hollywood and the Picture Colony," *McCall's*, Oct. 1925, 76.

10. Ibid.

11. Gene Stratton-Porter, "A New Day in Pictures," *McCall's*, Feb. 1923, 2.

12. Jeannette Porter Meehan, *The Lady of the Limberlost: The Life and Letters of Gene Stratton-Porter* (Garden City, N.Y.: Doubleday, Doran & Co., 1928), 285.

13. Ibid., 280.

14. Gene Stratton-Porter, "Gardens," *McCall's*, June 1926, 2.

15. Gene Stratton-Porter, "Individual Homes," *McCall's*, Nov. 1926, 2.

16. Ibid., 87.

17. Ibid.

18. Meehan, *Lady of the Limberlost*, 289.

19. Ibid., 292.

20. Gene Stratton-Porter, "Ramparts," *McCall's*, Aug. 1926, 2.

21. Letter from Frances Foster to Florence Compton dated 12 Dec. 1924, in possession of author.

Select Bibliography

The only bibliography of the works of Gene Stratton-Porter is *Gene Stratton-Porter: A Bibliography and Collector's Guide*, compiled by David G. MacLean (Decatur, Ind.: Americana Books, 1976). However, since the publication of this bibliography, new material has come to light. All new material not found in MacLean's bibliography is starred below with an asterisk. Works currently in print as listed in *Books in Print, 1989–90* are marked by a pound sign.

Only writings useful in the making of this book are listed here. A wide range of other works and records was examined to be certain that no significant information had been overlooked.

BOOKS AND SHORT STORIES BY GENE STRATTON-PORTER

*# *The Strike at Shane's: A Prize Story of Indiana.* Boston: American Humane Education Society, 1893. Reprint. Marietta, Ga.: Judith R. Long Antiquarian Books, 1984.
"Laddie, the Princess, and the Pie." *Metropolitan Magazine*, Sept. 1901, 416–21.
*"How Laddie and the Princess Spelled Down at the Christmas Bee." *Metropolitan Magazine*, Dec. 1901, 739–53.
"The Real Babes in the Woods." *Metropolitan Magazine*, Aug. 1902, 201–13.
*"Bob's Feathered Interloper." *Metropolitan Magazine*, Nov. 1903, (192)–202.

The Song of the Cardinal. Indianapolis: Bobbs-Merrill Co., 1903.
Reprint. New Orleans: River City Press, n.d.
Freckles. New York: Doubleday, Page & Co., 1904. Reprint. New
Orleans: River City Press, n.d.; Greenport, N.Y.: Harmony Raine
& Co., 1977; Cutchogue, N.Y.: Buccaneer Books, 1980;
Bloomington: Indiana University Press, 1986; New York: Dell
Publishing Co., Inc., 1988.
At the Foot of the Rainbow. New York: The Outing Publishing Co.,
1907. Reprint. New Orleans: River City Press, 1976.
What I Have Done with Birds. Indianapolis: Bobbs-Merrill Co., 1907.
Birds of the Bible. Cincinnati: Jennings and Graham, 1909. Reprint.
Cutchogue, N.Y.: Buccaneer Books, 1986.
A Girl of the Limberlost. New York: Doubleday, Page & Co., 1909.
Reprint. New Orleans: River City Press, n.d.; Bloomington:
Indiana University Press, 1984; New York: Dell Publishing Co.,
Inc., 1986.
Music of the Wild. Cincinnati: Jennings and Graham, 1910.
The Harvester. Garden City, N.Y.: Doubleday, Page & Co., 1911.
Reprint. New Orleans: River City Press, n.d.; Greenport, N.Y.:
Harmony Raine & Co., 1977; Bloomington: Indiana University
Press, 1984.
Moths of the Limberlost. Garden City, N.Y.: Doubleday, Page & Co.,
1912. Reprint. Greenport, N.Y.: Harmony Raine & Co., 1980;
Cutchogue, N.Y.: Buccaneer Books, 1986.
Laddie: A True Blue Story. Garden City, N.Y.: Doubleday, Page &
Co., 1913. Reprint. New Orleans: River City Press, n.d.;
Bloomington: Indiana University Press, 1988.
Michael O'Halloran. Garden City, N.Y.: Doubleday, Page & Co.,
1915. Reprint. New Orleans: River City Press, n.d.
Morning Face. Garden City, N.Y.: Doubleday, Page & Co., 1916.
Friends in Feathers. Garden City, N.Y.: Doubleday, Page & Co., 1917.
A Daughter of the Land. Garden City, N.Y.: Doubleday, Page & Co.,
1918. Reprint. New Orleans: River City Press, n.d.
Homing with the Birds. Garden City, N.Y.: Doubleday, Page & Co.,
1919. Reprint. Cutchogue, N.Y.: Buccaneer Books, 1986.
Her Father's Daughter. Garden City, N.Y.: Doubleday, Page & Co.,
1921. Reprint. New Orleans: River City Press, n.d.
The Fire Bird. Garden City, N.Y.: Doubleday, Page & Co., 1922.
The White Flag. Garden City, N.Y.: Doubleday, Page & Co., 1923.
Reprint. New Orleans: River City Press, 1976.
Jesus of the Emerald. Garden City, N.Y.: Doubleday, Page & Co., 1923.
The Keeper of the Bees. Garden City, N.Y.: Doubleday, Page & Co.,
1925. Reprint. New Orleans: River City Press, n.d.

MAGAZINE ARTICLES AND EDITORIALS BY GENE STRATTON-PORTER

"A New Experience in Millinery." *Recreation*, Feb. 1900, 115.

"Why the Biggest One Got Away." *Recreation*, Apr. 1900, 265–68.

"In the Camps of Croesus." *Recreation*, July 1900, 21–22.

*"From the Viewpoint of a Field Worker." In *The American Annual of Photography and Photographic Times Almanac for 1902*, edited by Walter E. Woodbury, 214–26. New York: Scoville Manufacturing Co., 1901.

"Bird Architecture." *Outing*, July 1901, 437–42.

"Photographing the Belted Kingfisher." *Outing*, Nov. 1901, 198–202.

"A Study of the Black Vulture." *Outing*, Dec. 1901, 279–83.

*"Under My Vine and Fig Tree." In *The American Annual of Photography and Photographic Times-Bulletin Almanac for 1903*, edited by W. I. Lincoln Adams, 24–34. New York: Scoville Manufacturing Co., 1902.

"The Birds' Kindergarten." *Outing*, Apr. 1902, 70–74.

*"When Luck Is Golden." *Metropolitan Magazine*, Apr. 1902, 440–45.

"Sight and Scent in Animals and Birds." *Outing*, June 1902, 295–98.

"The Music of the Marsh." *Outing*, Sept. 1902, 658–65.

*"The Camera in Ornithology." In *The American Annual of Photography and Photographic Times-Bulletin Almanac for 1904*, edited by W. I. Lincoln Adams, 51–68. New York: Scoville Manufacturing Co., 1903.

*"The Call of the Wayside." In *The American Annual of Photography and Photographic Times-Bulletin Almanac for 1906*, edited by W. I. Lincoln Adams, 186–92. New York: Scoville Manufacturing Co., 1905.

"The Making of a Great Ranch." *Country Life in America*, Jan. 1907, 298–302.

*"Character Sketches of Twelve Birds." In *Biennial Report of the Commissioner of Fisheries & Game for Indiana*. Indianapolis, 1908.

"Why I Wrote 'A Girl of the Limberlost.'" *World's Work*, Feb. 1910, 12545–47.

"The Gift of the Birds." *The Youth's Companion*. Part 1, 19 Mar. 1914, 147–48; Part 2, 26 Mar. 1914, 159–60.

"Hundred, Not Six." *New York Times Magazine*, 5 Sept. 1915, 14–15.

"My Life and My Books." *The Ladies' Home Journal*, Sept. 1916, 13, 80, 81.

"Why I Always Wear My Rose-Colored Glasses." *American Magazine*, Aug. 1919, 36–37, 112, 114, 117–19.

"My Ideal Home." Part 4. *Country Life of America*, Oct. 1921, 40–43.

"A New Year's Message." *McCall's*, Jan. 1922, 2, 25.

*"How to Make a Home." *McCall's*, May 1922, 2, 65.

"No Lazy Man Can Make a Garden." *McCall's*, June 1922, 2.

"Gene Stratton-Porter Calls on Our Government to Curb Indecent Literature." *McCall's*, July 1922, 1, 18.

*"Once It Was 'Home Sweet Home.'" *McCall's*, Aug. 1922, 2, 30.

"All Together, Heave!" *Izaak Walton League Monthly*, Dec. 1922, front cover.

*"A New Day in Pictures." *McCall's*, Feb. 1923, 2, 47, 89.

*"The Lost Talent in the World." *McCall's*, Mar. 1923, 2, 30, 96.

*"Shall We Save Natural Beauty?" *McCall's*, Apr. 1923, 2, 82.

*"Getting the Joy Out of Life." *McCall's*, May 1923, 2, 46.

*"Judy O'Grady and the Colonel's Lady." *McCall's*, Aug. 1923, 2.

*"Having Fun with Your Money." *McCall's*, Nov. 1923, 2, 38, 81.

*"Books for Busy People." *McCall's*, Jan. 1924, 2, 28, 74.

*"Ready!" *McCall's*, Apr. 1924, 2, 54, 78, 83.

"My Great Day." *Outdoor America*, June 1924, 12–14.

*"Educating Mother." *McCall's*, July 1924, 2, 39, 41, 77.

*"Helping Father." *McCall's*, Aug. 1924, 2, 38, 48.

*"By the People." *McCall's*, Oct. 1924, 2, 52, 62.

*"Our Thanks." *McCall's*, Nov. 1924, 2, 81, 82, 92.

*"Fixing Our Fences." *McCall's*, Feb. 1925, 2, 58, 62.

"What My Father Meant to Me." *American Magazine*, Feb. 1925, 23, 70, 72, 76.

"Let Us Go Back to Poetry." *Good Housekeeping*, Apr. 1925, 34-35, 194–96, 199–200.

*"The Bible in the Schools." *McCall's*, May 1925, 2, 78.

"Hollywood and the Picture Colony." *McCall's*, Oct. 1925, 2, 76.

"Making Your Vote Count for Something." *McCall's*, Nov. 1925, 2, 67.

"Religion as a Stimulus to Success." *McCall's*, Dec. 1925, 2.

"How I Write." *McCall's*, May 1926, 2, 117.

"Gardens." *McCall's*, June 1926, 2, 83.

"A Message to the Working Woman." *McCall's*, July 1926, 2, 68.

"Ramparts." *McCall's*, Aug. 1926, 2, 45.

"Choosing Words." *McCall's*, Oct. 1926, 2.

"Individual Homes." *McCall's*, Nov. 1926, 2, 87.

"Original Parties." *McCall's*, Dec. 1926, 2, 89.

"The Disadvantages of Authorship." *McCall's*, May 1927, 136.

"Personal Adventures as an Author." *McCall's*, June 1927, 2.

"Broken Promises." *McCall's*, July 1927, 100.

"Division of Labor in the Home." *McCall's*, Sept. 1927, 4.

"Do You Believe in Fairies?" *McCall's*, Oct. 1927, 4.

POEMS BY GENE STRATTON-PORTER

"Blue-Eyed Mary." *Good Housekeeping*, May 1921, 52.
"Euphorbia." *Good Housekeeping*. Part 1, Jan. 1923, 10–13; Part 2,
  Feb. 1923, 24–27; Part 3, Mar. 1923, 42–45.
"Symbols." *Good Housekeeping*, Jan. 1921, 12.

PUBLISHED INTERVIEWS WITH GENE STRATTON-PORTER

Interview by Emma Lindsay Squier. "The Lady from the
  Limberlost." *Los Angeles Times*, 11 June 1922.
Interview by Grace Wilcox. "Great Composers Stole Music from
  Bird Songs." *Los Angeles Times*, 19 Nov. 1922.
Interview by J. J. Lowman. "The Revolt." Published posthumously.
  Los Angeles Times, 6 Feb. 1925.
"How to Open Doors of Literary Fame." Reported posthumously
  without byline in the *Los Angeles Times*, 25 Apr. 1926.

BOOKS ABOUT GENE STRATTON-PORTER

In addition to David G. MacLean's bibliography cited above, there
have been four books about Gene Stratton-Porter. *Gene Stratton-Porter*
by Bertrand F. Richards (Boston: Twayne Publishers, 1980) is a volume
in Twayne's United States Authors Series and primarily a critical analysis of the subject's literary output. *Gene Stratton-Porter: A Lovely Light*
by Rollin King (Chicago: Adams Press, 1979) is a slim volume privately
published by an admirer. Neither of these works contain primary
source material. The third and fourth books about Gene Stratton-Porter
contain information useful in the making of this biography. They are
The Lady of the Limberlost: The Life and Letters of Gene Stratton-Porter
(Garden City, N.Y.: Doubleday, Doran & Co., 1928), a reminiscence
by Jeannette Porter Meehan, the only child of Gene Stratton-Porter,
and *Gene Stratton-Porter: A Little Story of the Life and Work and Ideals of
the Bird Woman* (Garden City, N.Y.: Doubleday, Page & Co., [1915]),
by S. F. E. [attributed to both Eugene Francis Saxton and Samuel F.
Ewart].

ARTICLES ABOUT GENE STRATTON-PORTER, INCLUDING REVIEWS OF HER WORK

Arena Magazine. Book review, Aug. 1903, 215.
Briggs, Margaret Day. "Gene Stratton-Porter." In *1872–1972 Geneva
  and Area Centennial*, edited by Alan S. Baumgartner, 44–49. N.p.,
  n.d. [Geneva, Ind., ca. 1972].

Cooper, Frederic Taber. "The Popularity of Gene Stratton-Porter."
    The Bookman, Aug. 1915, 671.
Elsasser, Glen. "Memories of Limberlost." *Indianapolis Star Magazine*,
    2 Sept. 1962.
"Gene Stratton-Porter: The Fourth in Our Series of Pictorial
    American Romances." *The Delineator*, May 1920, 24.
Independent. Book reviews. 2 July 1903, 1578; 30 Aug. 1915, 302.
"In Memoriam Gene Stratton-Porter." *McCall's*, Feb. 1925, 27.
Jones, Francis Arthur. "How They 'Broke Into Print.'" Part 2. *The
    Strand Magazine*, Sept. 1914, 166–67.
Nagley, Lester C. "Limberlost on Sylvan Lake." *Indianapolis Star
    Magazine*, 18 Nov. 1923.
Overton, Grant M. "Naturalist vs. Novelist: Gene Stratton-Porter."
    In *American Nights Entertainment*, 270–92. New York: D. Appleton
    & Co. [etc.], 1923.
Phelps, William Lyon. "The Why of the Best Seller." *The Bookman*,
    Dec. 1921, 298–302.
The Saturday Review of Literature. Book review. 12 Sept. 1925, 128.
The Spectator [London]. Book review. 9 Sept. 1911, 384–85.
Wallace, Frank N. "Afield with Gene Stratton-Porter." *McCall's*,
    June 1926, 10, 104.

GENERAL REFERENCES

Arlton, Alexander V. *Songs and Other Sounds of Birds*. Hoquiam,
    Wash.: Eklund, 1949.
Baker, Ronald L., and Marvin Carmony. *Indiana Place Names*.
    Bloomington: Indiana University Press, 1975.
Biographical and Historical Record of Adams and Wells Counties of Indiana.
    Chicago: Lewis Publishing Co., 1887.
"Canaan Cemetery." In *Wayne County, Ohio Burial Records*. Compiled
    by the Genealogical Section of the Wayne County Historical
    Society. [Wooster, Ohio]: The Society, 1975.
"The Clifton Springs Sanitarium & Clinic." Clifton Springs, N.Y.,
    [192?].
Commemorative Biographical Record of Wayne County, Ohio. Chicago:
    J. H. Beers & Co., 1889.
The Country Life Press. Garden City, N.Y.: Doubleday, Page & Co.,
    1929.
Curti, Merle. *The Growth of American Thought*. 2d ed. New York:
    Harper, 1951.
Dickinson, Asa Don. *The Best Books of Our Time, 1901–1925*. New
    York: The H. W. Wilson Co., 1928.

Doubleday, F. N. *The Memoirs of a Publisher.* Garden City, N.Y.: Doubleday, 1972.

Douglass, Ben. *History of Wayne County, Ohio, from the Days of the Pioneers and First Settlers to the Present Time.* Indianapolis: Robert Douglass, 1878.

Fatout, Paul. *Indiana Canals.* West Lafayette, Ind.: Purdue University Studies, 1972.

Gray, Ralph D. "The Canal Era in Indiana." In *Transportation and the Early Nation.* Indianapolis: Indiana Historical Society, 1982.

Hackett, Alice. *70 Years of Best Sellers, 1895–1965.* New York: R. R. Bowker Co., 1967.

Heizer, Robert F., and Alan F. Almquist. *The Other Californians.* Berkeley and Los Angeles: University of California Press, 1971.

Helm, T. B., ed. *History of Wabash County, Indiana.* Chicago: John Morris, 1884.

Herzberg, Max J. *The Reader's Encyclopedia of American Literature.* New York: Thomas V. Crowell, 1962.

Hockett, Leola. "The Wabash and Erie Canal in Wabash County." In *Indiana Magazine of History* 24 (Dec. 1928): 296–305.

Illustrated Historical Atlas of the State of Indiana. Chicago: Baskin, Forster & Co., 1876.

Johnson, Rossiter, ed. *A History of the World's Columbian Exposition Held in Chicago in 1893.* 4 vols. New York: D. Appleton & Co., 1897–98.

Los Angeles Today. Los Angeles Chamber of Commerce, 1920.

Lowe, David. *Lost Chicago.* Boston: Houghton Mifflin, 1975.

Ludlum, David M. *Early American Winters, 1604–1820.* Boston: American Meteorological Society, 1966.

Marshall, Thomas R. *Recollections of Thomas R. Marshall: A Hoosier Salad.* Indianapolis: Bobbs-Merrill, 1925.

Mott, Frank Luther. *Golden Multitudes: The Story of Best Sellers in the United States.* New York: Bowker, 1947.

Muir, John. *The Story of My Boyhood and Youth.* Boston: Houghton Mifflin Co., 1913.

Notovitch, Nicolas. *The Unknown Life of Jesus Christ.* Chicago: Rand, McNally & Co., 1894.

O'Hair, Mary C. *Slavery: The Underground Railroad Movement and Some History, as Related to Wabash County, Indiana.* 2 vols. Wabash, Ind.: Wabash County Historical Museum, 1964.

Owen, M. F. *History of Orange Township.* Rome City, Ind.: [American Legion Post 381, ca. 1930].

Pence, George, and Nellie C. Armstrong. *Indiana Boundaries: Territory, State and County.* 1933. Reprint. Indianapolis: Indiana Historical Bureau, 1967.

Pierrakos, John C. *The Energy Field in Man and Nature*. New York:
Institute of Bioenergetic Analysis, 1971.

Quinn, French. *A Short, Short Story of Adams County, Indiana*. Berne,
Ind.: Economy Printing Concern, [1945].

Robertson, Linda, ed. *Wabash County History Bicentennial Edition 1976,
Wabash, Indiana*. Marceline, Mo.: Walsworth Publishing Co., 1976.

Rowley, R. R. *The Geology of Pike County*. Missouri Bureau of
Geology and Mines, 2d ser., vol. 8. Jefferson City, Mo.: H.
Stephens Print. Co., 1907.

Schmitt, Peter J. *Back to Nature: The Arcadian Myth in Urban America*.
New York: Oxford University Press, 1969.

Shumaker, Arthur W. *A History of Indiana Literature*. Indianapolis:
Indiana Historical Bureau, 1962.

Siebert, Wilbur H. *The Underground Railroad from Slavery to Freedom*.
1898. Reprint. Gloucester, Mass.: P. Smith, 1968.

Snow, J. F. *Snow's History of Adams County, Indiana*. Indianapolis: B. F.
Bowen, 1907.

Stratton, Harriet Russell. *A Book of Strattons*. 2 vols. New York: The
Grafton Press, 1908; Frederick H. Hitchcock, 1918.

Swan, J. R. *Statutes of Ohio, 1841*. Columbus: S. Madary, 1841.

Tyndall, John W., and O. E. Lesh, eds. *Standard History of Adams &
Wells Counties, Indiana*. Chicago: Lewis Publishing Co., 1918.

Volney, C. F. *View of the Climate and Soil of the United States of America*.
London: J. Johnson, 1804.

Weesner, Clarkson, ed. *History of Wabash County, Indiana*. Vol. 2.
Chicago: Lewis Publishing Co., 1914.

Wilson, William E. *The Wabash*. New York: Farrar & Rinehart, 1940.

NEWSPAPERS

The Daily Sun. San Bernardino, Calif. 3 Apr. 1902.

Decatur Daily Democrat. Decatur, Ind. 4 Apr. 1884.

Geneva Herald. Geneva, Ind. Oct. 1893–Dec. 1894; May 1895–Aug.
1895; Mar. 1896–Aug. 1896; May 1907–Feb. 1909; Dec. 1911–Oct.
1912.

Indianapolis Star. Indianapolis. 11 Aug., 1 Dec. 1935; 16 Feb., 18 Oct.
1936; 12 Feb. 1939; 25 Feb. 1940.

Los Angeles Times. Los Angeles. Sec. 3, 14 Aug. 1921; Sec. 3, 12 Aug.
1923; Sec. 2, 27 Mar., Sec. 2, 2 Apr., Sec. 2, 27 Aug. 1924; Sec. 2,
13 Nov. 1925.

Our Dumb Animals. Boston. Vol. 24:10, Mar. 1892; Vol. 26:2, July,
Vol. 26:5, Oct. 1893.

The Shelby Democrat. Shelbyville, Ind. 6 Jan. 1916.
Wabash Plain Dealer. Wabash, Ind. Feb. 1872–July 1886; 17 Jan. 1890–
1908; 1 May 1912.

NATIONAL ARCHIVES

Bureau of the Census. Population Schedules 1830 through 1900.
Confirming names, whereabouts, occupations, and other data
essential to the narrative.
Bureau of Land Management. Wayne County, Ohio, patent records
1800–1820. Papers of Joseph Stratton and Jacob Shallenberger.
Bureau of Pensions. Applications and depositions. Papers of Lemon
M. Stratton.
Pension and Military Records. Papers of Thomas Stratton and John
Pomeroy Porter.
Cartographic Archives Division. New Jersey, Ohio, and Indiana field
notes and terrain/soil maps.

STATE ARCHIVES: INDIANA

Archives of Indiana United Methodism, Greencastle, Ind. Papers
clarifying the role of Mark Stratton, Gene Stratton-Porter's father,
as a local preacher.
Indiana State Library, Indiana Division
Biennial Reports of the Superintendent of Public Instruction 1868–
1876. Papers relating to the employment tenure of Irvin
Stratton.
Letters. By Gene Stratton-Porter. Five items.
Indiana Commission on Public Records, State Archives Division
Index. Wabash and Erie Canal Lands—Indiana. Papers relating to
canal land acquisition of Mark Stratton in 1850.
Indiana Department of Financial Institutions. Papers relating to
charter and annual statements of the Geneva Bank, founded by
Charles Porter in 1895.
U.S. Department of Veterans Affairs, Indianapolis Regional Office.
Pension records. Papers of Lemon M. Stratton.
Offices of the County Recorder and the Clerk of the Superior and
Circuit Courts of Adams, Allen, Kosciusko, Noble, Marion,
Shelby, and Wabash Counties. Deed, marriage, divorce, pension,
and probate records. Papers relating to Gene Stratton-Porter and
various members of her family, 1838–1924.

STATE ARCHIVES: CALIFORNIA

Office of the Secretary of State. Corporation papers. Gene Stratton-
  Porter, Inc., 1924–1940. Movie production papers.
Los Angeles County Hall of Records. Deed records. Papers relating
  to Gene Stratton-Porter, 1919–1924.
Clerk's Office of the Los Angeles Superior Court. Probate records.
  Gene Stratton-Porter, deceased.
Office of the Registrar-Recorder of Los Angeles County. Death
  certificates.

STATE ARCHIVES: OHIO

Office of the County Recorder, the Clerk of the Court of Common
  Pleas, and the Probate and Juvenile Court offices of Wayne and
  Wood Counties. Deed, marriage, guardianship, and probate
  records, 1820–1850. Papers relating to the maternal and paternal
  grandparents and aunts and uncles of Gene Stratton-Porter.

STATE ARCHIVES: NEW JERSEY

New Jersey State Library. Revolutionary War records. Papers of
  Thomas Stratton, great-uncle of Gene Stratton-Porter.
Clerk's Office, Sussex County. Papers in the name of Daniel Strattan
  [*sic*], Gene Stratton-Porter's paternal grandfather.

GENEALOGICAL ARCHIVES

The Church of Jesus Christ of Latter-Day Saints, Family History
  Library, Salt Lake City, Utah. Temple records, Stratton family.
Office of the Registrar General National Society Daughters of the
  American Revolution, Washington, D.C. Application papers of
  Florence Stratton Compton.

HOSPITAL ARCHIVES

Clifton Springs Sanitarium and Clinic, Clifton Springs, N.Y. Patient
  card index file relating to Gene Stratton-Porter.

OTHER SOURCES

Three letters written by Gene Stratton-Porter, copies in the
  possession of the author.
One letter written by Gene Stratton-Porter, in the possession of
  David C. Stratton.

Index

Designer: Tony Woodward

Typeface: Bembo

Typographer: Weimer Typesetting Co., Inc., Indianapolis, Indiana

Paper: 70-pound Glatfelter Offset B-32

Printer: Evangel Press, Nappanee, Indiana